IFIP Advances in Information and Communication Technology 422

IFIP – The International Federation for Information Processing

IFIP was founded in 1960 under the auspices of UNESCO, following the First World Computer Congress held in Paris the previous year. An umbrella organization for societies working in information processing, IFIP's aim is two-fold: to support information processing within its member countries and to encourage technology transfer to developing nations. As its mission statement clearly states,

> IFIP's mission is to be the leading, truly international, apolitical organization which encourages and assists in the development, exploitation and application of information technology for the bene t of all people.

IFIP is a non-profitmaking organization, run almost solely by 2500 volunteers. It operates through a number of technical committees, which organize events and publications. IFIP's events range from an international congress to local seminars, but the most important are:

- The IFIP World Computer Congress, held every second year;
- Open conferences;
- Working conferences.

The flagship event is the IFIP World Computer Congress, at which both invited and contributed papers are presented. Contributed papers are rigorously refereed and the rejection rate is high.

As with the Congress, participation in the open conferences is open to all and papers may be invited or submitted. Again, submitted papers are stringently refereed.

The working conferences are structured differently. They are usually run by a working group and attendance is small and by invitation only. Their purpose is to create an atmosphere conducive to innovation and development. Refereeing is also rigorous and papers are subjected to extensive group discussion.

Publications arising from IFIP events vary. The papers presented at the IFIP World Computer Congress and at open conferences are published as conference proceedings, while the results of the working conferences are often published as collections of selected and edited papers.

Any national society whose primary activity is about information processing may apply to become a full member of IFIP, although full membership is restricted to one society per country. Full members are entitled to vote at the annual General Assembly, National societies preferring a less committed involvement may apply for associate or corresponding membership. Associate members enjoy the same benefits as full members, but without voting rights. Corresponding members are not represented in IFIP bodies. Affiliated membership is open to non-national societies, and individual and honorary membership schemes are also offered.

Eunika Mercier-Laurent
Danielle Boulanger (Eds.)

Artificial Intelligence for Knowledge Management

First IFIP WG 12.6 International Workshop, AI4KM 2012
Held in Conjunction with ECAI 2012
Montpellier, France, August 28, 2012
Revised Selected Papers

 Springer

Volume Editors

Eunika Mercier-Laurent
Danielle Boulanger
Jean Moulin University Lyon 3
MODEME, Centre Magellan
6 cours Albert Thomas, 69355 Lyon Cedex 08, France
E-mail: {e.mercier-laurent, danielle.boulanger}@univ-lyon3.fr

ISSN 1868-4238   e-ISSN 1868-422X
ISBN 978-3-662-52566-1   e-ISBN 978-3-642-54897-0
DOI 10.1007/978-3-642-54897-0
Springer Heidelberg New York Dordrecht London

Typesetting: Camera-ready by author, data conversion by Scientific Publishing Services, Chennai, India

Printed on acid-free paper

Springer is part of Springer Science+Business Media (www.springer.com)

Preface

AI4KM (Artificial Intelligence for Knowledge Management) was the first workshop organized by IFIP (International Federation for Information Processing) group TC12.6 (Knowledge Management) in partnership with ECAI (European Conference on Artificial Intelligence).

TC12 is dedicated to the applications of artificial intelligence (AI) methods and techniques in all fields. The interest of TC12.6 members is in all aspects of knowledge management such as methods, knowledge models, techniques and tools, architecture of knowledge flows, specific solutions for problem solving in complex environments, knowledge acquisition and transfer methods etc.

The AI4KM workshop raised the interest of various research fields. AI is not split into symbolic and computational intelligence; often we need to combine both for the best results.

We would like to thank the members of the Program Committee, who gave up their valuable time to review the papers and helped put together an interesting program at Montpellier. We would also like to thank the invited speaker and authors. Finally, our thanks go out to the local Organizing Committee and all the supporting institutions and organizations.

This volume is a selection of improved papers presented during the workshop. After the workshop, the authors were asked to extend their proposals by highlighting their original thoughts. The selection focused on new contributions to the KM field and innovative aspects. An extended Program Committee then evaluated the last versions of the proposals, leading to these proceedings.

The proceedings begin with one of the invited talks:

"An Overview of AI Research History in URSS and in Ukraine. Up-to-date Just-In-Time Knowledge Concept."

It is followed by the contribution

"Artificial Intelligence for Knowledge Management with BPMN and Rules," which combines two approaches: BPMN as procedural knowledge representation and business rules offering specifications of knowledge in a declarative manner.

The next paper, "Validation Model for Discovered Web User Navigation Patterns," deals with Web usage mining considered as a complex process. It proposes an iterative and hybrid approach to discover user navigation patterns and design of a knowledge validation model as well.

"Kleenks: Linked Data with Applications in Research and Ambient Assisted Living" describes a new approach inspired by the success of Web 2.0 techniques such as wikis, blogs, and social networks, which allows both machines and humans (regular users) to combine efforts for the creation of more and better linked data. The concept of collaborative link "kleenk" contains unstructured data in addition to the classic RDF predicates. A free online platform, www.kleenk.com, implements the concept of kleenk in the scientific research domain.

"The Status Quo of Ontology Learning From Unstructured Knowledge Sources for Knowledge Management," presents a study of state-of-the-art research of ontology learning from unstructured knowledge sources for knowledge management. Nine approaches are identified based on statistics and natural language processing.

The next papers is titled "Knowledge Management Applied to Electronic Public Procurement." Electronic procurement aims at reducing the amount of paper, but also at quicker and more knowledgeable processing of proposals and decision taking. Procurement activity is a part of the global organizational knowledge flow. This work goal is to analyze the whole process, to identify the elements of knowledge necessary for successful purchase processing and to study the contribution of AI approaches and techniques to support the above elements. The goal is also to position e-procurement in the organizational knowledge flow.

"Distributed and Collaborative Knowledge Management Using an Ontology-Based System" is the next paper in the volume. The proposed system integrates a database and ontology for storing and inferring knowledge about traffic dangers in a given area. It allows storing of abstract data, shares them across several installations, and manages changes in a centralized way. A loose coupling of the ontology with a relational database allows storage of concrete data about a conceived area in a database, and populates the ontology with data instances during application run-time.

"Collective Intelligence for Evaluating Synergy in Collaborative Innovation" aims to present the *synergy index* as a multiplier of the innovation power of research partners to construct a successful collaboration.

Companies must innovate to be competitive; they are willing to collaborate for the unique product/processes/service only after defining the team with a bigger chance of success. Small and medium companies would like to gratify collaborative innovation with less risk. The paper proposes a new approach to measure synergy for collaboration, which is designed and achieved by using a brand new collective intelligence method.

"How to Understand Digital Studio Outputs: The Case of Digital Music Production" demonstrates how knowledge management principles and techniques could serve digital audio production workflow management, analysis, and preservation.

Knowledge management approaches for digital music production workflows could be of great utility at several time points: in the immediate time for production, in the intermediate time for collection, and in the long term for preservation.

The system combines a trace-based architecture and an ontology-driven knowledge management system, the latter being built on differential semantics theories.

"From Knowledge Transmission to Sign Sharing: Semiotic Web as a New Paradigm for Teaching and Learning in the Future Internet" focuses on the process of creating knowledge by sharing signs and significations (Semiotic Web) more than on knowledge transmission with intelligent object representations (Semantic Web). This way of sharing knowledge is illustrated with two examples issued from La Reunion Island projects in instrumental e-Learning (called @-MUSE) and biodiversity informatics (called IKBS).

We hope you will enjoy reading these papers.

November 2013

Eunika Mercier-Laurent
Danielle Boulanger

Organization

Co-editors

Eunika Mercier-Laurent   Jean Moulin University Lyon 3, France
Danielle Boulanger   Jean Moulin University Lyon 3, France

Program Committee

Danielle Boulanger   Jean Moulin University Lyon 3, France
Eunika Mercier-Laurent   Jean Moulin University Lyon 3, France
Nada Matta   Troyes Technical University, France
Mieczyslaw Lech Owoc   Wroclaw University of Economics, Poland
Anne Dourgnon   EDF Research Center, France
Otthein Herzog   Jacobs University, Bremen, Germany
Daniel O'Leary   USC Marshall School of Business, USA
Antoni Ligeza   University of Science and Technology, Krakow,
                            Poland
Helena Lindskog   Linköping University, Sweden
Gülgün Kayakutlu   Istanbul Technical University, Turkey
Knut Hinkelmann   University of Applied Sciences and Arts,
                            Switzerland
Vincent Ribière   Institute for Knowledge and Innovation,
                            Bangkok, Thailand
Jean Rohmer   Pole Leonard de Vinci, France
Inès Saad   Amiens School of Management, France
Frédérique Segond   Xerox Research Centre Europe, Grenoble,
                            France
Eric Tsui   Hong Kong Polytechnic University, SAR China

Local Organizing Committee

ECAI 2012 Montpellier – Christian Bessière, LIRMM, Université des Sciences et Techniques du Languedoc, France
Michele Sebag – LRI, Université Paris Sud of Orsay, France
Jerome Lang- IRIT, Université Paul Sabatier, France
Eunika Mercier-Laurent - Jean Moulin University Lyon 3, France

Table of Contents

Overview of AI Research History in USSR and Ukraine: Up-to-Date
Just-In-Time Knowledge Concept 1
    Konstantin M. Golubev

Artificial Intelligence for Knowledge Management with BPMN
and Rules 19
    Antoni Ligęza and Tomasz Potempa

Validation Model for Discovered Web User Navigation Patterns 38
    Mieczysław Owoc and Paweł Weichbroth

Kleenks: Linked Data with Applications in Research and Ambient
Assisted Living 53
    Andrei-Adnan Ismail, Razvan Dinu, Adina Magda Florea,
    Tiberiu Stratulat, and Jacques Ferber

The Status Quo of Ontology Learning from Unstructured Knowledge
Sources for Knowledge Management 72
    Andreas Scheuermann and Jens Obermann

Knowledge Management Applied to Electronic Public Procurement 95
    Helena Lindskog and Eunika Mercier-Laurent

Distributed and Collaborative Knowledge Management Using
an Ontology-Based System 112
    Weronika T. Adrian, Antoni Ligęza, Grzegorz J. Nalepa, and
    Krzysztof Kaczor

Collective Intelligence for Evaluating Synergy in Collaborative
Innovation 131
    Ayca Altay and Gulgun Kayakutlu

How to Understand Digital Studio Outputs: The Case of Digital Music
Production 151
    Karim Barkati and Francis Rousseaux

From Knowledge Transmission to Sign Sharing: Semiotic Web as a New
Paradigm for Teaching and Learning in the Future Internet 170
    Noël Conruyt, Véronique Sébastien, Olivier Sébastien,
    David Grosser, and Didier Sébastien

Author Index 189

Overview of AI Research History in USSR and Ukraine: Up-to-Date Just-In-Time Knowledge Concept

Konstantin M. Golubev[*]

General Knowledge Machine Research Group, Ukraine
gkm-ekp@users.sf.net

Abstract. This paper contains a short description of AI history in USSR and in Ukraine. It describes also a state-of-the-art approach to intellectual activity support called Adaptive Learning based on the Just-In-Time Knowledge concept. It's kind of the Artificial Intelligence and Knowledge Management fusion.

Keywords: artificial intelligence, USSR, Ukraine, adaptive learning, just-in-time knowledge, general knowledge machine, electronic knowledge publishing.

1 Introduction

The history of computing and Artificial Intelligence in particular in USSR and Ukraine is not widely known. One reason is the publication language which was mainly Russian. As not a historian by profession, but taking part in this research, we wish to share with the lecturers the contribution of remarkable people and ideas born in Soviet times in a hope that it could be interesting and inspiring.

It is followed by a description of the General Knowledge Machine Group research work, based on the previous experience and a new insight. It represents an original approach to knowledge presentation and learning developed in Kiev, Ukraine.

Excerpts and pictures from Website called "Development of Computer science and technologies in Ukraine" are included by permission from the International Charity Foundation for History and Development of Computer Science and Technique ICFCST http://www.icfcst.kiev.ua/MUSEUM/LEBEDEV/L_life.html

2 USSR AI Researchers and Their Work

2.1 Sergey Lebedev. Creator of the First Stored Program Computer in Continental Europe

Described by some as the "Soviet Alan Turing," Sergey Lebedev had been thinking about computing as far back as the 1930's, until interrupted by war. In 1946 he was made director of Kyiv's Institute of Electrical Engineering. After the second war some stories of "electronic brains" in the West began to circulate and his interest in computing re-vived.

---

[*] http://gkm-ekp.sf.net

E. Mercier-Laurent and D. Boulanger (Eds.): AI4KM 2012, IFIP AICT 422, pp. 1–18, 2014.
© IFIP International Federation for Information Processing 2014

Fig. 1. Sergey Lebedev (source ICFCST)

Initially, Lebedev's superiors were skeptical, and some in his team felt working on a "calculator"—how they thought of a computer—was a step backward compared to electrical and space systems research. Lebedev pressed on regardless, eventually finding funding from the Rocketry department and space to work in a derelict former monastery in Feofania, on the outskirts of Kyiv.

Work on MESM got going properly at the end of 1948 and, considering the challenges, the rate of progress was remarkable. Ukraine was still struggling to recover from the devastation of its occupation during WWII, and many of Kyiv's buildings were in ruins. The monastery in Feofania was among the buildings destroyed during the war, so the MESM team had to build their working quarters from scratch—the laboratory, metalworking shop, even the power station that would provide electricity. Although small—just 20 people—the team was extraordinarily committed. They worked in shifts 24 hours a day and many lived in rooms above the laboratory.

MESM ran its first program on November 6, 1950, and went into full-time operation in 1951. In 1952, MESM was used for top-secret calculations relating to rocketry and nuclear bombs, and continued to aid the Institute's research right up to 1957. By then, Lebedev had moved to Moscow to lead the construction of the next generation of Soviet supercomputers, cementing his place as a giant of European computing. As for MESM, it met a more prosaic fate—broken into parts and studied by engineering students in the labs at Kyiv's Polytechnic Institute".[9]

"Lebedev's interest in the digital computer engineering was not accidental. During the first 20 years of his creative career (until 1946) Lebedev worked in the field of power engineering and he constantly faced the necessity to do complex calculations. He successfully tried to automate them using analog devices, but quickly realized that the abilities of these techniques were limited.

Fig. 2. MESM and team members in 1951. From left to right: Lev Dashevsky, Zoya Zorina-Rapota, Lidiya Abalyshnikova, Tamara Petsukh, Evgeniy Dedeshko (source ICFCST).

His scientific work started with the vacuum tube machines that carried out ten thousands operations. At the time they were supercomputers. Computers M40 and M50, created in 1958 and 1959, were the most fast-acting computers in the world. With the advent of semiconductors and magnetic elements S.Lebedev switched to the elaboration of the second generation supercomputers. The 1967 BESM-6, with a million of operations per second efficiency, was manufactured for 17 years. The best computer facilities in the USSR were equipped with this machine. The BESM-6 took a worthy place in the world computer building. In 1972 London Museum of Science bought the machine to save it for the history. Lebedev's bright scientific career was concluded with construction of the supercomputers based on integrated circuits (microchip) devices that managed millions operations per second. Two of them after update are still in use in anti-missile and anti-airplane defense systems. Every computer was a new step in computer engineering. Every next one was more productive, more reliable and suitable in exploitation. The main principle of machines construction was paralleling of the calculation process. In MESM and BESM they used arithmetic parallel devices for this purpose. In M-20, M-40 and M-50 external devices worked in parallel with a processor. Conveyer calculation method (Lebedev called it water-pipe) was introduced into BESM-6. In the following computer models they used multiple processors and other improvements. All the machines projected under Lebedev's direction were on big serial production in the USSR.

The pioneering work of Lebedev contributed into the formation of powerful computer industry. The Institute of Precision Mechanics and Computer Engineering Academy of Science of the USSR, headed by Lebedev, became the leading one in the country. In 1950s - 1970s its achievements were as significant as ones of the American company IBM.

Characterizing scientific attainments of S.Lebedev, the President of National Academy of Science of Ukraine Boris Paton stressed out: "We would always be proud that in our very Academy of Science of Ukraine, in our beloved Kiev, the Lebedev's talent unfolded to become a prominent scientist in the field of computer engineering and mathematics, and the largest computer-based systems. He founded the famous school of thought in the field of computer science in Kiev. V.Glushkov carried on his work. And now we have productive V.Glushkov Institute of Cybernetics, NASU, one among the largest in the world.

One of Lebedev's wonderful qualities was his care of and trust to the youth. He put them in charge of solving the most difficult problems. He possessed an outstanding pedagogical talent. A lot of his disciples became prominent scientists. They developed their own scientific schools.

His whole life is a heroic example of the devotion to science and to his people. He always aspired to combine noble science with practice and engineering tasks.

He lived and worked in the period of stormy development of electronics, computer engineering, rocket production, space exploration and atomic energy. Being a patriot of his country, Lebedev participated in the biggest projects of I.Kurchatov, S.Korolyov and M.Keldysh, who created a reliable shield for the Motherland. In all these works the computers constructed by Lebedev played a special role.

His prominent works will enrich the treasury of the world science and technology, and his name will stand together with the names of the greatest scientists forever."

Due to the Lebedev's extraordinary modesty and classified nature of the significant part of his works, it is very little known in the western countries about this genius scientists. Until the end of 1990s there were almost no substantial publications. In the 1995 book "Computer Pioneers" by John Lee, which contains over 200 biographies of the scientists, Lebedev's name is not mentioned.

Only on 95th birthday anniversary his achievements were recognized abroad. He was recognized as a pioneer of computer engineering with a medal from the International Computer Society. Its legend states: "Sergei Alekseyevich Lebedev 1902-1974. Developer and designer of the first computer in the USSR. Founder of the Soviet computer building".[10]

2.2   Victor Glushkov. Institute of Cybernetics Founder

Victor Glushkov (August 24, 1923 – January 30, 1982) was the founding father of information technology in the Soviet Union (and specifically in Ukraine), and one of the founders of Cybernetics. He was born in Rostov-on-Don, Russian SFSR, in the family of a mining engineer. He was graduated from Rostov State University in 1948, and in 1952 has proposed solution to the Hilbert's fifth problem and defended his thesis in Lomonosov Moscow State University.

In 1956 he has started working in a computer science field in Kiev as a Director of the Computational Center of the Academy of Science of Ukraine.

He greatly influenced many other fields of theoretical computer science (including the theory of programming and artificial intelligence) as well as its applications in USSR.

Fig. 3. Victor Glushkov (source ICFCST)

Glushkov has founded a Kiev-based Chair of Theoretical Cybernetics and Methods of Optimal Control at the Moscow Institute of Physics and Technology in 1967 and a Chair of Theoretical Cybernetics at Kiev State University in 1969. The Institute of Cybernetics of National Academy of Science of Ukraine, which he has created in 1962, is named after him.

The significance of scientist's work is not always recognized fully by contemporaries. Real evaluation appears much later, when the scientific results and the expressed ideas are verified by the time. The prominent contribution of Victor Glushkov into mathematics, cybernetics and computer engineering was highly appreciated when he was still alive. But with the time passing by, it became evident that in the process of his creative activity he managed to stay ahead of time and oriented his Institute of Cybernetics of the Academy of Science of the Ukrainian SSR, which he founded and supervised, for the transition from computer engineering to computer science, and then - to information technologies (IT). V. Glushkov became a founder of this incredibly important field of science and technologies in Ukraine and in the former USSR. He has trained the necessary cohort of experts and created a powerful scientific school in this field.

The term "information technologies" appeared in science in the last years of XX century. Earlier the terms "informatics" or "computer engineering" were used, that defined narrower problem circle. Being high technologies, information technologies cover wide range of scientific, design, technological and industrial directions: design and construction of computers, periphery devices, elemental base, network equipment, system software, elaboration and creation of automated and automatic numeric systems of different destination and their application software. All these directions have been developed since 1960-70s in the Institute of Cybernetics of the Academy of Science of the Ukrainian SSR, created in 1962 by V. Glushkov". [11]

Author of this paper was working for the Institute of Cybernetics in 1980-86 and has started then General Knowledge Machine project.

Fig. 4. Cybernetic Center NASU planned by V.Glushkov in 1972 was organized in 1992. The main organization - V.Glushkov Institute of Cybernetics of the National Academy of Science of Ukraine, General Director of the Center and Director of the Institute - academician I.Sergienko (source ICFCST).

2.3   Nikolay Amosov. Founder of Bio-cybernetic Information Technologies

"The sphere of interests of outstanding surgeon Nikolai Mihailovich Amosov included not only medical problems, but also general human cognition problems. General system approach to understanding human nature has been reflected in the scientific directions initiated by N.M.Amosov in various areas of cybernetics: modeling of physiological functions of human organism (physiological biocybernetics), modeling of cognitive and psychological human functions (psychological biocybernetics), and modeling a man as a social creature (sociological biocybernetics). All these research directions have been represented in the Department of Biocybernetics founded in the Institute of Cybernetics by V.M.Glushkov and N.M.Amosov in 1961. Nikolai Mikhailovitch Amosov was the scientific leader of the Department since 1988.

In 1964 Nikolai Mikhailovitch Amosov formulated a hypothesis on the information processing mechanisms of the human brain. Within this hypothesis he expressed his system-level observations on the brain's structure and the mechanisms that are made operational by a human's mental functions. Of principal importance was the fact that it was not the separate structures, mechanisms or functions (such as memory, perception, learning and so on) that became the simulation object, but the brain of the human as a social being - the brain of homo sapiens. Such was the main idea of the monograph "Modeling of Thinking and of the Mind ", published in 1965, which for a couple of decades became the "bible" for several generations of Department's researchers (and not only for them).

The ideas, which N.M.Amosov put forward in his book "Modeling of Thinking and of the Mind" were further developed in his subsequent works "Modeling of Complex Systems ", "Artificial Intelligence ", "Algorithms of the Mind " and "Human Nature ".

On a theoretical level, two main features characterize the research of Amosov School.

Fig. 5. The founder of bio-cybernetics in Ukraine Nikolay Amosov at the seminar in the Institute of Cybernetics, AS Ukr.SSR. 70th of XX century (source ICFCST).

The first feature is that not an individual neuron, but a set of neurons organized in a particular way - neuron assembly - is considered to be the core functional element of a neural network, its "principal character ". Given this, the neural network appears now as a structure consisting of a multitude of interacting assemblies, each of which corresponds (and this is a very important point) to some individual image or concept out of a set of images and concepts that participates in forming integrative mental functions realized by the brain. That is, this set participates in the thought process. Thus the neural network turns out to be a network with semantics (a special kind of a semantic network). The origins of the present approach can be traced to the early works of a well-known physiologist D.Hebb, whose main study was published as early as in 1949.An important characteristic of this kind of network is that all of its elements at any point in time are active to some degree. The magnitude of this activity varies in time, reflecting the interaction of concepts represented by the network's nodes.

The second feature of Amosov school research concerns the introduction of the notion of a specific system for reinforcement and inhibition (SRI) to scientific use. This system is an integral neural network attribute, and it plays a role comparable to that of functions of attention in the thought processes in network functioning. The idea of SRI is entirely original. Using this system allows to introduce a direction component into neural network information processing, and, what is very important, to use value characteristics of information in organizing this processing.

Dr.Alexander Kasatkin, Dr.Lora Kasatkina International Research and Training Center of Information Technologies and Systems of National Academia of Sciences of the Ukraine [12]

2.4   Dmitry Pospelov. Russian Artificial Intelligence Association Founder

Dmitry Pospelov, born 19.XII.1932 , Moscow.Technical Sciences Doctor, Professor, Member of Russian Academy of Natural Sciences (10.X.1990).

Pospelov was graduated from Lomonosov Moscow State University as a Computational Mathematics specialist. He was heading Artificial Intelligence Problems Department at the Computer Center of Russian Academy of Sciences named after A.A. Dorodnitsin.

He was Head of International UNESCO Artificial Intelligence Laboratory and Head of "Intellectual Systems" division of Russian Academy of Sciences.

Fig. 6. Dmitry Pospelov. Head of International UNESCO Artificial Intelligence Laboratory. Head of "Intellectual Systems" division of Russian Academy of Sciences (source ICFCST)

Pospelov was a founder of Russian (Soviet) Artificial Intelligence Association (www.raai.org).

The small parts from a paper "Universal Scales to Systems of Communicating Contextual Systems" by Irina Ezhkova are quoted [14].

"It was more than four decades ago when Dmitry Pospelov began his inspiring study of the Semiotic Systems, Situated Logics, Universal Scales and Spaces. His interest in psychology and neurology, in mathematical logics and fuzzy sets, in linguistics and behavior sciences had been stimulated the blossoming tree of a broad Russian school of AI. His typical way of approaching constructive model was formalized as a cortege, or train (or even a simple list) of elements, each of which then may be represented well in a traditional way. This reflected his original flexibility, profound vision and interdisciplinary views.

His intuition was deeply based on a belief that Osgood scales and related spaces may lead to a better understanding of semantically grounded systems. This finally has lead to a discovery and development of the Universal Scales. Latter research in this direction allowed development of the unified integrating framework for modeling a diversity of cognitive and complex real phenomenon. The basic principles of Cognitive Relativity, Rationality and Clarity were crystallized to underline this direction of the Russian school of thought. It became clear that both views can be integrated on the basis of these principles. The mathematical theory of Systems of Communicating Contextual Systems is based on recursive mechanisms of theorem proving and constraints recognition and satisfaction, the first elements of which were also developed in 1974-1978 under the supervision of Dmitry Pospelov, and in a productive collaboration with other Russian mathematical schools such as of Prof. Maslov and of Prof. Kotov.

The Contextual theory of Cognitive States and the Systems of Communicating Contextual Systems (C2S) suggest a unified framework for modeling life-cycles of patterns, representations, and of possible ways of their construction, generation, interaction and transformation. This framework allows modeling complex center-activated or distributed self-organizing phenomenon, which may have centered or distributed cognition. It allows invention of a new kind of AI systems, Evolutionary Evolving Intelligent Systems (EI), which are based on what we call by λ-Intelligence, and which are principally open and flexible, continuously learning, self organized, cognitively tailored and collectively adaptive systems "[13].

2.5   Mikhail N. Livanov. Spatial Organization of Cerebral Processes Research

Mikhail Nikolaevich Livanov, born October 7, 1907 in Kazan was graduated from Kazan state University in 1931 as physiologist and became academician of the Academy of Sciences of the USSR in 1970.

Fig. 7. Mikhail N. Livanov, the Soviet physiologist, academician of the Academy of Sciences of the USSR   (source ICFCST)

He was the Head of laboratories at the Moscow Institute of a brain (1933-1947), Institute of pathology and therapy of intoxication of the AMS of the USSR (1947-1949), Institute of Biophysics of the Academy of medical Sciences of the USSR (1949-61). From 1961 he was with the Institute of higher nervous activity and neurophysiology of the USSR Academy of Sciences.

His major works were on the study of bioelectrical phenomena in the cortex of large hemispheres in norm and pathology. Livanov first applied the methods of the mathematical analysis to bioelectrical fluctuations in the cortex of the brain. He was one of the founders of electroencephalography in the USSR. It shows the functional significance of individual frequency components of the EEG and the role of the spatial distribution of them by the cortex of large hemispheres. Theoretical research and methodological techniques developed by Livanov, are used for the diagnosis of diseases in neuropsychological clinic, are used in the space and aviation medicine. He was awarded 4 orders and medals. His work on spatial organization of cerebral processes is described in [3].

The small description of the paper by V. N. Dumenko "The phenomenon of spatial synchronization of the brain potentials in a broad frequency band 1-250 Hz" is quoted in [15].

"The article dedicated to the centenary of academician Mikhail Nikolaevich Livanov briefly outlines the history of development of his original concept of the functional significance of the brain potential's spatial synchronization phenomenon as a possible way of studying systemic organization of the brain electrical activity. The new parameter of "space" introduced into neurophysiology by M. N. Livanov made it possible to research the earlier unknown aspect of the brain activity. Livanov's ideas have been developed in many studies of the late decades of the XX century. In the review, much attention is given to specific functional significance of this phenomenon in a broad frequency band 1-250 Hz, especially, during instrumental learning. Energy (power spectra) and coherent-phase characteristics of cortical potentials in traditional (1-30 Hz), gamma-(30-80 Hz) and high-frequency (80-250 Hz) bands are compared. The problem of linear and nonlinear processes in the organization of the brain potentials is mentioned".[14]

All these people's works influenced and inspired the creation and activity of General Knowledge Machine Research Group.

3   General Knowledge Machine Research Group

General Knowledge Machine Research Group was founded in 1986 in Kiev, Ukraine, as informal institution by mathematicians and IT experts. It counts 11 members including sponsors, developers and thinkers. The author of this paper has generated initial ideas, coordinates activities and plays all roles needed for the show.

3.1   Just In Time Knowledge Concept

The term "JIT Knowledge" was introduced in the paper "Traditional + Adaptive learning = broad way to knowledge" by K.M. Golubev [5]

Knowledge is can be considered a set of holistic items directing our behavior including descriptions of typical situations and proposed actions. We should learn continuously to be able to apply our knowledge in present and in the future. In a case of knowledge items traditional search engines are inefficient due to impossibility to distinguish knowledge items from full text.

General Knowledge Machine works on an intelligent e-knowledge base engine for any kind of knowledge-based applications supporting effective knowledge presentation, precise knowledge search, adaptive learning and immediate consulting.

Example of Learning Processes

Dialog Professor – student during an exam:

Prof.: You are looking very worried. Any problems with exams questions?
Stud.: Oh, no! Questions are OK. It is the answers that I worry about.

Traditional learning

Traditional learning is based on a linear process, when students must learn all proposed knowledge, topic by topic. After that students must pass exams to get acknowledgement from professors that they acquired the related knowledge. There are many exams, sometimes very difficult, having significant influence on the life of students. But all this very hard work does not guarantee that students have all or even greater part of knowledge needed to solve problems which arise in their post-school activity, in the real world life.

Adaptive Learning

Adaptive Learning is based on a concept called Just- In-Time Knowledge (JIT-Knowledge). Total amount of external sources of knowledge, even in the specific areas, becomes greater all the time. It is not possible, taking into account limitations of human brain, to learn it with Traditional Learning, topic by topic. It means that in reality significant part of knowledge is not used by anyone, and many problems are not solved because no one learns needed knowledge. The Electronic Knowledge Publishing based on General Knowledge Machine power, called GKM-EKP technology, allows to find and to learn knowledge relevant to existing problems.

Table 1. Comparison of AI Expert Systems and Electronic Knowledge Systems

AI Expert Systems	Electronic Knowledge Systems
Intended to replace human experts	Intended to assist human intellect
Based primarily on mathematics	Based on neurophysiology, psychology, knowledge management theory and mathematics
It is practically impossible to transform directly external knowledge sources to expert systems	It is further advancement of a traditional publishing – external knowledge sources (books, articles etc) may be transformed into e-knowledge systems .
Based on the decision rules concept	Based on the general knowledge concept using approach developed by Academician of USSR M.N.Livanov
It is relatively hard work to incorporate an expert system into other information systems due to sequential nature of data input and output	E-knowledge system may be easily incorporated into any kind of information system due to support of wide range of data input and output sources
It is practically impossible to use expert systems for learning, because they are not based on human knowledge	It may be used for Adaptive Learning applications, based on the Just-In-Time Knowledge concept

3.2   Steps of Intellectual Activity

The expert's activity is similar to work of Mr. Sherlock Holmes [17], and consist in following tasks:

- Observation
- Producing propositions, based on a knowledge
- Elimination of impossible propositions
- Selection and verification of the most appropriate propositions

Thus, if we want to help human intellect, to make it more powerful and more creative, we should make a knowledge machine which could assist during these steps. Let's name demands to such a machine.

11 Demands to Knowledge Machine

Step 1 - Observation
    1. Knowledge machine should have maximum possible information about a case before a judgment.

Step 2 - Producing propositions, based on knowledge

2. Knowledge machine should possess maximum possible knowledge in a sphere of implementation.

3. Knowledge machine should possess no excessive knowledge, should have nothing but the tools which may help in doing work.

4. Getting indication of the course of events, knowledge machine should be able to guide itself by other similar cases which occur to its memory.

5. Knowledge machine should have an ability to take into account not only descriptions of situations in its memory but results as well, providing a possibility to reconstruct a description from a result, i.e. if you told it a result, it would be able to evolve what the steps were which led up to that result.

6. Possessing information about the great number of cases, knowledge machine should have an ability to find a strong family resemblance about them, i.e. to find templates of typical cases.

7. Knowledge machine should have an ability to explain the grounds of its conclusion.

8. Knowledge machine should arrive at the conclusion for a few seconds after getting a description of case.

9. Knowledge machine should focus on the most unusual in descriptions of situations.

Step 3 - Elimination of impossible propositions

10. Knowledge machine should have an ability to point out all impossible propositions.

Step 4 - Selection and verification of the most appropriate propositions.

11. Knowledge machine should estimate a level of a confidence of its propositions.

We think that there are many possible solutions for estimation, but we have developed our own Proposition Value Index, based on idea of member of USSR Academy of Science M. N. Livanov from Russia that the essence of memory associations is a spatial-temporal coherence of narrow-band periodical oscillations of central neurons sets activity (see [15]).

AI Expert Systems and Neural Networks

Expert system, as we understand, is based on the idea of decision tree, when, with every answer to a program's question, a direction of moving through a tree changes until a final leaf (decision) will be reached [1].

- So not all possible questions will be asked, and not maximum information will be received.
- The key elements are decision rules, but no knowledge itself. Not a word about the thousands of other similar cases, about typical cases.

- As we see, expert systems originally were designed to be deduction machines. But it is not very reliable to entrust to machine deciding what is absolutely impossible. We think that more fruitful approach is to show what reasons to consider some hypotheses as impossible. And only man should make the final decision.

It is not amazing that development and implementation of a successful expert system is very hard work, because experts cannot think, as a rule, in terms of decision trees, and the mathematical theory of probability have a little in common with a feeling of a confidence of an expert.

Neural network is based, as we know, on the idea of teaching of set of elements (neurons), controlling conductivity between them (see [2]). Teaching is going under control of expert, which defines whether attempt is successful. This is more merciful towards expert - nobody is trying to make him feel himself deficient asking: what is the probability of this conclusion when that parameter's value is present. But there are some difficulties, not outdone yet.

- A neural network is oriented on decision rules rather than on knowledge itself. So there are no thousands of other similar cases in memory of neural network.
- A neural network cannot explain reasons of own conclusion in terms that people can understand. So it is very hard to verify its activity and, therefore, to believe.

An expert system is an example of a 'top-down' approach when particular instances of intelligent behavior selected and an attempt to design machines that can replicate that behavior was made. A neural network is an example of 'bottom-up' approach when there is an attempt to study the biological mechanisms that underlie human intelligence and to build machines, which work on similar principles.

GKM-EKP technology is based on principles uniting both 'top-down' and 'bottom-up' approaches.

3.3   Building Knowledge Machine

And if we could build a knowledge machine satisfying 11 demands, it should mean that we could introduce a new kind of publishing - publishing of knowledge itself.

How to build such a knowledge machine?

Famous experts in Artificial Intelligence (AI) Alan Newell and Herbert Simon, developers of General Problem Solver, proposed to define memory elements as rules called 'Productions' of the following type 'If-Situation-Then-Action'. We have a right to suppose, taking into account this definition and opinion of Mr. Sherlock Holmes, that big part of knowledge consists of following 3-parts elements:

(*Description of real problem-Name-Action-Result*), that is called a concrete knowledge, or (*Description of template of problem-Name-Action-Result*), that is called an abstract knowledge (we think that this kind of knowledge appears of a concrete knowledge for a long lifetime).

Let's consider the following example. It is a try to develop a knowledge machine for pictures authors' recognition assistance. We pick up a fragment from "Renaissance painting from Brueghel to El Greco" by Lionello Venturi [16].

"Like the Florentines, a Parma artist Francesco Mazzola (1503-1540), known as Parmigianino (i.e. little Parmesan), tended to the use of abstract forms, but, less doctrinaire in his abstractionism than such man as Rosso and Pontormo, he achieved a fragile grace and delicacy, reminiscent of Raphael and Corregio. His universal popularity contributed largely to the spread of mannerism in Europe.

The Madonna of the Long Neck (Uffizi, Florence) illustrates to perfection of his aesthetic. Here elegance replaces beauty and the somewhat abstract treatment of the figure gives it an immaterial charm. His sfumato, his discreet allusions to reality, the elongation of proportions and the sinuous movement of his figures were enthusiastically followed up by many painters in the second half of Cinquecento."[16]

Let's try to formalize it in a form (*Description of template of problem-Name-Action- Result*), because it is an abstract knowledge.

Description of problem consists of sentences that we call description signs.

"Tendency to the use of abstract forms; Fragile grace and delicacy; Elegance replaces beauty; Sfumato; Elongation of proportions; Sinuous movement of figures"

Name

"Possible author is Francesco Mazzola (Parmigianino) from Parma, Italy (1503-1540)."

Action and Result

Description of action consists of sequence of sentences that we call action signs.
In our case there are no action signs.

Description of result consists of sequence of sentences that we call result signs.
In our case result sign could be: "Possible author is Francesco Mazzola (Parmigianino) from Parma, Italy (1503-1540)."

Step 1 - Observation

We gather all description signs from all elements of knowledge eliminating synonyms and duplicates, and numerate signs and their grades. Signs numeration sequence doesn't matter. As a result we get a chapter of problem's description input form called (*1.Descriptions signs*). The second part of problem's description input form chapter (*2.Actions signs*) consists of action signs, arranged in a way similar to description signs. The third part of input form chapter (*3.Results signs*) consists of result signs, arranged in a way similar to description signs.

Problem's Description Input Form

1.Descriptions signs
   1.Tendency to the use of abstract forms
   ...
   2.Actions signs
   None
   3.Results signs
   200.Possible author is Francesco Mazzola (Parmigianino) from Parma, Italy (1503-1540)
   ...

Step 2 - Producing propositions, based on knowledge

Initially, we should numerate *Name* parts of knowledge elements that will be used as propositions, just for convenient reference. It will look like:

   1. Francesco Mazzola (Parmigianino) from Parma, Italy (1503-1540)
   ...

Every proposition is accompanied with a list of numbers of signs and grades from problem's description input form.

Getting the most possibly full description of problem, we could build a list of elements of knowledge with the most similar descriptions. It could be presented in a menu-like list of propositions, sorted according to indexes, which present value index depended on degree of similarity.

The highly valuable propositions
Index Number Proposition
90 % 1) Francesco Mazzola (Parmigianino) from Parma, Italy (1503-1540)
...
We have developed our own Proposition Value Index, based on ideas of member of USSR Academy of Science M. N. Livanov (see [15]).

Step 3 - Elimination of impossible propositions

So there's a possibility to verify manually - are there any objections against our favorite propositions?

Step 4 - Selection and verification of the most appropriate propositions

If we choose some proposition from list to get additional information, we should get a list of signs on which proposition is based and its description. In our case, if we select the proposition:

90 % 1 Francesco Mazzola (Parmigianino) from Parma, Italy (1503-1540),

Then we would get the following:

Proposition was made according to the following signs
4.Sfumato.
...
Francesco Mazzola (Parmigianino) from Parma, Italy (1503-1540)
Tendency to the use of abstract forms
...

And we have a possibility for additional verification.

Knowledge system on Renaissance Painting may be found at Web address:
     `http://gkm-ekp.sf.net/IVP-Portal.html`

3.4   Results

Early versions of General Knowledge Machine were developed for UNIX, MS-DOS, Windows operating systems. The latest version supports all platforms of GNU compiler options (any Windows, Linux, UNIX ...).

There are working products which can be presented to experts in corresponding areas.

Products were tested in various environments – business, medicine, arts. Papers were published in Russia, Italy and UK. The work was featured in the 2006-2007 Edition of the Marquis Who's Who in Science and Engineering as a pioneer research.

4   Conclusion and Perspectives

Some people say about a crisis of Artificial Intelligence. But is this crisis of human intellect? Of course, not. May be it's a crisis of human self-confidence. In the beginning there were many promises to built machines more intelligent than people. And those machines should use advanced principles of work, much better than obsolete human intellect [5]. Instead of help to human intellect there were attempts to replace it. But those, who read works of academician V. Vernadsky from Ukraine [6], E. Le Roy [7] and P. Teilhard de Chardin from France [8], know that the main result of evolution on Earth is creation of Noosphere - a sphere of intellect. And, in this case, it is very interesting what can be called an intellect, but is based on other principles than developed by evolution?

References

1. Alty, J.L., Coombs, M.J.: Expert systems. Concepts and examples. The National Computing Centre Limited (1984)
2. Hinton, G.E.: Learning in parallel networks. Byte. McGraw-Hill, Inc., New York (1985)
3. Livanov, M.N.: Spatial Organization of Cerebral Processes. John Wiley & Sons, Chichester (1977)
4. Golubev, K.M.: Adaptive learning with e-knowledge systems. IJTM 25(6/7) (2003)
5. Golubev, K.M.: Traditional + Adaptive learning = broad way to knowledge. In: ISPIM (1999), http://www.ispim.org/files/ ISPIM_1999_Conference_Programme.pdf
6. Schank, R., Hunter, L.: The quest to understand thinking. Byte. McGraw-Hill, Inc., New York (1985)
7. Vernadsky, V.I.: The Biosphere. Copernicus, New York (1998); Langmuir, D.B. (tr.), McMenamin, M.A.S. (ed.)
8. Le Roy, E.: Les origines humaines et l'evolution de l'intelligence, Paris (1928)
9. Teilhard de Chardin, P.: La place de l'homme dans la nature. Éditions du Seuil, Paris (1956)
10. Google blog posted by Marina Tarasova, Communications Associate, Ukraine, http://googleblog.blogspot.com/2011/12/ remembering-remarkable-soviet-computing.html
11. Development of Computer science and technologies in Ukraine, International Charity Foundation for History and Development of Computer Science and Technique, ICFCST, http://www.icfcst.kiev.ua/MUSEUM/LEBEDEV/L_life.html
12. Development of Computer science and technologies in Ukraine, International Charity Foundation for History and Development of Computer Science and Technique, ICFCST, http://www.icfcst.kiev.ua/MUSEUM/GL_HALL2/1f5_9.html#1f5_9-1
13. Development of Computer science and technologies in Ukraine, International Charity Foundation for History and Development of Computer Science and Technique, ICFCST, http://www.icfcst.kiev.ua/MUSEUM/Amosov.html
14. Ezhkova, I.: Universal Scales to Systems of Communicating Contextual Systems, http://posp.raai.org/data/posp2005/Ezhkova/ezhkova.html
15. Dumenko, V.N.: The phenomenon of spatial synchronization of the brain potentials in a broad frequency band 1-250 Hz, http://lib.bioinfo.pl/paper:18064890
16. Oshe, V.K.: A role of operative memory in solving of tasks of visual interpolation of linear intervals. In: Psychophysiological Regularities of Perception and Memory, Nauka, Moscow, Russia (1985)
17. Venturi, L.: Renaissance painting from Breughel to El Greco. Gilbert, S. (trans.). Editions d'Art Albert Skira S.A., Geneva (1979)
18. Doyle, A.C.: The Penguin Complete Sherlock Holmes. With a preface of Christopher Morley. Penguin Books (1981)

Artificial Intelligence for Knowledge Management with BPMN and Rules

Antoni Ligęza[1] and Tomasz Potempa[2]

[1] AGH University of Science and Technology, Krakow, Poland
ligeza@agh.edu.pl
[2] Higher School of Tarnów, Tarnow, Poland
t_potempa@pwsztar.edu.pl

Abstract. This paper presents a framework combining BPMN and BR as a tool for Knowledge Management (KM). An attempt at providing a common model supported with Artificial Intelligence (AI) techniques and tools is put forward. Through an extended example it is shown how to combine BPMN and BR and how to pass to semantic level enabling building executable specifications and knowledge analysis. Some of the problems concerning these two approaches can be to certain degree overcome thanks to their complementary nature. We only deal with a restricted view of Knowledge Management, where knowledge can be modeled explicitly in a formal representation, and it does not take into account the hidden, personal knowledge.

1 Introduction

Design, development and analysis of progressively more and more complex business processes require advanced methods and tools. Apart from variety of classical Artificial Intelligence (AI) stuff, two generic modern approaches to modeling such processes have recently gained wider popularity; these are: *Business Process Model and Notation* (BPMN) [1] and *Business Rules* (BR) [2,3]. Although aimed at a common target, both of these approaches are rather mutually complementary and offer distinctive features enabling process modeling.

BPMN constitutes a set of graphical symbols, such as links modeling workflow, various splits and joins, events and boxes representing data processing activities. It is a transparent visual tool for modeling complex processes promoted by OMG [1]. What is worth underlying is the expressive power of current BPMN; unfortunately, it is restricted to the visual layer with no clear semantics. BPMN allows for visual modeling conditional operations, loops, event-triggered actions, splits and joins of data flow paths and communication among processes. Moreover, modeling can take into account several levels of abstraction enabling a hierarchical approach.

BPMN can be considered as *procedural knowledge representation*; a BPMN diagram represents in fact a set of interconnected procedures. Although BPMN provides transparent, visual representation of the process, due to lack of formal model semantics it makes attempts at more rigorous analysis problematic. Further, even relatively simple inference requires a lot of space for representation; there is no easy way to specify declarative knowledge, e.g. in the form of rules.

E. Mercier-Laurent and D. Boulanger (Eds.): AI4KM 2012, IFIP AICT 422, pp. 19–37, 2014.

Business Rules, also promoted by OMG [4,5], offer an approach to specification of knowledge in a *declarative* manner. The way the rules are applied is left over to the user when it comes to rule execution. Hence, rules can be considered as *declarative knowledge specification*; inference control, however, is not covered by basic rules. Hence, the same set of rules can be used in numerous ways, and it may become problematic to *find* a solution even having at hand all the necessary rules.

Note that these two approaches are to certain degree complementary: BR provide declarative specification of domain knowledge, which can be encoded into a BPMN model. On the other hand, BPMN diagram can be used as procedural specification of the workflow, including inference control [6]. However, BPMN lacks of a *formal declarative model* defining the semantics and logic behind the diagram. Hence, defining and analyzing correctness of BPMN diagrams is a hard task. There are papers undertaking the issues of analysis and verification of BPMN diagrams [7,8,9,10]. However, the analysis is performed mostly at the *structural* level and does not take into account the semantics of dataflow and control knowledge.

In this position paper, we follow the ideas initially presented in [11]. An attempt at defining foundations for a more formal, logical, declarative model of the most crucial elements of BPMN diagrams combined with BR is undertaken. We pass from logical analysis of BPMN component to their logical models, properties and representation in PROLOG [12]. The model is aimed at enabling definition and further analysis of selected formal properties of a class of restricted BPMN diagrams. The analysis should take into account properties constituting reasonable criteria of correctness. The focus is on development of a formal, declarative model of BPMN components and its overall structure. In fact, a combination of the recent approaches to development and verification of rule-based systems [13,14,15,16,17] seems to have potential influence on the BPMN analysis.

2 Motivation

Knowledge has become a valuable resource and a decisive factor for successful operation of organizations, companies and societies. As vast amounts of knowledge are in use, tools supporting Knowledge Management (KM) are inevitable support for Decision Makers. Such tools can be roughly classified into the following categories:

- *Conceptual Models* — various symbolic and visual ways of Knowledge Representation (KR), analysis, and supporting design of knowledge-intensive systems and applications; as an example one can mention various schemes, graphs, networks and diagrams, with UML [18] and BPMN [19] being some perfect examples,
- *Logical Models* — more formal KR and knowledge processing (reasoning, inference) tools, supporting both *representation* and *application* of knowledge [20,21]. It is important that such models typically support also *semantic* issues; as an example one can mention various types of logics and logic-derived formalisms including rules and Business Rules (BR) as some perfect examples.
- *Functional and Procedural Models* — these include all algorithmic-type recipes for performing operations; some typical examples may vary from linguistically represented procedures, e.g. ISO, to programs encoded with any programming languages.

When speaking about Conceptual Models one usually assumes more or less informal, abstract, illustrative presentation of concepts, relations, activities, etc. In case of Logical Models, clear syntax and semantic rules are in background; this assures possibility of identification and verification of properties, such as (i) *consistency*, (ii) *completeness*, (also: coverage), (iii) *unique interpretation* (lack of ambiguity), (iv) *efficiency* (minimal representation, lack of redundancy, efficient operation), (v) *processability*. Some further requirements may refer to: readability and transparency, easy modifications and extensionability, support for knowledge acquisition and encoding, etc.

The above-mentioned models are used to represent, analyze, process and optimize knowledge. Note that there are at least the following types of knowledge aimed at separate goals and requiring different way of processing:

- *typological* or *taxonometric* knowledge (e.g. a taxonomy in typed logics and languages or TBox in Description Logics),
- *factographic* knowledge representing facts and relations about object (e.g. a set of the FOPC atomic formulae or ABox in DL),
- *inferential* or *transformation* knowledge — specification of legal knowledge rewriting rules or production rules,
- *integrity and constraints* knowledge on what is impossible, not allowed, etc.
- *meta-knowledge* — all about how to use the basic knowledge (e.g. inference control rules).

Now, most typical KM activities require solving such issues as:

1. Knowledge Representation,
2. Inference — knowledge processing rules,
3. Inference Control — principles on how to apply inference rules in a correct and efficient manner,
4. Knowledge Acquisition and Updating,
5. Knowledge Analysis and Verification,
6. Friendly User Interface,
7. Generalization and Learning.

A tool, or a set of tools, for efficient Knowledge Management should support as many KM activities in a smooth way and deserve handling as many types of knowledge within a single framework.

2.1   BPMN as a Tool for Knowledge Management

BPMN [1] appears to be an effective choice for Knowledge Management tasks. It offers a wide spectrum of graphical elements for visualizing of events, activities, workflow splits and merges, etc. It can be classified as Conceptual Modeling tool of high expressive power, practically useful and still readable to public.

Let us briefly analyze the strengths and weaknesses of BPMN as a KM tool. It is mostly a way of *procedural knowledge specification*, so it supports p. 3 above, but neither p. 1 nor 2. Certainly, referring to p. 6 its user interface is nice. An important issue about BPMN is that it covers three important aspects of knowledge processing; these are:

- *inference control* or *workflow control*, including diagrammatic specification of the process with partial ordering, switching and merging of flow,
- *data processing* or *data flow* specification, including input, output and internal data processing,
- *structural representation* of the process as a whole, allowing for visual representation at several levels of hierarchy.

Some more serious weakness issues concerning characteristics and activities presented in Section 2 are as follows:

- BPMN — being a Conceptual Modeling tool — does not provide formal semantics,
- it is inadequate for knowledge analysis and verification (p. 5),
- it neither support declarative representation of taxonometric, factographic, nor integrity knowledge.

A further issue is that BPMN does not support oparation planning, and does not take into account neither cost nor temporal constraints nor uncertainty, which are important factors for real-world plan operations [22]. However, some of these weaknesses can be overcome by combination of BPMN with Business Rules.

2.2 Business Rules as a Tool for Knowledge Management

Business Rules (BR) can be classified as Logical Model for Knowledge Representation (KR). They constitute a declarative specification of knowledge. There can be different types of BR serving different purposes; in fact all the types of knowledge (taxonometric, factographic, transformation, integrity, and meta) can be encoded with BR.

A closer look at foundations of Rule-Based Systems [23] shows that rules can:

- have high expressive power depending on the logic in use,
- provide elements of procedural control,
- undergo formal analysis.

Some modern classification cover the following types of rules:

- facts – rules defining true statement (with no conditional part),
- definition rules – for defining terms and notions in use,
- integrity rules – rules defining integrity constraints,
- production rules – for derivation of new facts,
- reaction rules – rules triggered by events, reactive rules or ECA rules,
- transformation rules – rules defining possible transformations, term-rewriting rules; they may include numerical recipe rules,
- data processing rules – rules defining how particular data are to be transformed; these include numerical processing rules,
- control rules – in fact meta rules used for inference process control,
- meta rules – other rules defining how to use basic rules.

An interesting pattern of rules are the exclusion rules discussed in [24].

Rules, especially when grouped into decision modules (such as decision tables) [25], are easier to analyze. However, the possibility of analysis depends on the accepted *knowledge representation language*, and in fact – the logic in use. Formal models of rule-based systems and analysis issues are discussed in detail in [23]. An interesting, new tool for such analysis — the Alvis language — is promoted in [17].

The main weakness of BR consists in lack of procedural (inference control) specification and transparent knowledge visualization. However, these issues can be solved at the BPMN level.

2.3 BPMN and BR: Towards an Integration Framework

In order to integrate BPMN and BR, a framework combining and representing intrinsic mechanisms of these two approaches is under development. It should be composed of the following elements:

- Workflow Structure/Sequence Graph (WSG) — an AND-OR graph representing a workflow structure at abstract level,
- Logical Specification of Control (LSC) — logical labels for WSG,
- Dataflow Sequence Graph (DSG) — a DFD-type graph showing the flow of data,
- Logical Specification of Data (LSD) — constraints imposed on data being input, output or processed at some nodes.
- Temporal Constraint Specification (TCS) — not discussed in this paper.

3 Workflow Structural Graph for BPMN

Workflow Structure/Sequence Graph (WSG) is in fact a simplified structural model of BPMN diagrams. It constitutes a restricted abstraction of crucial intrinsic workflow components. As for events, only start and termination events are taken into account. Main knowledge processing units are activities (or tasks). Workflow control is modeled by two subtypes of gateways: split and join operations. Finally, workflow sequence is modeled by directed links. No time or temporal aspect is considered.

The following elements will be taken into consideration [11]:

- $\mathbb{S}$ — a non-empty set of *start events* (possibly composed of a single element),
- $\mathbb{E}$ — a non-empty set of *end events* (possibly composed of a single element),
- $\mathbb{T}$ — a set of *activities* (or *tasks*); a task $T \in \mathbb{T}$ is a finite process with single input and single output, to be executed within a finite interval of time,
- $\mathbb{G}$ — a set of *split gateways* or *splits*, where branching of the workflow takes place; three disjoint subtypes of splits are considered:
  - $\mathbb{GX}$ — a set of *exclusive splits* where one and only one alternative path can be followed (a split of the $EX - OR$ type),
  - $\mathbb{GP}$ — a set of *parallel splits* where all the paths of the workflow are to be followed (a split of the AND type or a *fork*), and
  - $\mathbb{GO}$ — a set of *inclusive splits* where one or more paths should be followed (a split of the OR type).

- $\mathbb{M}$ — a set of *merge gateways* or *joins*, where two or more paths meet; three disjoint subtypes of merge (join) nodes are considered:
  - $\mathbb{MX}$ — a set of *exclusive merge* nodes where one and only one input path is taken into account (a merge of the $EX - OR$ type),
  - $\mathbb{MP}$ — a set of *parallel merge* nodes where all the paths are combined together (a merge of the AND type), and
  - $\mathbb{MO}$ — a set of *inclusive merge* nodes where one or more paths influence the subsequent item (a merge of the OR type).
- $\mathbb{F}$ — a set of workflow links, $\mathbb{F} \subseteq \mathbb{O} \times \mathbb{O}$, where $\mathbb{O} = \mathbb{S} \cup \mathbb{E} \cup \mathbb{T} \cup \mathbb{G} \cup \mathbb{M}$ is the join set of objects. All the component sets are pairwise disjoint.

The splits and joins depend on logical conditions assigned to particular branches. It is assumed that there is defined a partial function Cond: $\mathbb{F} \to \mathbb{C}$ assigning logical formulae to links. In particular, the function is defined for links belonging to $\mathbb{G} \times \mathbb{O} \cup \mathbb{O} \times \mathbb{M}$, i.e. outgoing links of split nodes and incoming links of merge nodes. The conditions are responsible for workflow control. For intuition, an exemplary simple BPMN diagram is presented in Fig. 1.

In order to assure *structural correctness* of BPMN diagrams a set of restrictions on the overall diagram structure is typically defined; they determine the so-called *well-formed diagram* [9]. Classical AI graph search methods can be applied for analysis. Note however, that a well-formed diagram does not assure that for any input knowledge the process can be executed leading to a (unique) solution. This further depends on the particular input data, its transformation during processing, correct work of particular objects, and correct control defined by the branching/merging conditions assigned to links.

The further issues, i.e. Logical Specification of Control (LSC), Dataflow Sequence Graph (DSG), and Logical Specification of Data (LSD) will be analyzed on the base of an example presented below.

4 BPMN and BR Example: The Thermostat Case

In order to provide intuitions, the theoretical considerations will be illustrated with a simple exemplary process. The process goal is to establish the so-called *set-point* temperature for a thermostat system [26]. The selection of the particular value depends on the season, whether it is a working day or not, and the time of the day.

Consider the following set of declarative rules specifying the process. There are eighteen inference rules (production rules):

Rule 1: $aDD \in \{monday, tuesday, wednesday, thursday, friday\} \longrightarrow aTD = wd.$
Rule 2: $aDD \in \{saturday, sunday\} \longrightarrow aTD = wk.$
Rule 3: $aTD = wd \wedge aTM \in (9, 17) \longrightarrow aOP = dbh.$
Rule 4: $aTD = wd \wedge aTM \in (0, 8) \longrightarrow aOP = ndbh.$
Rule 5: $aTD = wd \wedge aTM \in (18, 24) \longrightarrow aOP = ndbh.$
Rule 6: $aTD = wk \longrightarrow aOP = ndbh.$
Rule 7: $aMO \in \{january, february, december\} \longrightarrow aSE = sum.$
Rule 8: $aMO \in \{march, april, may\} \longrightarrow aSE = aut.$
Rule 9: $aMO \in \{june, july, august\} \longrightarrow aSE = win.$

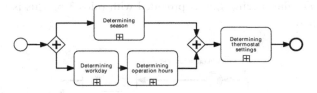

Fig. 1. An example BPMN diagram — top-level specification of the thermostat system

Rule 10: $aMO \in \{september, october, november\} \longrightarrow aSE = spr$.
Rule 11: $aSE = spr \wedge aOP = dbh \longrightarrow aTHS = 20$.
Rule 12: $aSE = spr \wedge aOP = ndbh \longrightarrow aTHS = 15$.
Rule 13: $aSE = sum \wedge aOP = dbh \longrightarrow aTHS = 24$.
Rule 14: $aSE = sum \wedge aOP = ndbh \longrightarrow aTHS = 17$.
Rule 15: $aSE = aut \wedge aOP = dbh \longrightarrow aTHS = 20$.
Rule 16: $aSE = aut \wedge aOP = ndbh \longrightarrow aTHS = 16$.
Rule 17: $aSE = win \wedge aOP = dbh \longrightarrow aTHS = 18$.
Rule 18: $aSE = win \wedge aOP = ndbh \longrightarrow aTHS = 14$.

Let us briefly explain these rules. The first two rules define if we have today (aTD) a workday (wd) or a weekend day (wk). Rules 3-6 define if the operation hours (aOP) are during business hours (dbh) or not during business hours ($ndbh$); they take into account the workday/weekend condition and the current time (hour). Rules 7-10 define the season (aSE) is summer (sum), autumn (aut), winter (win) or spring (spr). Finally, rules 11-18 define the precise setting of the thermostat ($aTHS$). Observe that the set of rules is flat; basically no control knowledge is provided.

Now, let us attempt to visualize a business process defined with these rules. A BPMN diagram of the process is presented in Fig. 1.

After start, the process is split into two independent paths of activities. The upper path is aimed at determining the current season (aSE; it can take one of the values $\{sum, aut, win, spr\}$; the detailed specification is provided with rules 7-10). A visual specification of this activity with an appropriate set of rules is shown in Fig. 2.

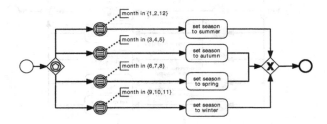

Fig. 2. An example BPMN diagram — detailed specification a BPMN task

The lower path determines whether the day (aDD) is a workday ($aTD = wd$) or a weekend day ($aTD = wk$), both specifying the value of today (aTD; specification provided with rules 1 and 2), and then, taking into account the current time (aTM), whether the operation (aOP) is during business hours ($aOP = dbh$) or not

($aOP = ndbh$); the specification is provided with rules 3-6. This is illustrated with Fig. 3 and Fig. 4.

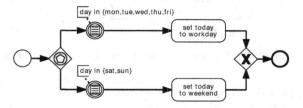

Fig. 3. An example BPMN diagram — detailed specification of determining the day task

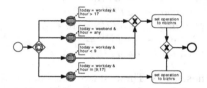

Fig. 4. An example BPMN diagram — detailed specification of working hours task

Finally, the results are merged together, and the final activity consists in determining the thermostat settings ($aTHS$) for particular season (aSE) and time (aTM) (the specification is provided with rules 11-18). This is illustrated with Fig. 5.

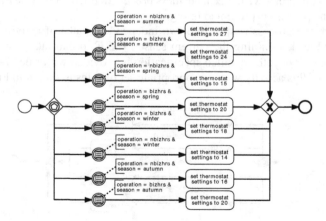

Fig. 5. An example BPMN diagram — detailed specification of the final thermostat setting task

Even in this simple example, answers to the following important questions are not obvious:

1. *Data flow correctness*: Is any of the four tasks/activities specified in a correct way? Will each task end with producing desired output for any admissible input data?

2. *Split consistency*: Will the workflow possibly explore all the paths after a split? Will it always explore at least one?
3. *Merge consistency*: Will it be always possible to merge knowledge coming from different sources at the merge node?
4. *Termination/completeness*: Does the specification assure that the system will always terminate producing some temperature specification for *any* admissible input data?
5. *Determinism*: Will the output setting be determined in a unique way?

Note that we do not ask about *correctness* of the result; in fact, the rules embedded into a BPMN diagram provide a kind of *executable specification*, so there is no reference point to claim that final output is correct or not.

5   Logical Specification of Control

This section is devoted to analysis of logical specification of control. In fact, two types of control elements are analyzed: split nodes and merge nodes.

5.1   Analysis of Split Conditions

An exclusive split $GX(q_1, q_2, \ldots q_k) \in \mathbb{GX}$ with k outgoing links is modeled by a fork structure assigned excluding alternative of the form:

$$q_1 \veebar q_2 \veebar \ldots \veebar q_k,$$

where $q_i \wedge q_j$ is always false for $i \neq j$. An exclusive split can be considered correct if and only if at least one of the alternative conditions is satisfied. We have the following logical requirement:

$$\models q_1 \vee q_2 \vee \ldots \vee q_k, \tag{1}$$

i.e. the disjunction is in fact a tautology. In practice, to assure (1), a predefined exclusive set of conditions is completed with a default q_0 condition defined as $q_0 = \neg q_1 \wedge \neg q_2 \wedge \ldots \wedge \neg q_k$; obviously, the formula $q_0 \vee q_1 \vee q_2 \vee \ldots \vee q_k$ is a tautology.

Note that in case when an input restriction formula ϕ is specified, the above requirement given by (1) can be relaxed to:

$$\phi \models q_1 \vee q_2 \vee \ldots \vee q_k. \tag{2}$$

An inclusive split $GO(q_1, q_2, \ldots q_k) \in \mathbb{GO}$ is modeled as disjunction of the form:

$$q_1 \vee q_2 \vee \ldots \vee q_k,$$

An inclusive split to be considered correct must also satisfy formula (1), or at least (2). As before, this can be achieved through completing it with the q_0 default formula.

A parallel split $GP(q_1, q_2, \ldots q_k) \in \mathbb{GP}$ is referring to a fork-like structure, where all the outgoing links should be followed in any case. For simplicity, it can be considered as an inclusive one, where all the conditions assigned to outgoing links are set to *true*.

Note that, if ϕ is the restriction formula valid for data at the input of the split, then any of the output restriction formula is defined as $\phi \wedge q_i$ for any of the outgoing link i, $i = 1, 2, \ldots, k$.

5.2 Analysis of Merge Conditions

Consider a workflow merge node, where k knowledge inputs satisfying restrictions $\phi_1, \phi_2, \ldots, \phi_k$ respectively meet together, while the selection of particular input is conditioned by formulae $p_1, p_2, \ldots, p_k$, respectively.

An exclusive merge $MX(p_1, p_2, \ldots, p_k) \in \mathbb{MX}$ of k inputs is considered correct if and only if the conditions are pairwise disjoint, i.e.

$$\not\models p_i \wedge p_j \tag{3}$$

for any $i \neq j$, $i, j \in \{1, 2, \ldots, k\}$. Moreover, to assure that the merge works, at least one of the conditions should hold:

$$\models p_1 \vee p_2 \vee \ldots \vee p_k, \tag{4}$$

i.e. the disjunction is in fact a tautology. If the input restrictions $\phi_1, \phi_2, \ldots, \phi_k$ are known, condition (4) might possibly be replaced by $\models (p_1 \wedge \phi_1) \vee (p_2 \wedge \phi_2) \vee \ldots \vee (p_k \wedge \phi_k)$.

Note that in case a join input restriction formula ϕ is specified, the above requirement can be relaxed to:

$$\phi \models p_1 \vee p_2 \vee \ldots \vee p_k, \tag{5}$$

and if the input restrictions $\phi_1, \phi_2, \ldots, \phi_k$ are known, it should be replaced by $\phi \models (p_1 \wedge \phi_1) \vee (p_2 \wedge \phi_2) \vee \ldots \vee (p_k \wedge \phi_k)$.

An inclusive merge $MO(p_1, p_2, \ldots, p_k) \in \mathbb{MO}$ of k inputs is considered correct if one is assured that the merge works — condition (4) or (5) hold.

A parallel merge $MP \in \mathbb{MP}$ of k inputs is considered correct by default. However, if the input restrictions $\phi_1, \phi_2, \ldots, \phi_k$ are known, a consistency requirement for the combined out takes the form that ϕ must be consistent (satisfiable), where:

$$\phi = \phi_1 \wedge \phi_2 \wedge \ldots \wedge \phi_k \tag{6}$$

An analogous requirement can be put forward for the active links of an inclusive merge.

$$\models p_1 \wedge p_2 \wedge \ldots \wedge p_k, \tag{7}$$

i.e. the conjunction is in fact a tautology, or at least

$$\phi \models p_1 \wedge p_2 \wedge \ldots \wedge p_k. \tag{8}$$

In general, parallel merge can be made correct in a trivial way by putting $p_1 = p_2 = \ldots = p_k = true$.

Note that even correct merge leading to a satisfiable formula assure only passing the merge node; the funnel principle must further be satisfied with respect to the following-in-line object. To illustrate that consider the input of the component determining thermostat setting (see Fig. 1). This is the case of parallel merge of two inputs. The joint formula defining the restrictions on combined output of the components for determining season and determining operation hours is of the form:

$$\phi = (aSE = sum \vee aSE = aut \vee aSE = win \vee \\ aSE = spr) \wedge (aOP = dbh \vee aOP = ndbh).$$

A simple check of all possible combinations of season and operation hours shows that all the eight possibilities are covered by preconditions of rules 11-18; hence the funnel condition (11) holds.

6 Dataflow Sequence Graph

A Dataflow Sequence Graph (DSG) can be any DFD-type graph showing the flow of data that specifies the data transfers among data processing components. It shows that data produced by certain components should be sent to some next-in-chain ones. In the case of our thermostat example, it happens that the DSG can be represented with the graph shown in Fig. 1 — the workflow and the dataflow structure are the same.

7 Logical Specification of Data

Logical Specification of Data (LSD) are constraints on data being input, output or processed at some nodes.

7.1 Logical Constraints on Component Behavior

In this section we put forward some minimal requirements defining correct work of rule-based process components performing BPMN activities. Each such component is composed of a set of inference rules, designed to work within the same context; in fact, preconditions of the rules incorporate the same attributes. In our example, we have four such components: determining workday (rules 1-2), determining operation hours (rules 3-6), determining season (rules 7-10) and determining the thermostat setting (rules 11-18).

In general, the outermost logical model of a component T performing some activity/task can be defined as a triple of the form:

$$T = (\psi_T, \varphi_T, \mathcal{A}), \tag{9}$$

where ψ_T is a formula defining the restrictions on the component input, φ_T defines the restrictions for component output, and $\mathcal{A}$ is an algorithm which for a given input satisfying ψ_T produces an (desirably uniquely defined) output, satisfying φ_T. For intuition, ψ_T and φ_T define a kind of a 'logical tube' — for every input data satisfying ψ_T (located at the entry of the tube), the component will produce and output satisfying φ_T (still located within the tube at its output). The precise recipe for data processing is given by algorithm $\mathcal{A}$.

The specification of a rule-based process component given by (9) is considered *correct*, if and only if for any input data satisfying ψ_T the algorithm $\mathcal{A}$ produces an output satisfying φ_T. It is further *deterministic* (unambiguous) if the generated output is unique for any admissible input.

For example, consider the component determining operation hours. Its input restriction formula ψ_T is the disjunction of precondition formulae $\psi_3 \vee \psi_4 \vee \psi_5 \vee \psi_6$, where

ψ_i is a precondition formula for rule i. We have $\psi_T = ((aTD = wd) \wedge (aTM \in [0,8] \vee aTM \in [9,17] \vee aTM \in [18,24])) \vee (aTD = wk)$. The output restriction formula is given by $\varphi_T = (aOP = dbh) \vee (aOP = ndbh)$. The algorithm is specified directly by the rules; rules are in fact a kind of *executable specification*.

In order to be sure that the produced output is unique, the following *mutual exclusion* condition should hold:

$$\not\models \psi_i \wedge \psi_j \tag{10}$$

for any $i \neq j$, $i, j \in \{1, 2, \ldots, k\}$. A simple analysis shows that the four rules have mutually exclusive preconditions, and the joint precondition formula ψ_T covers any admissible combination of input parameters; in fact, the subset of rules is locally *complete* and *deterministic* [23].

7.2 Logical Specification of Data Flow

In our example we consider only rule-based components. Let ϕ define the context of operation, i.e. a formula defining some restrictions over the current state of the knowledge-base that must be satisfied before the rules of a component are explored. For example, ϕ may be given by $\varphi_{T'}$ of a component T' directly preceding the current one. Further, let there be k rules in the current component, and let ψ_i denote the joint precondition formula (a conjunction of atoms) of rule i, $i = 1, 2, \ldots, k$. In order to be sure that at least one of the rules will be fired, the following condition must hold:

$$\phi \models \psi_T, \tag{11}$$

where $\psi_T = \psi_1 \vee \psi_2 \vee \ldots \vee \psi_k$ is the disjunction of all precondition formulae of the component rules. The above restriction will be called the *funnel principle*. For intuition, if the current knowledge specification satisfies restriction defined by ϕ, then at least one of the formula preconditions must be satisfied as well.

For example, consider the connection between the component determining workday and the following it component determining operation hours. After leaving the former one, we have that $aTD = wd \vee aTD = wk$. Assuming that the time can always be read as an input value, we have $\phi = (aTD = wd \vee aTD = wk) \wedge aTM \in [0,24]$. On the other hand, the disjunction of precondition formulae $\psi_3 \vee \psi_4 \vee \psi_5 \vee \psi_6$ is given by $\psi_T = ((aTD = wd) \wedge (aTM \in [0,8] \vee aTM \in [9,17] \vee aTM \in [18,24])) \vee aTD = wk$. Obviously, the funnel condition given by (11) holds.

8   Anomalies

Answering questions about essential properties of the model, such as correctness, consistency, termination/completeness requires at the very beginning verification whether the model contains any anomalies. These anomalies may appear in the model in all five layers of the framework proposed in section 2.3. Proper detection of an anomaly can in simple case use information delivered and available within single layer of the framework, but in more complex cases it must utilize information which are derived from two or even more layers. An example of the former is deterministic deadlock (XOR split gateway followed by an AND join gateway) where only graph structure determines occurrence of an anomaly in control flow, whereas an example of the latter is potential livelock (model with infinite cycle, AND split gateway followed by OR join gateway) where besides specific graph structure also some control flow preconditions must be satisfied.

Essential anomalies which can be detected by framework are as follows:

1. Within Workflow Structure/Sequence Graph and Logical Specification of Control:
   - deadlocks;
   - livelocks;
   - races;
   - lacks of synchronization;
   - dead tasks/nodes;
   - starvation.
2. Within Dataflow Sequence Graph and Logical Specification of Data:
   - too restrictive preconditions;
   - implicit routing;
   - implicit constraints on the execution order.

Business process is *deadlocked* if activities, which are on path to the end event, are waiting infinitely for a token that can only be passed by another activity in the process. In such situation, all activities of business process are put into idle state, therefore none operations of business process are carried out. Common example of an anti-pattern where deadlock can occur is construction consisting of an XOR/OR split together with an AND join. In such anti-pattern XOR/OR split creates alternative paths that are later joined by an AND join causing that eventually process cannot make any forward progress. Examples of deterministic and potential *deadlock* are illustrated with Fig. 6 and Fig. 7.

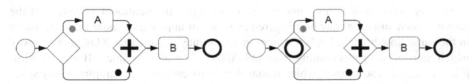

Fig. 6. *Deterministic deadlock*   **Fig. 7.** *Potential deadlock*

In the literature numerous different descriptions of *livelock* have been used, however taking into consideration business processes, only one of them can be applied, i.e. infinite execution. Infinite execution would occur in business process diagram when the individual activities of a business process model are running successfully but the model as a whole remains stuck in a loop. Such erroneous situation may occurs, in trivial case, when activity A always passes token to activity B that similarly, continuously passes a token back to process A. A *livelock* is very similar to a *deadlock*, with an exception that the states of the processes participating in the livelock continually change with regard to one another without any progress [27]. Common, significant property which joins

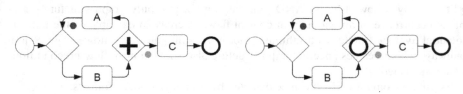

Fig. 8. *Deterministic livelock*   **Fig. 9.** *Potential livelock*

definitions of deadlock and livelock is impossibility to maintain liveness of a business process model. Examples of deterministic and potential *livelock* are illustrated with Fig. 8 and Fig. 9.

Race in business process means situation when result of the execution of business process depends on order in which activities are performed. In model depicted in Fig. 10 when the former token is before split gateway *s2* and the latter one before merge gateway *j2*, gateway *j2* is allowed to be activated since there exists direct path from gateway *s2* to gateway *j2*. Alternatively, when tokens are respectively before merge gateway *j2* and before split gateway *s3*, gateway *j2* cannot be activated unless token will leave gateway *j3*. Such two scenarios lead to totally different execution of the business process.

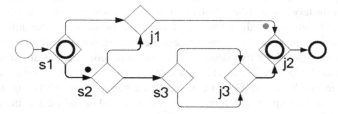

Fig. 10. Races

Lack of synchronization occurs in case of multiple, unintentional activation of the activity. Such situation may be triggered as result of appearance more than one token in the same flow branch. *Lack of synchronization* may occurs after XOR join gateway which merges two paths coming from OR/AND split gateway. Since BPMN uses implicit termination semantics, which means that a process instance completes only when each token existing in the model reaches an end event, *lack of synchronization* does not trigger *multiple termination* anomaly.

Dead task within BPMN model is an activity that can never be reached and executed. Occurrence of *dead task* is always connected with existence of *dead transition*. This anomaly could occur because of some specific input preconditions, that would always route control flow omitting one of all possible flows Fig. 14 or in simple case there is no path from start to task/node or no path from task/node to the end Fig. 13.

Starvation anomaly can be observed in message flow when specific task is waiting infinitely for a message from another task. This anomaly may arise because of existence of dead tasks in process or simply because of specific control flow which omits task responsible for sending messages between pools.

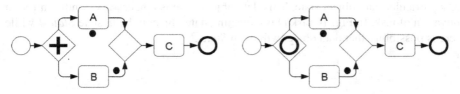

Fig. 11. Deterministic lack of synchronization   **Fig. 12.** Potential lack of synchronization

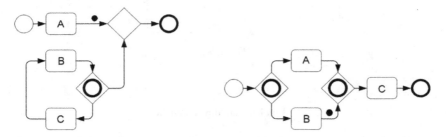

Fig. 13. Dead tasks   **Fig. 14.** Potential dead task

Fig. 15 depicts case when task *B1* of *Pool 1* potentially cannot make any forward progress due to specific input precondition which route control flow omitting task *A2* of *Pool 2*. Although control flow in *Pool 1* seems to be correct the whole process cannot be terminated. In contrast to deadlock and livelock which can be considered only within single pool, starvation is a consequence of improper interactions between pools.

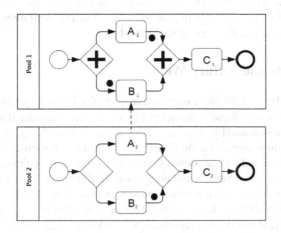

Fig. 15. Starvation

Too restrictive preconditions [28] is an error that occurs when task which is ready for for an execution from a flow control perspective is put into idle state because of waiting for a particular data object state. This data object state is a necessary condition for an activation of task. In Fig. 16 task *D* is expecting data object to be in state *State 4* while there is possibility that data object will be in *State 3*.

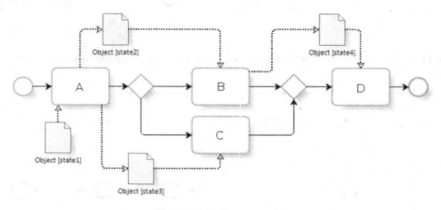

Fig. 16. Data flow anomalies

Implicit routing is an anomaly which causes that some necessary data preconditions are omitted during execution of the process. Such situation can happen in model with XOR/OR split gateway where improper path is selected, eventually resulting in omitting some data object. Although process still can be continued, final result may be wrong. Example of this problem is depicted in Fig. 16 where task *A* can change data object's state to *State 2* whereas the control flow could be still routed to task *C* by XOR split gateway. Such anomaly could be considered as a specific variant of *too restrictive precondition* error.

Implicit constraints on the execution order anomaly takes into account situations when two concurrent activities share preconditions. The problem may occur when one of these activities updates the state of the data object.

9   Conclusions and Future Work

In this paper, BPMN and BR were explored as tools for Knowledge Management. It is argued that integration of these approaches can overcome some disadvantages of these approaches when considered in separate. Four areas of knowledge specification were put forward: Workflow Specification Graph, Logical Specification of Control (missing in current BPMN), Dataflow Sequence Graph and Logical specification of Data. The ideas of knowledge representation and analysis were illustrated with an example.

The original contribution of our work consists in presenting a framework combining BPMN and BR as a tool for Knowledge Management. The papers only deals with a restricted view of Knowledge Management, where knowledge can be modeled explicitly in a formal representation, and it does not take into account any implicit or hidden knowledge.

As future work, a more complex modeling and verification approach is considered. In the case of modeling issue, we plan to implement this approach by extending one of the existing BPMN tools in order to integrate it with the HeKatE Qt Editor (HQEd) for XTT2-based Business Rules [29]. XTT2 [15] constitutes a formalized attributive language for representing rules in decision tables. Thus, the XTT2 rules (and tables) can be formally analyzed using the so-called verification HalVA framework [19] Although table-level verification can be performed with HalVA [30], the global verification is a more complex issue [31]. Our preliminary works on global verification have been presented in [32].

References

1. OMG: Business Process Model and Notation (BPMN): Version 2.0 specification. Technical Report formal/2011-01-03, Object Management Group (2011)
2. Ambler, S.W.: Business Rules (2003), http://www.agilemodeling.com/artifacts/businessRule.htm
3. Giurca, A., Gašević, D., Taveter, K. (eds.): Handbook of Research on Emerging Rule-Based Languages and Technologies: Open Solutions and Approaches. Information Science Reference, Hershey (2009)
4. OMG: Production Rule Representation RFP. Technical report, Object Management Group (2003)
5. OMG: Semantics of Business Vocabulary and Business Rules (SBVR). Technical Report dtc/06-03-02, Object Management Group (2006)
6. Kluza, K., Nalepa, G.J., Łysik, Ł.: Visual inference specification methods for modularized rulebases. Overview and integration proposal. In: Nalepa, G.J., Baumeister, J. (eds.) Proceedings of the 6th Workshop on Knowledge Engineering and Software Engineering (KESE6) at the 33rd German Conference on Artificial Intelligence, Karlsruhe, Germany, September 21, pp. 6–17 (2010)
7. Dijkman, R.M., Dumas, M., Ouyang, C.: Formal semantics and automated analysis of BPMN process models. Preprint 7115. Technical report, Queensland University of Technology, Brisbane, Australia (2007)
8. Lam, V.S.W.: Formal analysis of BPMN models: a NuSMV-based approach. International Journal of Software Engineering and Knowledge Engineering 20, 987–1023 (2010)
9. Ouyang, C., van der Aalst, W.M.P., Dumas, M., ter Hofstede, A.H.: Translating BPMN to BPEL. Technical report, Faculty of Information Technology, Queensland University of Technology, GPO Box 2434, Brisbane QLD 4001, Australia Department of Technology Management, Eindhoven University of Technolog y, GPO Box 513, NL-5600 MB, The Netherlands (2006)
10. Wynn, M., Verbeek, H., van der Aalst, W.M.P., ter Hofstede, A.H., Edmond, D.: Business process verification – finally a reality! Business Process Management Journal 1, 74–92 (2009)
11. Ligęza, A.: BPMN – a logical model and property analysis. Decision Making in Manufacturing and Services 5(1-2), 57–67 (2011)
12. Ligęza, A., Nalepa, G.J.: Knowledge representation with granular attributive logic for XTT-based expert systems. In: Wilson, D.C., Sutcliffe, G.C.J., FLAIRS (eds.) FLAIRS-20: Proceedings of the 20th International Florida Artificial Intelligence Research Society Conference: Key West, Florida, May 7-9, pp. 530–535. Florida Artificial Intelligence Research Society, AAAI Press, Menlo Park, California (2007)

13. Ligęza, A., Nalepa, G.J.: A study of methodological issues in design and development of rule-based systems: proposal of a new approach. Wiley Interdisciplinary Reviews: Data Mining and Knowledge Discovery 1, 117–137 (2011)
14. Nalepa, G.J.: Semantic Knowledge Engineering. A Rule-Based Approach. Wydawnictwa AGH, Kraków (2011)
15. Nalepa, G.J., Ligęza, A.: HeKatE methodology, hybrid engineering of intelligent systems. International Journal of Applied Mathematics and Computer Science 20, 35–53 (2010)
16. Szpyrka, M.: Design and analysis of rule-based systems with adder designer. In: Cotta, C., Reich, S., Schaefer, R., Ligęza, A. (eds.) Knowledge-Driven Computing: Knowledge Engineering and Intelligent Computations. SCI, vol. 102, pp. 255–271. Springer, Heidelberg (2008)
17. Szpyrka, M., Szmuc, T.: Design and verification of rule-based systems for Alvis models. In: Skowron, A., Suraj, Z. (eds.) Rough Sets and Intelligent Systems. ISRL, vol. 43, pp. 539–558. Springer, Heidelberg (2013)
18. Nalepa, G.J., Kluza, K.: UML representation for rule-based application models with XTT2-based business rules. International Journal of Software Engineering and Knowledge Engineering (IJSEKE) 22, 485–524 (2012)
19. Kluza, K., Maślanka, T., Nalepa, G.J., Ligęza, A.: Proposal of representing BPMN diagrams with XTT2-based business rules. In: Brazier, F.M.T., Nieuwenhuis, K., Pavlin, G., Warnier, M., Badica, C. (eds.) Intelligent Distributed Computing V. SCI, vol. 382, pp. 243–248. Springer, Heidelberg (2011)
20. Bobek, S., Kaczor, K., Nalepa, G.J.: Overview of rule inference algorithms for structured rule bases. Gdansk University of Technology Faculty of ETI Annals 18, 57–62 (2010)
21. Nalepa, G.J., Bobek, S., Ligęza, A., Kaczor, K.: Algorithms for rule inference in modularized rule bases. In: Bassiliades, N., Governatori, G., Paschke, A. (eds.) RuleML 2011 - Europe. LNCS, vol. 6826, pp. 305–312. Springer, Heidelberg (2011)
22. Baki, B., Bouzid, M., Ligeza, A., Mouaddib, A.I.: A centralized planning technique with temporal constraints and uncertainty for multi-agent systems. J. Exp. Theor. Artif. Intell. 18, 331–364 (2006)
23. Ligęza, A.: Logical Foundations for Rule-Based Systems. Springer, Heidelberg (2006)
24. Szpyrka, M.: Exclusion rule-based systems – case study. In: International Multiconference on Computer Science and Information Technology, Wisla, Poland, vol. 3, pp. 237–242 (2008)
25. Ligęza, A., Szpyrka, M.: Reduction of tabular systems. In: Rutkowski, L., Siekmann, J.H., Tadeusiewicz, R., Zadeh, L.A. (eds.) ICAISC 2004. LNCS (LNAI), vol. 3070, pp. 903–908. Springer, Heidelberg (2004)
26. Negnevitsky, M.: Artificial Intelligence. A Guide to Intelligent Systems. Addison-Wesley, Harlow (2002) ISBN 0-201-71159-1
27. Mogul, J.C., Ramakrishnan, K.K.: Eliminating receive livelock in an interrupt-driven kernel. ACM Trans. Comput. Syst. 15, 217–252 (1997)
28. Awad, A., Decker, G., Lohmann, N.: Diagnosing and repairing data anomalies in process models. In: Rinderle-Ma, S., Sadiq, S., Leymann, F. (eds.) BPM 2009. LNBIP, vol. 43, pp. 5–16. Springer, Heidelberg (2010)
29. Kluza, K., Kaczor, K., Nalepa, G.J.: Enriching business processes with rules using the Oryx BPMN editor. In: Rutkowski, L., Korytkowski, M., Scherer, R., Tadeusiewicz, R., Zadeh, L.A., Zurada, J.M. (eds.) ICAISC 2012, Part II. LNCS, vol. 7268, pp. 573–581. Springer, Heidelberg (2012)
30. Nalepa, G.J., Bobek, S., Ligęza, A., Kaczor, K.: HalVA - rule analysis framework for XTT2 rules. In: Bassiliades, N., Governatori, G., Paschke, A. (eds.) RuleML 2011 - Europe. LNCS, vol. 6826, pp. 337–344. Springer, Heidelberg (2011)

31. Kluza, K., Nalepa, G.J., Szpyrka, M., Ligęza, A.: Proposal of a hierarchical approach to formal verification of BPMN models using Alvis and XTT2 methods. In: Canadas, J., Nalepa, G.J., Baumeister, J. (eds.) 7th Workshop on Knowledge Engineering and Software Engineering (KESE 2011) at the Conference of the Spanish Association for Artificial Intelligence (CAEPIA 2011), La Laguna (Tenerife), Spain, November 10, pp. 15–23 (2011)
32. Szpyrka, M., Nalepa, G.J., Ligęza, A., Kluza, K.: Proposal of formal verification of selected BPMN models with Alvis modeling language. In: Brazier, F.M.T., Nieuwenhuis, K., Pavlin, G., Warnier, M., Badica, C. (eds.) Intelligent Distributed Computing V. SCI, vol. 382, pp. 249–255. Springer, Heidelberg (2011)

Validation Model for Discovered
Web User Navigation Patterns

Mieczysław Owoc[1] and Paweł Weichbroth[2]

[1] Wroclaw University of Economics, Department of Artificial Intelligence Systems, Poland
mieczyslaw.owoc@ue.wroc.pl
[2] University of Economics in Katowice, Department of Knowledge Engineering, Poland
pawel1739@gmail.com

Abstract. Information society with huge number of everyday acting partici-pants becomes valuable source of surfer behavior research. Especially web server logs can be used for discovering knowledge useful in different areas. Knowledge acquired from web server logs in order to generate solutions has to be validated. The aim of this paper is presentation of web usage mining as a rather complex process and in this context elaboration of validation model. On a basis of iterative and hybrid approach to discover user navigation patterns the concept of generated knowledge validation model is proposed. Some experi-ments on real website allow to define a new method of generated association rules refinement including specific knowledge validation techniques. Some con-straints as discovered knowledge validation criteria are defined.

1 Introduction

Evolution of designing and developing Web sites from static to dynamic approach has enabled easy updates. Furthermore, intensive development and proliferation of WWW network resulted in other new modeling methods. It's obvious - being recognized and visited in the Web means that the content is up-to-date and satisfies its visitors. Wide-spread scope of content topics shared and presented on the Web site affects the size and depth level of its structures. This results in negative impression of presented con-tent and weaker usability.

Usability of delivered information and knowledge depends on dynamically created user profiles as a result of Web mining and particularly user navigation patterns dis-covery process. Knowledge acquired from web server log files in order to generate navigation patterns embraces useful as well as non-relevant association rules and has to be validated. Therefore the ultimate   goal of this research is presentation of the method allowing for generated knowledge refinement.

These are very specific features of Web Mining procedures: temporal and massive data input, big differentiation of user types. They have direct impact on generated knowledge about website content and forms and in turn should be considered in Knowledge Validation (KV) framework. List of constrains useful in knowledge vali-dation processes includes: page-view duration, total session time, include and exclude items, support and confidence and time and date. All the mentioned constraints should

E. Mercier-Laurent and D. Boulanger (Eds.): AI4KM 2012, IFIP AICT 422, pp. 38–52, 2014.

be considered as potential criteria of discovered knowledge about web surfer navigation patterns. On the other hand the considered constraints are useful in search space reduction in a case of frequent files. Actually the application supporting the discussed problem with mentioned above constraints has been implemented.

The paper is structured as follows. After presentation of related work, crucial definitions essential for this survey are proposed. Results of prepared experiments consisting of relationships between components are demonstrated in the next section. Crucial procedure for formulating knowledge discovery in such environment is investigated later. The paper ends with itemizing of conclusions and considering future research.

2   Related Works

Recommendation systems help to address information overload by using discovered web users navigation patterns knowledge gained from web server log files. A problem for association rule recommendation systems (RS) is placed in dataset. It is often sparse because for any given user visit or object rank, it is difficult to find a sufficient number of common items in multiple user profiles. As a consequence, a RPS system has difficulty to generate recommendations, especially in collaborative filtering applications.

In [1] to solve above problem, some standard dimensionality reduction techniques were applied due to improved performance. This paper presents two different experiments. Sarwar et al. have explored one technology called Singular Value Decomposition (SVD) to reduce the dimensionality of recommender system databases. The second experiment compares the effectiveness of the two recommender systems at predicting *top-n* lists, based on a real-life customer purchase database from an *e*-Commerce site. Finally, results suggest that SVD can meet many of the challenges of recommender systems, under certain conditions.

Ad hoc exclusion of some potential useful items can be one of known deficiencies of this and other reduction of dimensions solutions hence they will not appear in the final results. Two solutions that address this problem were proposed by Fu et al. in [2]. The first solution assumes to rank all the discovered rules based on the degree of intersection between the left-hand side (antecedent) and active session of the user. Then, the *SurfLen* (client-server system) generates the top *k* recommendations. In addition to deal with sparse datasets - if users browsing histories intersect rarely, the system is unable to produce recommendations - the algorithm for ranking association rules was presented. The second solution takes advantage of collaborative filtering. The system is able to find "close neighbors" who represent similar interest to an active user. Then, based on that, a list of recommendations is generated.

Many collaborative filtering systems have few user ranks (opinions) compared to the large number of available documents. In this paper [3], Sarwar et al. define and implement a integration model for content-based ranks into a collaborative filtering. In addition, metrics for assessing the effectiveness filter bots and a system were identified and evaluated.

In the paper [4], Lin et al. a collaborative recommendation system based on association rules framework was proposed. The framework provides two measures for evaluating the association expressed by a rule: confidence and support. Moreover, the system generates association rules among users as well as among items.

3   Definitions

The web site space can be considered as universe U which consists of a sequential sets (P_i) where $i=1...M$. Each of sets P_i corresponds to unique user session where as each element of P_i is user's request for single page shared by a web site. We consider only such subsets A of P_i ($A \subseteq P_i \subseteq U$) which appeared often enough. The frequency of subset A is defined as *support* (or support ratio) denoted as $support(A)=|\{i ; A \subseteq P_i\}| / M$. A "frequent" set is a set which support satisfies the minimum support value, denoted as *minsupport*. It is a user dependent value, often defined as cut-off as well.

We developed and applied an Apriori-like algorithm to mine frequent itemsets that is based on level-wise search. It scans a database recursively – a growing collections A are generated using smaller collections, especially the subsets of A of cardinality $|A|-1$, called hipersubsets. Formally, a set B is a hipersubset of a set A if and only if $\exists_{a \in A} A = B \cup \{a\}$.

An *association rule* is an implication of the form $A \rightarrow B$, where $B \subseteq P_i \subseteq U$ and $A \cap B = \emptyset$. The support of a rule is the percentage sessions in P that contains $A \cup B$. It can be seen as an estimate of the probability $Pr(A \cup B)$. The rule support is computed as follows: $support(A \rightarrow B) = support(A \cup B) / M$. The confidence of a rule $A \rightarrow B$ is the percentage of sessions in P that contain A also contain B. It can be seen as an estimate of the conditional probability $Pr(B \backslash A)$. The rule confidence is computed as follows: $confidence(A \rightarrow B) = support(A \cup B) / support(A)$. Confidence of the disjoint couple of sets $\{A,B\}$ can be read B under the condition A. If its value exceeds an arbitrarily determined level of minimum confidence (also defined by user), denoted as minconfidence, the pair $\{A,B\}$ will express an association rule $A \rightarrow B$.

Given a session data set D, the problem of mining association rules is to discover *relevant* (or *strong*) association rules in D which satisfy support and confidence greater than (or equal) to the user-specified minimum support and minimum confidence. Here, the keyword is "relevant" (or "strong") which means, taking into account a user's point of view, association rule mining process is complete.

Theorem 1: *Each subset of the frequent set is a frequent set.*

Proof 1: Let A be an arbitrary frequent set and $B \subseteq A$ be a subset of A. The set A is frequent, thus $support(A)=|\{i ; A \subseteq P_i\}| / M \geq$ minsupport. Since B is a subset of A, we have that $A \subseteq P_i \Rightarrow B \subseteq P_i$, thus $support(B) = |\{i ; B \subseteq P_i\}| / M \geq |\{i ; A \subseteq P_i\}| / M \geq$ *minsupport*. Therefore the set B is also frequent which ends the proof.   □

Theorem 2: *If $A \rightarrow B \cup C$ is a relevant association rule (A, B, C – pair wise distinct), then also $A \rightarrow B$, $A \rightarrow C$, $A \cup B \rightarrow C$ and $A \cup C \rightarrow B$ are relevant association rules.*

Proof 2: Let $A{\rightarrow}B \cup C$ be an user- relevant association rule. Then *minconfidence* $\leq$ *confidence*(A,B$\cup$C) = *support*(A$\cup$B$\cup$C) / *support*(A).   □

Let us consider $A{\cup}B \subseteq A{\cup}B{\cup}C$. Having in mind theorem 1, we get *support*(A) $\geq$ *support*(A$\cup$B) $\geq$ *support*(A$\cup$B$\cup$C). As a result, *confidence*(A,B) = *support*(A$\cup$B) / *support*(A) $\geq$ *support* {A$\cup$B$\cup$C} / *support*(A) $\geq$ *minconfidence*. The set {$A{\cup}B$} is frequent, so $A{\rightarrow}B$ is a relevant association rule. On the other hand, *confidence*(A$\cup$B,C) = *support*(A$\cup$B$\cup$C) /*support*(A$\cup$B) $\geq$ *support* {A$\cup$B$\cup$C}/*support*(A) $\geq$ *minconfidence*, because of a frequency of a set A$\cup$B$\cup$C, A$\cup$B$\rightarrow$C is also a relevant association rule. Consequently, proofs for rules $A{\rightarrow}C$ and $A{\cup}C{\rightarrow}B$ are similar.

Two additional interpretation of introduced earlier constraints should be presented: page view duration and total session time. *Page view duration* is calculated as a difference between the page view start time of the next page minus the page view start of the previous page. *Total session time* is calculated as a sum of duration times referencing to particular elements of frequent sets without the last element.

4   Phases of Web Usage Mining Process

Tools commonly used in data mining are applied in Web Internet resources analysis. The main fundamental task is pattern usage discovering available in the Internet. Such knowledge can be the basics of recommendation systems in order to improve functionality (cross-selling) and usability (easier access) to Internet portals and services. First holistic and integrated (incl. different KDD steps) model of Web Usage Mining process was proposed by Cooley et al. in [5]. Afterwards, Srivastava et al. in [6] extended this model and apparently distinguished three phases: (*1*) preprocessing, (*2*) pattern discovery and (*3*) pattern analysis. This model has been widely applied – the references can be found e.g. in [7-14].

This model is complex and practice- oriented solution of solving problem of knowledge discovery from Web data repositories. The following particular tasks are subordinated to the mentioned phases. It allows for clear defining of user requirements from its point of view including data format and expected analysis results. However it seems to be reasonable to extend the model by data collection (see Fig. 1). During this phase data sources are defined based on data entry type and the same selection of necessary variables necessary variables including planned analysis are performed.

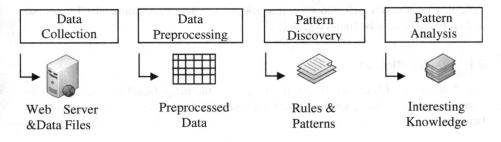

Fig. 1. Extended Web Usage Mining process

Two dimensions can be defined in this model: e.g.:

- phase – definition of data-oriented actions (tasks),
- object – definition of data types.

The whole process consists of the four phases; first three can be considered as machine-aided while the last one is human - expert oriented. In this frames, similarly to CRISP-DM, specialized tasks are separate. We can distinguish four phases in web usage mining process:

1. Data collection, usage data can be collected from various sources like Web Server (e.g. log files), Client side (e.g. cookie files) or proxy servers.
2. Data preprocessing, this phase concerns raw data files which often includes web server log files. There can be distinguish following tasks: (a) data cleaning and filtering, (b) de-spidering, (c) user identification, (d) session identification and (e) path completion.
3. Pattern discovery, it can be seen as the data mining step when comparing to KDD. The following methods and techniques can be applied: (a) statistical techniques, (b) association rules, (c) sequential patterns, (d) clustering and (e) classification.
4. Pattern analysis, where domain expert evaluates discovered knowledge and optionally does performance assessment. If necessary, some modeling methods and techniques can be applied, such as clustering and classification.

In the next section, we refer to each phase briefly, emphasizing the most important issues which can be seen as a part of knowledge validation challenge.

5   Experiments on Real Web Sources

In Web Usage Mining the major sources of data are Web Server and application server log files. We only used Web Server log files which are a set of Web users' activity record, registered by onet.pl - one of the most recognized Web portals in Poland. Web Server log files contain full history of access requests to files, shared on the Web Server. Usually, http server vendors apply Common Log Format (CLF) to the log files associated with http protocol service. This format was developed by CERN and NCSA as the component of http protocol. According to this format, there are seven variables which were selected to be recorded. Complete description of CLF format and its variables can be found e.g. in [15].

5.1   Data Collection

The data format of Web Server log files is specific in onet.pl (see Tab. 1) and includes seven variables. Sample entries, which represent Web users' activity, are presented below.

Table 1. The structure of raw Web Server log files

Row	Variable					
	$\Diamond$	$\spadesuit$	$\circ$	$\square$	$\triangle$	$\clubsuit$
1	140229	8654	2166	2	5723	724
2	140229	8654	2166	2	5723	725
3	140229	8655	2227	124	5086	8052
4	140229	8641	2310	26	1587	1007
5	140229	8654	2227	124	5086	8151

$\Diamond$ time of the session, $\spadesuit$ session ID, $\circ$ user ID, $\square$ service ID, $\triangle$ subservice ID, $\clubsuit$ html file ID.

In our research, we used a web server log file which covers five hours of system activity - from 2PM to 7PM on 29th December 2008. We also want to notice the fact that dedicated solutions (e.g. scripts, services) on the Web Server side were implemented. They were intended to reduce globally useless data (e.g. spiders activity). In this case, we can determine that in the phase of data collection, some preprocessing tasks took(or have taken) place.

5.2   Data Preprocessing

We used Linux operating system to operate on the raw data. To carry out this phase, a simple script in awk language was implemented to process the log files. Firstly, from six available variables just two were selected ($\spadesuit$ $\clubsuit$) and separated from others. Secondly, these two were sorted accordingly to the session time ($\Diamond$) and session identifier ($\spadesuit$). Thirdly, the sessions, where only one html page was requested by the users, were deleted from the log files. In such way, there were 2.132.581 unique sessions observed which would be taken into account in our experiments. The size of the log file was reduced from 4.018.853 KB to 512.934 KB. Again, it can be noticed that necessary tasks which typically had to be performed in the second phase were very limited. In addition, the source data was supplemented with text files which contained dictionaries corresponding to the URL name (e.g. 724 denotes to [www]). Finally, the processed file had the following format (session id, URL name):

- 8654 [www]
- 8654 [sport.html]
- 8654 [games.html]

5.3   Pattern Discovery

In this phase, frequent Web users' access patterns are discovered from sessions. A few algorithms have been proposed to discover frequent itemsets. During the literature study of KDD, we came across the algorithms such as AprioriAll [16], GSP [17], SPADE [18], PrefixSpan [19], ItemsetCode [20].

We have decided to use Apriori algorithm, although it is not the most efficient and recent one. It is suitable solution for our problem since we can make it more efficient by pruning most of the candidate sequences generated in each iteration. This can be done because of given constraints and requirements. We cannot assume that for every subsequent pair of pages in a sequence the former one must have a hyperlink to the latter one. The justification of that assumption is the fact that we do not have full access to the Web Server repository. Some files could have been deleted, moved to the archives or simply changed by the provider. On the other hand, the frequency of content update can be seen as very high - we have to keep in mind that approximately 7 million users per day visit this Web portal. So, it is obvious that the content hosted on the portal must be up-to-date. Furthermore and what seems to be the most important, the engine of recommendation system is able to generate links directly on web pages and does not require knowledge of inner-oriented structure and relationships of individual web pages.

Let $P = \{p_1, p_2, \dots, p_m\}$ be a set of web pages, called items. Database D represents a set of reconstructed sessions $S = \{s_1, s_2, \dots, s_n\}$. Each session s_n is a subset of P where $s_n \subseteq P$, called itemset.

We implemented Apriori algorithm (Algorithm 1) where input is a database of sessions D and output is a set of frequent sequences L.

```
(1)  L₁ = find_frequent_1-itemsets(D);
(2)  for (k = 2; L_{k-1} = ∅; k++) {
(3)      C_k = apriori_gen(L_{k-1});
(4)      for each transaction T ∈ D
(5)          C_t = subset(C_k, t);
(6)          for each candidate c ∈ C_t
(7)              c.count++; }
(8)      L_k = {c ∈ C_k | c.count ≥ min_sup} }
(9)  return L = U_k L_k
```

```
procedure apriori_gen(L_{k-1} : frequent(k - 1) -itemsets
(1) for each itemset l₁ ∈ L_{k-1} and
(2) for each itemset l₂ ∈ L_{k-1}
(3)     if(l₁[1] = l₂[1]) ∧ (l₁[2] = l₂[2]) ∧...∧ (l₁[k - 2] =
l₂[k - 2]) ∧ (l₁[k - 1] < l₂[k - 1])
(4)     then {
(5)         c = l₁ ⊠ l₂;
(6)         if has_infrequent_subset(c, L_{k-1}) then
(7)             delete c;
(8)         else add c to C_k; }
(9) return C_k;
```

```
procedure has_infrequent_subset(c: candidate k- itemset);
L_{k-1}: frequent(k - 1)- itemsets;
(1)     for each(k - 1)-subset s ∈ c
(2)         if s ∉ L_{k-1} then
(3)             return True else
(4)             return False;
```

As a result the program returns frequent sequences with support for each. A simple example of a three element sequence is given below.

[www];[info]/science/item.html;[info]/world/item.html;0,02011

Interpretation of this particular sequence may be expressed in these words: *"Over 2 percent of anonymous users between 2PM and 7PM on 29th December 2008, first requested access to the home page, next opened science section then world section".*

Based on the set of frequent sequences L we are able to generate sequential association rules (SAR). In this scenario, a simple algorithm was developed (Algorithm 2). Let $R = \{ r_1, r_2, \dots , r_m \}$ be a set of SAR. In each rule antecedent (body of the rule, left side) and consequent (head of the rule, right side) must not be replaced. In other words, it guarantees the precise order of each element in the sequence. Also, a user is requested to provide the minimum confidence (*minconfidence*) threshold.

```
(1)  R={}
(2)  for all I ∈ L do
(3)     R = R ∪ I →{}
(4)     C₁ = {{i} | i ∈ I};
(5)     k:= 1;
(6)     while Cₖ ≠ {} do
(7)        //extract all consequents of confident association
rules
(8)        Hₖ := {X ∈ Cₖ | confidence(I \ X ⇒ X, D) ≥
min_conf}
(9)        //generate new candidate consequents
(10)       for all X, Y ∈ Hₖ, X[i] = Y[i] for 1 ≤ i ≤ k - 1
and X[k] < Y[k] do
(11)          I = X ∪ {Y[k]}
(12)          if ∀J ⊂ I, |J| = k : J ∈ Hₖ then
(13)             Cₖ₊₁ = Cₖ₊₁ ∪ I
(14)          end if
(15)       end for
(16)       k++
(17)    end while
(18)    //cumulate all association rules
(19)    R := R ∪ {I \ X →X | X ∈ H₁ ∪ ⋯ ∪ Hₖ}
(20) end for
```

The set of sequential association rules R is achieved as a result. We give a simple example of such results, based on previously given frequent sequence.

r_1:{www};{science.html}→{world.html}; 0,02011; 0,964

r_2:{www}→{science.html}{world.html}; 0,02011; 0,652

r_3:{www}→{science.html}; 0,0305; 0,00209

r_4:{www}→{world.html}; 0,0294; 0,00152

Interpretation of the first rule may be expressed in these words: *"There is a 96,4% chance that a user who visited {www} and {science.html} pages, after them would also visit {world.html}"*. In other words, the value of confidence ratio shows degree of rule reliability.

In this way we have shown that attractiveness of discovered knowledge is evaluated by two measures: support and confidence ratio. They are both specified by a user - it guarantees a definitive result.

5.4   Results of Pattern Analysis

The aim of the research was to discover frequent sequences which represent web user navigation paths. In first iteration the level of support and confidence ration was respectively 0,01 and 0,9. Table 2 shows top ten (taking into account the highest support, denoted by percentage) one element frequent itemsets.

Table 2. Itemsets and its support

Itemset	Support	Itemset	Support
www	78.48%	email/logout.html	14,09%
email/login.html	27.08%	email/folder/delete.html	10,80%
email/folder.html	25.49%	sport/football/news.html	10,22%
info/world/item.html	20.27%	sport/formula one/news.html	9,88%
email/folder/open.html	15,01%	info/homeland/item.html	9,18%

For instance, human interpretation of such knowledge might be expressed in these words: "Over 27 percent of sessions include a page enabling user to log on the email service".

Entire volume of frequent sequences draws picture of the most popular content of the web portal. First conclusion which arises from this analysis to divide and group discovered knowledge to two different categories: (1) service- oriented and (2) content- oriented. First category relates to the hosted services via the web portal like email, advertisements, auctions, games, video on demand, dates. Second category relates to the shared content like information, news and plots. In this kind of the web portal, we are not able to recommend anything on the home page unless we violate user's privacy. On the other hand, keeping in mind high level of usability and visibility, the objects' arrangement should remain static. Therefore service- oriented content will not be considered to be recommended. Also, over 60% of discovered knowledge concerns users' actions while using email service. As an example let us deliberate on sequence below:

- [www];[email]/login.html;[email]/inbox.html;[email]/new-message.html;[email]/logout.html

Such knowledge is useless for recommendation engine since it simply presents obvious and feasible actions during common session, restricted to single service. In this case, we decided to decrease the confidence ratio to four additional levels: 0,8; 0,7; 0,6 and 0,5. Table 3 shows the volume of discovered sequential association rules for five different levels of confidence ratio.

Table 3. The volume of SAR

| Number of items | Number of SAR | | | | |
| | Confidence | | | | |
	◊	□	○	θ	⌂
2	65	79	95	118	142
3	169	197	254	349	430
4	196	225	315	480	585
5	114	132	209	328	407
6	28	32	68	111	146
total	**572**	**665**	**941**	**1386**	**1710**

minimum confidence: ◊ 0.9 □ 0.8 ○ 0.7 θ 0.6 ⌂ 0.5

It can be noticed easily that simple and apparent indication has occurred - on every lower level of confidence the number of rules have increased. Finally, for 0,5 confidence more than 1710 rules were discovered. These 1138 rules (difference between 0,5 and 0,9 confidence) are not likely to bring further knowledge of web data usage. Nevertheless, some interesting itemset groups were observed which will be added to knowledge base. An example of useful sequence is presented below:

• [www];[sport/football/news.html];[sport/formula one/news.html];[info/homeland/item.html]

At this point, previously undiscovered knowledge shall be reviewed and compared to that, which is already stored in knowledge base. Moreover, if discovered knowledge was transferred to knowledge base and its resources are engaged by recommendation engine, we are able to track the process of knowledge validation. It means that two measures recall and precision will determine degree of knowledge adequacy. In other words, we are able to determine quality of recommendations produced by the system.

Another step, which is possible to undertake and promises to discover new rules, is to decrease the value of the minimum support. There is no general instruction with suggested value in any scenario. It is a subjective issue and relies on expert intuition and experience. In the next two iterations, we set up the value of minimum support respectively on 0,05 and 0,001. In our opinion it should be compromise between time-consumption and hardware requirements constraints.

Table 4. Frequent sequences for three different minimum support values

| Number of items | Frequent sequences | | | | |
| | Quantity | | | Change ($◊$=100) | |
	$◊$	$□$	$○$	$□$	$○$
1	64	103	276	61%	331%
2	167	307	1522	84%	811%
3	177	438	3279	147%	1753%
4	418	338	3768	-19%	801%
5	40	154	2625	285%	6463%
6	14	44	1193	214%	8421%
7	0	6	373	-	-
8	0	0	73	-	-
9	0	0	5	-	-
total	**880**	**1390**	**13114**	**58%**	**1390%**

minimum support: $◊$ 0.01 $□$ 0.005 $○$ 0.001

The program was executed under Eclipse environment with Java version 1.6.0 on IBM PC x86 computer with an Intel Core2 Quad processor 2.4 GHz and 2 GB Random Access Memory. Execution times are 55 minutes, 2 hours 30 minutes and 28 hours 16 minutes respectively to lower value of the minimum support. The determination of the factors influencing on the effectiveness of algorithm covers an remarkable research question. Unfortunately, we are not able to put forward straightforward answers.

Let us examine new sequences discovered throughout these two independent iterations. Though, we only focus on the set ($○$) because it is a superset of the other two sets ($◊$ and $□$). First of all, we can notice a enormous growth - almost 14 times larger set of frequent sequences was discovered, when value of minimum support was set up on 0,001 comparing to 0,01. This fact is worth deep consideration however our attention would be focused on the longest nine- items sequences which one of them is presented below:

- [www];
- [dates]/visitors.html; [dates]/email.html; [dates]/email/new.html;
  [dates]/index.html; [dates]/user-page/index.html; [dates]/user-page/index/k.html;
  [dates]/user-page/album.html;   [dates]/album.html

We can definitely state that the results are unsatisfactory. The longest sequences present the interactions within one hosted service. The same situation can be observed taking into account eight- and seven- items sequences. Just six sequences in the latter one would possibly classified to be added to the knowledge base. These sequences present interesting navigation paths like:

- [www];
- [business]/pap.html; [business]/news.html; [business]/company/market.html;
- [info]/homeland/item.html;   [info]/world/item.html;   [business]/stock   market/news.html

We asked ourselves: was it necessary to decrease value of minimum support having in mind program time-consumption? Even some portion of discovered knowledge might be useful, there is a great risk that it would become inadequate. This situation happens when the content update is very often. Discovered sequences are not longer available to reach because its items (represented by links) are simply replaced by others.

In our approach we anticipated the last step which can help to discover relevant knowledge from web server log files. The assumption is simple: the domain expert shall determine service- oriented itemsets and any other irrelevant items and exclude them from the data. Then, the data is preprocessed again and process of web usage mining starts one more. Preliminary experiments have confirmed presented model in the next section.

6   A Concept of a Validation Procedure

In this section, we present an iterative model for discovering and validating web user navigation patterns. General assumptions of this procedure are as follows:

- Input data are the results of the previous described steps (data are collected then preprocessed to allow for discovering patterns).
- The procedure consists of four steps where defined confidence and support parameters are changed in order to exclude irrelevant sets.
- A domain expert is responsible for the validation generated knowledge base. He plays crucial role in order to exclude irrelevant sets – furthermore called also as an user.
- The procedure is iterative what denotes active participant of the expert on different steps of validation with possibility of starting the procedure from the beginning.

The graphical form of the procedure is presented in Figure 2.

In the first step, initial values for minimum support and confidence are set by a user. Next, the pattern discovery process is performed and thus analyzed and evaluated by a user. Positively assessed knowledge is put into the knowledge base from where inference engine produces a list of recommendations to active user sessions. The effectiveness of this process can be measured by two metrics: recall and precision. Therefore the knowledge base is validated by them, expressing the degree of its adequacy. If the values of metrics are not satisfied, in the second step the confidence value is decreased.

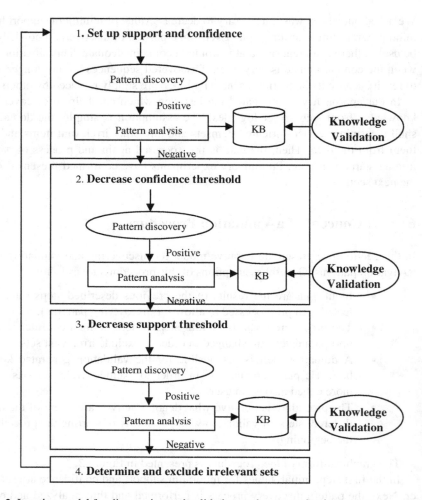

Fig. 2. Iterative model for discovering and validating web user navigation patterns

Similarly, in the third step, a user can decrease the minimum support value. If even in this case, values of evaluation metrics are not satisfied, a user specifies additional constraint by excluding sets which are irrelevant. If results are not satisfactory, the process can be started from the beginning.

7   Conclusions

In this paper, we introduced an interactive a user-driven model which addresses problem of validating web user navigation patterns. Experiments performed on web server file logs show that the model is useful and in some circumstances can be used in large-scale web site environments.

Conclusions based on our presented results can be divided into two groups. In the first group we have the confirmation of the general properties of the method of association rules, and detailed observations of Agrawal and Srikant algorithm and its implementation in the form of application.

Thanks to the cut-off at the level of support we discovered only the strong association rules. The number and size of the discovered association rules increase with the growth of the minimal support ratio. Cutting off the irrelevant sets of frequent factor support was implemented to be done at first, so that level has decisive influence on the uptime. Confidence factor, which determines the level at which the second cut-off is made after pruning of low-level support sets, has a significant impact on the final number of the rules, but the change of this factor does not affect the uptime. Number of the elements of the association rules determines the strength of correlation (the more elements in the antecedent of a rule, the correlation is weaker, the more elements in the consequent of a rule, the correlation is stronger). This, in addition to the actual values of support and confidence, has a decisive influence on ordering rules in the final results.

The second group of the conclusions concerns the study – particular data that have been examined and usage of a multistage pruning. The primary study revealed structure of the portal. In particular, there were extracted two independent services which have extremely strong, static navigation paths. These services have their own audience and introduce artifacts which hinders the proper analysis. Furthermore, the hierarchical structure of information service is reflected in the extracted association rules.

Despite the relatively slight reduction in the size of data, allows to significantly reduce the parameters in the secondary study and obtain more relevant knowledge. In summary, the multistage pruning seems to be accurate for use in the analysis that uses method of association rules. In addition, the method itself seems to give satisfactory results in discovering web users' navigation paths.

References

1. Sarwar, B., Karypis, G., Konstan, J., Riedl, J.: Application of Dimensionality Reduction in Recommender System - A Case Study. In: ACM WEBKDD Workshop. ACM (2000)
2. Fu, X., Budzik, J., Hammond, K.J.: Mining navigation history for recommendation. In: Proceedings of the 5th International Conference on Intelligent User Interfaces, pp. 106–112. ACM, New Orleans (2000)
3. Sarwar, B.M., Konstan, J.A., Borchers, A., Herlocker, J., Miller, B., Riedl, J.: Using filtering agents to improve prediction quality in the GroupLens research collaborative filtering system. In: Proceedings of the 1998 ACM Conference on Computer Supported Cooperative Work, pp. 345–354. ACM, Seattle (1998)
4. Lin, W., Alvarez, S.A., Ruiz, C.: Efficient Adaptive-Support Association Rule Mining for Recommender Systems. Data Mining and Knowledge Discovery 6, 83–105 (2002)
5. Cooley, R., Mobasher, B., Srivastava, J.: Web Mining: Information and Pattern Discovery on the World Wide Web. In: Proceedings of the 9th International Conference on Tools with Artificial Intelligence. IEEE Computer Society (1997)

6. Srivastava, J., Cooley, R., Deshpande, M., Tan, P.N.: Web usage mining: discovery and applications of usage patterns from web data. ACM SIGKDD Explorations Newsletter 1, 12–23 (2000)
7. Kosala, R., Blockel, H.: Web mining research: A survey. Newsletter of the Special Interest Group (SIG) on Knowledge Discovery and Data Mininig SIGKDD: GKDD Explorations 1 (2000)
8. Eirinaki, M., Vazirgiannis, M.: Web mining for web personalization. ACM Trans. Internet Technology 3, 1–27 (2003)
9. Mobasher, B., Dai, H., Luo, T., Nakagawa, M.: Discovery and Evaluation of Aggregate Usage Profiles for Web Personalization. Data Mining and Knowledge Discovery 6, 61–82 (2002)
10. Pierrakos, D., Paliouras, G., Papatheodorou, C., Spyropoulos, C.D.: Web Usage Mining as a Tool for Personalization: A Survey. User Modeling and User-Adapted Interaction 13, 311–372 (2003)
11. Facca, F.M., Lanzi, P.L.: Mining interesting knowledge from weblogs: a survey. Data Knowledge Engineering 53, 225–241 (2005)
12. Bayir, M.A., Toroslu, I.H., Cosar, A., Fidan, G.: Smart Miner: a new framework for mining large scale web usage data. In: Proceedings of the 18th International Conference on World Wide Web, pp. 161–170. ACM, Madrid (2009)
13. Staś, T.: Wykorzystanie algorytmów mrowiskowych w procesie doskonalenia portali korporacyjnych. Rozprawa doktorska. Akademia Ekonomiczna im. Karola Adamieckiego w Katowicach, Katowice (2008) (in Polish): Staś, T.: The Usage of Ant Colony in the Improvement of corporate portals process. Ph.D. Dissertation. University of Economics in Katowice, Katowice (2008)
14. Markellou, P., Rigou, M., Sirmakessis, S.: Mining for Web Personalization. In: Scime, A. (ed.) Web Mininig: Applications and Techniques, pp. 27–49. Idea Group Reference, USA (2005)
15. http://www.w3.org/Daemon/User/Config/ Logging.html#common-logfile-format
16. Agrawal, R., Srikant, R.: Mining Sequential Patterns. In: Proceedings of the Eleventh International Conference on Data Engineering, pp. 3–14. IEEE Computer Society (1995)
17. Srikant, R., Agrawal, R.: Mining Sequential Patterns: Generalizations and Performance Improvements. In: Apers, P.M.G., Bouzeghoub, M., Gardarin, G. (eds.) EDBT 1996. LNCS, vol. 1057, pp. 3–17. Springer, Heidelberg (1996)
18. Zaki, M.J.: SPADE: An Efficient Algorithm for Mining Frequent Sequences. Machine Learning 42, 31–60 (2001)
19. Pei, J., Han, J., Mortazavi-Asl, B., Wang, J., Pinto, H., Chen, Q., Dayal, U., Hsu, M.-C.: Mining Sequential Patterns by Pattern-Growth: The PrefixSpan Approach. IEEE Transactions on Knowledge and Data Engineering 16, 1424–1440 (2004)
20. Ivancsy, R., Vajk, I.: Frequent pattern mining in web log data. Acta Polytechnica Hungarica 3, 77–90 (2006)

Kleenks: Linked Data with Applications in Research and Ambient Assisted Living

Andrei-Adnan Ismail[1], Razvan Dinu[2]
Adina Magda Florea[1], Tiberiu Stratulat[2], and Jacques Ferber[2]

[1] University Politehnica of Bucharest, 060042, 313 Splaiul Independentei
`andrei.ismail@cs.pub.ro`
`http://aimas.cs.pub.ro/people/andrei.ismail`
[2] University of Montpellier 2, UMR 5506 - CC477, 161 rue Ada, Montpelllier, France
`dinu@lirmm.fr`
`http://www.lirmm.fr/~dinu/`

Abstract. In the spirit of the Linked Data initiative pioneered by Tim Berners-Lee, we propose a new type of link between entities identified by URIs named kleenk. This new type of link bridges the gap between the classical structured data published as RDF and the semi-structured data formats pushed by social networks such as Facebook and Twitter.

Unlike previously published work on RDF and its extensions, our proposal promotes links to a first-class citizenship in the world of a semantic web: a kleenk has a content of itself, can be linked to recursively, and both people and machines can harmoniously collaborate in creating, evaluating and extending them.

We discuss the theoretical model of the kleenk and how it can be built on top of existing frameworks such as RDF, and identify the main challenges for adoption of the new model.

Finally, we validate our model with two real-world implementations: an online platform for spreading research results between researchers and an ambient intelligence elder tracking scenario where kleenks are used to perform sensor fusion between heterogeneous data sources.

Keywords: linked data, ambient intelligence, RDF.

1 Introduction

"This is what Linked Data is all about: it's about people doing their bit to produce a little bit, and it's all connecting.,, - Tim Berners-Lee, TED 2009.

Linked data is a movement trying to expose the world's data in a structured format and to link it all together in meaningful ways. This concept has been gaining traction as more and more organizations are starting to expose their data in a structured, computer-understandable format, besides the traditional website. Until recent, the habit was this: if an organization owned some data and it wanted to expose it to the public, it created a website allowing users to explore it. However, it soon became obvious that this was not enough; humans were not the only ones interested in working with this data, sometimes even computers or software agents delegated by humans should be able to manipulate

E. Mercier-Laurent and D. Boulanger (Eds.): AI4KM 2012, IFIP AICT 422, pp. 53–71, 2014.

it. In the dawn of this era, the web crawling[14] and screen scraping [15] concepts appeared. Programs that contained specific parsing code for extracting specific knowledge out of raw HTML emerged, and they were named crawlers or scrapers. Due to the technical difficulties of doing NLP (Natural Language Processing), these programs would use the underlying regularities in the HTML structure to parse the structured data. Soon, a war broke out between content owners who did not want to expose their data to machines and humans aiding the machines in extracting the data by continuously adapting the parsers to changes in HTML structure and to security additions aimed at differentiating humans from crawlers.

In the center of this war comes Berners-Lee's concept of Linked Data. Linked data is no longer data exposed by machines for machines, but it is data exposed by humans for their fellow machines. The Linked Open Data (LOD) project is leading this movement of encouraging people to expose their data to machines in a meaningful format. Most of the projects put forward by LOD are projects in which humans are in the center of the process of generating linked data. Big names in the internet industry such as Facebook agree with this vision, as confirmed by the launch of Facebook Open Graph v2 initiative at the F8 conference in 2011[1]. This announcement is about making the transition from the singular "like" action that users could perform on the social platform to a multitude of actions, even custom ones definable by application developers: read, watch, listen, cook, try out, and so on. Given the large amount of data continuously generated by users on their social networks, this step will finally expose all that data internally as structured data.

While academia has taken the pure path towards linked data adoption, industry has done the exact opposite. Social networking giants have convinced their users to first produce data in the form of small snippets of unstructured text, and then slowly introduced structure into the produced data, while keeping a vigilant eye on engagement metrics. Nowadays, users reference hashtags and other users in their tweets, allow applications to geotag their tweets in order to include location information, share pictures on Facebook and tag faces in them. While industrial examples of linked data are well-known and famous, we would like to give credit to some of the most important academic initiatives in exposing linked data:

– DBPedia[2] is a community effort to write parsers that extract structured information from Wikipedia infoboxes which are found on most pages. Triples in this database are kept in sync by using a subscription to a live feed of modifications, and they are created by automated programs as an indirect consequence of people's actions.
– Freebase [3] is an initiative supported by Google to apply the wiki concept to the world's knowledge. A user interface and a RESTful API are provided to users in order to be able to collaboratively edit a database of triples spanning more than 125 million triples, linked by over 4000 types of links, from domains as diverse as science, arts & entertainment, sports or time and space.

Domains such as information retrieval and ambient intelligence, with a huge impact in the socio-economic domains would benefit immensely from a larger adoption of linked data. In this paper we propose the **kleenk** concept, a link between two entities that is

---

[1] https://f8.facebook.com/

compatible with both academic and industrial approaches. Not only this model is able to leverage all existing produced data by both environments, but it is built in such a way that users and machines can both work together to build a larger graph of linked data.

This paper is organized as follows: in section 2 we formally define the problem kleenks are trying to solve: bridging the gap between generating structured data using machines and semi-structured data using social interactions. In section 3, we present related works in both the area of formal modelling of online knowledge and in ambient intelligence. In section 4, we contribute 2 scenarios that have been implemented by the authors in order to validate the kleenk model. In section 5, we present the formal Kleenk model and how it can be built on top of other existing models such as RDF and RDFS. In section 6 we present `http://kleenk.com`, a novel platform for spreading research results and linking between them based on the kleenk paradigm. In section 7 we present ElderMonitor, a novel distributed person tracking platform for building ambient intelligence applications. We show how the kleenk concept can be successfully applied to storing and processing sensor data in real-time in order to determine the location of the person. In section 8 we draw conclusions and expand on future research directions for the kleenk concept.

2   Problem Statement

As we have seen in the previous section, there is a growing need for exposing the world's data in a structured format, as confirmed by industry giants and academia alike. There are a number of efforts trying to bridge this gap. Only to name a few:

- crowd-sourcing structured data from users; examples are Freebase and OpenStreetMap
- crowd-sourcing unstructured data from users, in a nearly-structured format; examples are Wikipedia and Facebook before the launching of Facebook Open Graph v2
- crawling / scraping data from unstructured data; this includes shopping, travel and news aggregators
- extracting entities and links from unstructured text using NLP (Natural Langauge Processing); one eloquent example of this is OpenCalais [2]

However, current efforts for structuring the web's data are mostly concentrated around describing entities and their properties, as shown in [2]. This is also the nature of the information usually found in web pages: in Wikipedia, each page is dedicated to one entity, and none to relations between entities. Also, most of the current approaches generate data through automated means, by parsing online data sources or exposing legacy databases in RDF format. This has two shortcomings: the only relations present in Linked Data are those detectable by a computer program (so only explicit relations can be detected), and also the decision of whether the data is correct or not is left to the computer. Moreover, the current quantity of available linked data in the largest such database was 4.7 billion RDF triples [2], compared to over 1 trillion of web pages in

---

[2] `http://www.opencalais.com/`

2008 [3]. This tells us that the current approach of exposing the web's data in a structured form is not scalable enough when compared to the explosive growth of social content since the advent of Web 2.0 and the social web: tweets, statuses, blogs, wikis and forums are all very hard to understand for a computer program.

Therefore, it is our strongly held belief that general linked data would benefit from a social component, allowing creation and editing to be crowdsourced among enthusiasts. This way, people and machines can collaborate in order to generate more semi-structured content of better quality (because it has been validated by both parties).

We envision that people should be able to easily create links between any two online entities identifiable by a unique URI and to associate extra information to these links (note that online does not necessarily mean public in this case). The current process of creating linked data lacks transparency into the process, evaluation of the results by human beings, and human contributions. If people can create such links easily in the same format as machines do, an interesting validation phenomena can happen:

- humans can validate the content generated by machines
- machines can validate the content generated by humans by using different correlation and information retrieval algorithms

The key difference between our proposal and existing crowd-sourcing approaches is that the dual feedback cycle (human $\rightarrow$ machine $\rightarrow$ human) allows scaling the generation of content while maintaining good quality. We will showcase the importance of this feedback mechanism in both proposed scenarios. We have chosen the Ambient Intelligence in order to validate our model outside the classical applications of linked data for several reasons:

- sensor data is inherently linked and correlated; however, usually machine learning algorithms are used to detect correlations between this data
- such automatically detected correlations always need human feedback (as showcased by any online recommendation system: they all have a feedback mechanism such as vote up/down)
- sensor data can be easily accessed online by using identifiers; a recent development in this direction is http://www.pachube.com; humans should be able to link sensor data together as well, and machines can use this as training data

Our scenario is related to the Ambient Assisted Living[5] paradigm, the vision that elders should be assisted by equipment integrated seamlessly into their homes in order to prolong their independent healthy life as much as possible.

To sum up, the problem the **kleenk** is trying to solve is **scalable generation of linked data content by machines and humans collaborating together**.

3   Related Works

Here, we have chosen a few relevant works that treat the same problems as mentioned previously: adding a social dimension to the web of data, using crowdsourcing to build

---

[3] http://googleblog.blogspot.com/2008/07/we-knew-web-was-big.html

up the web of data, or ways to open up linked data to the big public, which might be the only fighting chance of keeping up with the growth rate of online content.

ConceptWiki[4] tries to apply the wiki concept to linked data. It contains a list of concepts as specific as "an unit of thought". Any person with an account on the website can edit the concepts and there are two main sections on the website right now: WikiProteins (which contains information about proteins) and WikiPeople (which contains information about authors in the PubMed database). The WikiPeople exemplifies the importance of automatically generated data in bootstrapping a human community. However, due to slow human adoption, the machine-extracted data is not proving to be enough.

OpenStreetMap[8] is a success story in machine-generated data from public sources complemented by communities of enthusiasts around the world wishing to create an open and accessible geographical database. A notable design choice in this community was to only enable contributions from registered users, the opposite of Wikipedia. In addition to geographical coordinates of important landmarks, the database stores key-value pairs for each graphical coordinate.

Facebook Open Graph (v2) is a recent development of the social networking giant, allowing people to publish their online social activity as something very similar to RDF triples. They can now connect themselves to other entities by verbs like watch, read and listen, instead of the traditional like. Friends can afterwards rate and comment these actions, therefore this approach has also a very strong community evaluation component. However, this platform lacks in two respects: the first is generality, as it only connects people with entities, and through a pretty limited amount of actions (Facebook has to approve all new actions, giving it complete control over the ontology of predicates that appear); the second is aggregated visualisation capabilities, which is actually what makes the web of data interesting for the regular user: the ability to discover new content by navigating from content to content.

Pachube[9] is a platform for recording and distributing sensor data from around the world. It is based on a set of APIs that are used to store and retrieve sensory data from the selected feeds. Thousands of enthusiasts have connected sensor for temperature, wind speed and many others and are feeding data into this online sensor data brokerage platform. This platform, developed by a successful startup, exemplifies the importance of linked data in all sensor-related activities, including Ambient Intelligence.

SensorML[4] is an approved Open Geospatial Consortium standard. It provides models and encoding schemes (for example, XML) that can be used for describing process measurements in an interoperable way. It supports a wide range of sensors, on both stationary and dynamic platforms.

The Semantic Sensor Web[19] is an initiative aiming to integrate and adnotate data sources around the web in order to make up for a machine query-able and discoverable array of measurements that can be integrated with other data sources. Interestingly enough, this is similar to our proposed application in Ambient Intelligence, with the observation that it lacks the double feedback loop we're proposing in order to scale the meta-data of the system and ensure its correctness.

---

[4] http://conceptwiki.org/

The fact that there are a number of projects solving the same problem as us, some even approached by internet giants or academia gives us the strength to believe that we are working on the right problem. However, our proposed solution is unique, in that it lets both humans and machines users easily create their own linked data, both in structured and semi-structured format, with a great potential for powerful visualisations, as we will shortly see in the next sections.

4   Working Scenarios

We will use two scenarios in this article: one is related to discovery of scientific articles by a young researchers, and one is related to tracking a single elder living at home, a scenario prototyped at University Politehnica of Bucharest[11].

4.1   Research Discovery

Rob is a PhD student in computer science and he is reading a lot of books and papers related to his subject, which is artificial intelligence. He is testing applications and algorithms to see how they perform in different scenarios. He would like to discuss his findings with other researchers to have their opinions and also make his results easily accessible. In addition to discussing with his friends, he publishes multiple articles, but he feels that the feedback is limited and delayed (at least a few months from an article submission to its publication). Rob also has some younger friends that study the same topic. Whenever they find a new interesting article or application they ask Rob about it: What's important about this article? How does this application relate to application Y? Rob could tell them to read his articles but that may take a lot more time and his friends may get confused and get lost in other information they might not need. He gives them the answer but he knows that there may be more students out there that would benefit from those answers. How can he structure this information, and where to put it, so that it can be easily found by all interested researchers?

4.2   Elder Tracking

Mary is 80 years old and has been retired for a decade. Her children have moved to the U.S. to found a successful start-up and her husband recently died of a heart-attack. Now she is alone but doesn't want to leave the house she has lived in for all her life. Also, she doesn't want to ask her children to come back to Europe and take care of her. So she is researching on the internet for a system that is able to monitor her vital signs non- intrusively and alert her physician in case of danger. The system should not require her to wear any equipment , and would ideally allow her to easily communicate with her children without having to use an actual computer. Also, it's very important that the system works well at night, since her vision is weakened and sometimes stumbles against the furniture. How can sensors together with linked data processed in a private cloud ensure that she is safe and sound? Also, her physician and children need to be able to look into the insights drawn by the system, visualize them in an intuitive way, and provide corrections as training data. (This is actually the double feedback loop we were mentioning earlier on).

5   Kleenks

In this section we will propose a solution to the problem stated in section 2. We start by considering a simplified model of the Web of Data which allows us to explain the role of our approach and how it fits in the existing landscape. We finish by identifying the main challenges for implementing our proposal.

5.1   Web of Data

We consider a simplified model for the Web of Data which consists of the following elements: *contents, entities, links, software agents, humans* and *ontologies.*

Contents represent any type of unstructured data such as text, images, sounds or videos and they may, or may not have, an URI that uniquely identifies them. Entities can represent anything such as places, people or articles and they are uniquely identified by URIs. Links connect two entities, have an associated type and they can represent any relation between entities. By software agent we understand any software application (desktop, web or mobile) that uses the Web of Data. Also, we consider that humans can access entities and links directly, making abstraction of the browser or any application in between. Finally, ontologies can be used by both humans and software agents to understand the links between entities.

5.2   A New Perspective, a New Type of Links

Inspired by the explosion of content in Web 2.0, we believe that the Web of Data could also use an internal perspective in which links are first class citizens, and not just express a relationship between content. This would create an interesting phenomena, where links can be part of other links as either the target or the source. We believe that the Web of Data needs a new social, unstructured and collaborative dimension that would bring people, unstructured content, entities and links closer to each other (Figure 1).

We argue that this can be achieved through a new type of links, that we call *kleenks* (pronounced "clinks"), which are collaborative links created, evaluated and consumed by the users of the Web of Data in collaboration with machines (just like in the example ofOpenStreetMap, where some public data was automatically imported in the system and afterwards enhanced by users). A kleenk (Figure 2) is a directed connection and consists of the following (below the words "entity", "content" and "link" have the meaning considered in the simplified model of the Web of Data from the beginning of this section):

1. **Source.** The source of a kleenk is an entity.
2. **Target.** The target of a kleenk is another entity.
3. **Type.** The type is a verb or expression that summarizes the link from the source to the target.
4. **Contents.** The contents represents the most important elements of a kleenk and they can have different roles:
   - *Description.* Descriptive contents can be simple text paragraphs, other media contents such as images and videos or even domain specific. They provide more details about the connection and they are added by the creator of a kleenk.

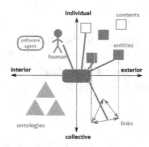

Fig. 1. Social, Unstructured, Collaborative dimension to the Web of Data

- *Feedback.* As with descriptive contents, feedback contents can take any form but they are added by other participants to the kleenk (other people or software agents).
- *Evaluation.* Evaluation contents must provide means to obtain quantitative data about the quality of a kleenk and they can take the form of ratings, like or thumb up/down buttons etc.

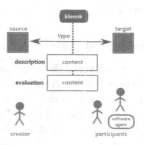

Fig. 2. Elements of a kleenk

Kleenks are collaborative links because new content can be added to a kleenk at any time by its creator or by another participant (be it human or machine).. Kleenks have an unstructured dimension because the content added to a kleenk is in an unstructured form. Finally, a kleenk is social because it provides a mechanism for users to express their position (like, agree, disagree, etc.) with respect to it. One important point is that this position can even be expressed by automated means: for example, a spam filtering module could vote with "disagree" on a content created by a human.

The term "kleenk" is actually a short version for collaborative link with a slightly different spelling since the term "clink" has been used in other works such as Project Xanadu [5] and we wanted to avoid confusion.

Let's take an example. Rob, from our first working scenario, reads a paper X that talks about an efficient implementation of an algorithm described in another paper Y. He will create a kleenk from the article X to article Y with the type "efficient implementation of". Also, if the implementation is accessible on the internet he can also create

---

[5] http://www.xanadu.com

a second kleenk from X to the implementation with the type "implemented here". As a description of the first kleenk he will provide a few details about what exactly makes the implementation efficient. Other researchers can express their opinion about the implementation directly on the kleenk, and comment for instance that the performance improvement is visible only on a particular class of input data. Other implementations can be kleenked to the same article X and the implementations can also be kleenked between them. Now, whenever an younger friend of Rob finds paper X he will quickly see the most important implementations of the algorithm and the relations with other important papers and they can continue their research without interruption.

Also, in order to get the community started on the usage of Kleenks (so that Rob can explore something that already exists), a large body of "A cites B" type of kleenks can be created automatically by scanning all the papers in the domain and importing them as kleenks. As the content of these kleenks, the paragraph in which the citation occurs can be used, so that people can rate on the relevance of the citation itself or not. This could also lead to interesting research in the scientometry field, where citations from a paper to another usually cannot be distinguished by importance.

5.3 Benefits and Quality of Kleenks

One main feature of kleenks is the ability to add unstructured content, in any form, to structured links. They are therefore compatible with both the existing RDF databases already available online and the semi-structured content added by users in social networking websites. As a side-note, in this section, we will mainly insist on the advantages of humans finally being able to contribute links between content in an easy way; the advantages of machines already doing that are well known.

Kleenks have multiple benefits for both the user and the Web of Data. First because kleenks are richer in content than simple links, this makes them important on their own. Up until now, in the Web of Data, it is rare that links are very important on their own but rather in sets that describe an entity or a topic. We believe that making each link important on its own will engage people more in creating meaningful links. Second, allowing people to create links with content will also facilitate the apparition of new links of high abstraction level that otherwise would have been impossible to extract automatically.

Allowing people to contribute to existing kleenks with new content is meant to make kleenks become more accurate and complete. However, as it has been seen in many projects such as Wikipedia and StackOverflow, an explicit evaluation system for user contributed content is necessary. The design of rating systems has been widely studied in computer science [12]. An overview of techniques that can be used to heuristically assess the relevance, quality and trustworthiness of data is given in [1]. This automatic rating system which also takes into account human intervention is what can close the feedback loop. An important note is that in the absence of human feedback (which can be scarce on some deep topics, just like those found in scientific research), an automatic algorithm has to complement this lack of feedback.

Also, allowing social validation through mechanisms such as likes, agree/disagree or ratings allows important kleenks to step ahead of the less important ones guiding the users through what is important and what is less important. Of course, the best way to validate a content can differ from domain to domain and each platforms that uses kleenks is free to choose the method that is more suitable.

5.4 Challenges

Implementing a system based on kleenks, be it targeted to a specific domain or as a general platform, raises a few challenges that must be properly addressed in order to be successfully used.

Access to Entities. A kleenk, as an RDF triple, is a link that connects two entities and in addition it adds more content to the link. Letting regular users create such kleenks raises an important question: *"How will a user quickly select the entities he's interested in kleenking?"*.

The answer to this question depends on the type of platform: domain specific or general. In case of a domain specific platform it means that the user will kleenk entities he's working with. Usually these entities are already gathered in some databases and the kleenk platform only needs to integrate with these databases to provide quick search of the entities the user wants to kleenk.

On the other hand, a general platform is faced with a much more difficult question due to inherent ambiguities. If a user wants to use "Boston" as the source of a kleenk the platform has to decide whether it's about the city, the band or the basketball team. In this context we believe that semantic searches and large open databases such as DBpedia and Freebase will help in the disambiguation process.

Also, the user might want to kleenk things that don't yet have an URI and the platform must be able to create such URI's on the fly.

The Ontologies for Kleenks. Even though kleenks contain unstructured content, their type, as with RDF links, will still be a predicate in an ontology, allowing computers to have at least a basic understanding of what a kleenk means and use them in new ways. However, allowing users to create any type of links between entities means that it is very hard to develop a comprehensive ontology from the start. A kleenk platform would have to provide a mechanism that would allow users to define ontologies, such as in Freebase, or it must integrate with platforms that allow users to build ontologies such as MyOntology.

Also, for kleenks automatically created by machines, these ontologies should serve as the authoritative sources of types of kleenks available. Humans create the ontologies, machines use types from the ontologies to create kleenks automatically, humans evaluate the kleenks by providing rating and feedback, and machines take as much feedback as they can (and understand) and make sure that in the future they create better kleenks. In this respect, kleenks can serve as a semi-structured way for humans to interact with machines.

Visualization and Privacy. Allowing users to create kleenks between any two entities has the potential of creating a very big number of kleenks. Users must be able to handle a big number of kleenks related to the entities that are of interest to them. Since kleenks form a graph structure, we can use visualisation techniques for graphs and create interactive ways of navigating the kleenks. We believe that since kleenks contain more content on the "edges" between the nodes, than just a simple predicate, more interactive and engaging visualizations can be built.

Since kleenks contain more content than simple RDF links and since most of this content will be based on the user's experience, the problem of the visibility of a kleenk must not be neglected. A user might want to create a kleenk between two entities and allow only a limited number of persons to see it. Also, kleenks can be used to collaboratively build some data (i.e. state of the art on a topic) which might, at least on its early stages, be visible only to a limited number of people. So, a kleenk platform must also provide proper mechanisms for kleenks' visibility.

Also, in our scenario regarding elder tracking, we are referring to kleenks extracted in real-time from sensor data and processed within a private cloud. This means that not only the kleenks themselves can be private or public, but also the kleenk platform themselves.

5.5 Modeling Kleenks

In this section we will look at the theoretical and technical aspects of modeling kleenks using existing techniques in semantic web. We will first analyze different alternatives and motivate our chose for one of them. Finally, we will give an example of what a kleenk might look like.

Theoretical Model. Basically, the kleenk model could be seen as an extension of the RDF model with support for unstructured data. In the semantic web many extensions of the RDF model have been proposed during the last years. There are extensions dealing with temporal aspects [7], with imprecise information [13], provenance of data [6] or trust [18]. In [21] a general model based on annotation is proposed which generalizes most of the previous models.

All the above mentioned techniques are based on the named graph data model, a well known technique in semantic web to attach meta-information to a set of RDF triples. Even though these techniques could be applied to model kleenks, that would require that each kleenk has its own named graph (with its own URI), in order to associate the unstructured content with it.

A different technique, known under the name of RDF Reification, is described in the RDF specification [10]. This technique has well known limitations and weak points such as triple bloat and the fact that SPARQL queries need to be modified in order to work with reified statements. However, we believe that this techniques is the most suitable for modeling kleenks because a kleenk needs many different types of meta-information associated with it: creator, description content, feedback content (i.e. comments), evaluation content (i.e. ratings) and possibly other domain specific data.

Next, we provide an example kleenk by using reification:

```
kleenk:123   rdf:type        rdf:Statement
kleenk:123   rdf:subject     entity:234
kleenk:123   rdf:predicate   research:implements
kleenk:123   rdf:object      entity:444
```

```
kleenk:123   klnk:description   "Some text describing
 in detail the link between the source and
 the target. This can be used in order to motivate
 the chosen type for the kleenk."

kleenk:123   klnk:creator          user:33

kleenk:123   klnk:comment          comment:1023
comment:123 klnk-comment:txt  "The opinion of a
 user about the kleenk"
comment:123 klnk:creator          user:123

kleenk:123   klnk:rating           rating:2231
rating:2231 klnk-rating:txt    "4.5"^^xds:decimal
rating:2231 klnk:creator           user:344
```

We believe that modeling kleenks this way provides maximum interoperability with existing infrastructures and allows kleenks to be implemented on top of practically any triple store.

6   kleenk.com

6.1   Description

kleenk.com [6] is an online collaborative platform for linking scientific content. The project's motto is: "Smart-connecting scientific content". It is allows users to link scientific contents, revealing other relations than citations, such as:

- paper P1 implements the algorithm in paper P2 (relation: "implements algorithm in")
- diagram D1 is an explanation for the theory in paper P2 (relation: "explains the theory in")
- algorithms A1 and A2 solve the same problem (relation: "solves the same problem as")

This kind of relation is not easy to extract neither by an automated program, and nor by humans that are just starting their research in a certain area. That is why it is crucial that these two means complement each other. In Europe, the first year of a PhD program is usually dedicated to researching the state of the art, which consists of reading many scientific contributions by other authors and creating mental links like those mentioned previously. Given the exploding number of scientific works, conferences and journals it is hard to keep up-to-date even for a scientific advisor, which makes the work of a starting researcher even harder. Kleenk actually solves this problem by allowing the community to create and visualise kleenks between the contents. Machines aid in this process by automatically extracting relationships between papers in the following ways:

---

[6] http://app.kleenk.com

- extract citations automatically between different papers - this will ensure a healthy amount of content for the community to get started and to suggest possible pairs of papers that might be interconnected in other ways, not just by way of citation
- extract n-grams automatically from different papers and create links between papers that speak about the same concepts, especially when the elements of the n-grams are very rare

While the machine-extracted content is surely limited in quality, making sure that machines aggresively generate kleenks of "good enough" quality that are afterwards reviewed by the community is key for this platform's adoption. Given the observation found during the development of OpenStreetMap[8], that up to 99.8% users of a wiki will only consume its content, making sure that the rest of 0.2% users are encouraged to easily contribute is key to the success of a wiki.

This platform is aimed at the following groups of persons:

- PhD students which need community guidance in order to read the most relevant and up-to-date materials related to their subject
- professional researchers who need to stay in touch with the vibrant scientific community's developments
- other people interested in quickly gaining an overview of a scientific domain

The platform allows the easy selection of content to kleenk from a number of sources by manually adding it, importing it from web pages (such as ACM or IEEE public pages of articles) and even by importing BibTeX bibliography files. Once all the content a user wants to kleenk is available in the platform, the user can start creating kleenks by selecting a source and destination content.

After they are created, kleenks can be shared with research fellows or made public, and grouped around meaningful ideas using tags. Every time a new content is created or updated, the interested users are notified using their personal news feed. Therefore, changes to a kleenk or any comment reach out across the entire community instantly.

Authors have the chance to kleenk their own papers to existing ones, and by subjecting these kleenks to the community scrutiny, the platform makes it possible for them to obtain early feedback for their ideas. In today's society, when the internet allows information to be propagated from one end of the world to another in seconds, the traditional peer review system is becoming more and more criticized due to the number of months passed from submitting the work to actual post-publication feedback from the scientific community. Our service aims to complement the quality and thoroughness of the peer review system with the opinion of the crowd. One important observation is that the opinion of the crowd is not necessarily misinformed, as proven lately by the tremendously successful service for programmers StackOverflow [7]. This website is a collaborative question answering system, with world renown experts easily connecting and answering each others' questions. We think that the scientific community would benefit from a low-latency alternative to obtaining feedback for a piece of work.

---

[7] http://www.stackoverflow.com

6.2   Implementation of the Theoretical Framework

Having earlier detailed the kleenk model and characteristics, we will now underline which instantiation of the general principles was used in order to implement this knowledge sharing platform. First of all, in our particular case, the kleenk has the following elements:

- **the source, destination and type** - these are also present in the general model
- **the description** - this is specific to this pair of content, and represents a more detailed explanation of the type. It should be used in order to motivate the choice of type and to give more relevant results
- **comments** - since each kleenk has its own set of comments, these can be used in order to discuss the relevance of the link and to give extra information by anyone who can see it. These are similar to Wikipedia's talk pages, which are used by contributors to clarify informations in the main page
- **ratings** - together with ratings, these allow the community to evaluate the quality of a kleenk. In the visualisation, kleenks with better community score (which is computed from the ratings, number of comments, number of views and a number of other metrics) are displayed with a thicker connecting line, signifying a greater importance. Ideally, an user who is interesting in exploring the web of scientific articles will first navigate the most important kleenks.
- **privacy level** - as already mentioned in the general model, there should be a privacy setting associated with each kleenk. This allows users to first try out their own ideas in a personal incubator before promoting them to the whole community. In our implementation, there are 3 privacy levels: private (visible only to the owner), public (visible to anyone) and shared (visible to research fellows, which can be added through a dedicated page, given that they also agree).
- **tags** - each kleenk can be part of one or more tags. This is actually a mechanism for grouping tags related to the same idea or topic under a single name. For example, when writing this article, the authors created a "Kleenk Article" tag which contained the relevant bibliographic items and the kleenks between them.

The visualisation of the graph induced by the kleenks is done, as mentioned in the description of the general model, using consacrated layout methods. Specifically, in our case, we use an attraction-force model.

kleenk.com is a linked data application, conforming to Berner-Lee's vision of the future of the web. Contents, kleenks and tags all have persistent URIs that can be dereferenced in order to obtain linked data. One other interesting side-effect of this is that interesting scientific applications can emerge on top on the data contributed by the users to kleenk. For example, new scientometric indicators based on kleenks could be computed by a 3rd party application.

6.3   Use Case Example

Obtaining Feedback for a Recently Published Article. Alice is a fresh PhD student in Semantic Web, who is overwhelmed by the vast amount of publications on this topic. Being a first year student, she has to complete a document describing the state of the art by the end of the year. As a Facebook user, it's easy for her to create an account using one click on kleenk.com, since it features integration with Facebook's login service. Once logged in, she adds her colleagues who already have a Kleenk account as research fellows and now can easily see their shared tags. She studies the visualisations and grows to see a few important articles which are in the center of most tags, and starts reading them. Since she pays close attention to her news feed, she can easily see in real time what connections her colleagues are creating, and they all obtain quick feedback from their advisor, via comments and ratings.

Since she will be writing a survey article as well, she started creating a tag specifically for the bibliography of the article. First, the tag is private, since it is a work in progress and she doesn't want to share it with anyone. As the text of the article and the bibliography mature, she changes the visibility of the tag from private to shared, so that her research fellows can express their opinion on the connections she is making. After receiving the final approval for publication, she makes the tag public and includes the visualisation of the bibliography in a presentation for her department.

7   ElderMonitor - Real-Time Kleenk Creation in a Private Cloud

We have implemented the concept of Kleenk in a prototype distributed tracking system of an elder, inside a lab of University Politehnica of Bucharest. This system uses a number of 9 Microsoft Kinect[20] and 20 Arduino [17] boards equipped with microphones, light and proximity sensors in order to track an elder living alone at home[11]. This system consumes raw sensor data and turns it into kleenks by using a data structure named the **Database of Trajectories**. This data structure is comprised of tuples (x, y, z, t) together with some associated information, presented as one or more kleenks, having this tuple as the source. (x, y, z) refers to the position of the person, while t refers to the timestamp when the system has determined that the person was at the position (x, y, z). Because the system can track more persons, but only one single person at a time, a first information attached to this tuple would be the identity of the person:

```
kleenk:123   rdf:type           rdf:Statement
kleenk:123   rdf:subject        andrei.ismail@cs.pub.ro
kleenk:123   rdf:predicate      ami:has_position
kleenk:123   rdf:object         (x,y,z,t)

kleenk:123   klnk:description   "This has been automatically
                                determined by node 13, based
                                on the image 24."

kleenk:123   klnk:creator       node:13.

kleenk:123   klnk:comment       comment:1024
comment:123  klnk-comment:txt   "Caregiver A doesn't this this
                                represents a valid position
                                determination based on images
                                25 and 26"
comment:123  klnk:creator       user:123
```

```
kleenk:123   klnk:rating        rating:2231
rating:2231  klnk-rating:txt    "4.5"^^xds:decimal .
rating:2231  klnk:creator       user:344
```

Secondly, to such an (x, y, z, t) tuple, the Database of Trajectories allows association of proof based on which the machine algorithms have determined this position. Such proof consists of imagery, sound samples, and sensor positions and physical parameters. For example, the proof for one particular location might be comprised of:

- 6 sound samples from 3 different pairs of microphones and their physical positions (based on which the sound source position - the person - has been triangulated)
- RGB and depth imagery from a Kinect which confirms the same position by using skeleton data derived from the depth image in order to estimate the relative position of the person to the kinect

This can be represented using kleenks as following:

```
kleenk:124   rdf:type           rdf:Statement
kleenk:124   rdf:subject        kleenk:123
kleenk:124   rdf:predicate      ami:proof_for
kleenk:124   rdf:object         img:456

kleenk:124   klnk:description   "Image with id 456 is a proof
                                that kleenk with id 123
                                represents a correct information"

kleenk:124   klnk:creator       node:13 .
```

Attaching proof to the user localization has several benefits:

- interesting queries can be formulated against the Database of Trajectories: "give me the images that serve as proof that the person Y was near the kitchen in the night of 27th of May". Given that the data can be exposed in an RDF format, it can be queried using the SPARQL[16] language.
- information can be spatially and temporally correlated more easily. For example, if a person enters the room but has a new haircut and some glasses, and the system doesn't recognize the person for the first 300 seconds, but recognizes it when the person answers the phone using the voice, all the imagery samples related to the anonymous-until-then person can be fed to the system as training samples. This will ensure that the system is permanently adapted to the changing physiognomy of its users.
- proof can be manually validated by both caregivers and experts helping to train the system, introducing the double-feedback mechanism mentioned before. It is assumed that the deployment of such a system includes a training phase in which the sensors are calibrated by specialized personnel and the algorithms' training data tweaked to the specific location. If needed, specialized personnel and caregivers can intervene and manually create kleenks in order to supply further training data to the system (except for the training data it is able to generate for itself).

One interesting aspect of the usage of kleenks in this case is that it naturally uses "recursive" kleenks (that have another kleenk as the source) in order to represent semi-structured data retrieved by machine learning algorithms. Specialized users are able to provide feedback to the system, which in turn grows more and more able to generate samples for itself by using the data structure. This is a perfect exemplification of how human and machine efforts can complement each other in order to reach unprecedented scale in producing linked data.

Just like in the `kleenk.com` use-case, privacy is of utmost importance. Kleenks created by the nodes of the system are private and processed within a private cloud running a private kleenk system. The kleenk system provides creation, discovery and feedback mechanisms for its users, with the sole purpose of scaling the quantity and quality of linked data.

8   Conclusions and Future Works

This article discusses the current context of the Web of Data, analyzes a few of its current limitations and focuses on the need to scale linked data generation with respect to the quantity of raw data available. We propose a new approach inspired by the success of Web 2.0 techniques such as wikis, blogs and social networks, that allows both machines and humans to combine efforts into creating more and better linked data.

The main contribution of this paper is the concept of *kleenk* which is a collaborative link that contains unstructured data in addition to the classical RDF predicate. We discuss the importance of allowing users to add unstructured data to the Web of Data and how this approach could lead to the creation of links which would otherwise be impossible to automatically parse from existing datasets. In the ElderMonitor use-case, we clearly exemplify how machines can benefit from this new linked data to parse even more linked data, leading to a spiraled evolution. What is most important about kleenks, they can be evaluated, manually or automatically (by software similar to spam filters), in order to control its influence in generating further linked data based on it.

We also identify the main challenges of a platform allowing users to create kleenks: access to entities, collaborative ontology creation, visualization of kleenks and privacy. These challenges have to be properly addressed for a system to succeed in applying kleenks. We introduce two already implemented platforms that have kleenks at their core:

- `kleenk.com`, a novel platform for spreading research results and obtaining feedback on insights extracted from them in real-time. Insights are represented here as kleenks between papers, that can be grouped together by tagging them with common tags. Kleenks have privacy levels and users can view newly created kleenks by following a newsfeed similar to that of many social networks.
- ElderMonitor, a state-of-the-art distributed indoor tracking system for single elders living at home. This system has been prototyped at University Politehnica of Bucharest [11] and uses kleenks as the backbone of its high-level information extracted from raw sensor data.

In both systems, we highlight the importance of kleenks in generation of more linked data, and the importance of both the social and unstructured aspects of our proposal.

As an extension to the already implemented systems and to our proposed kleenk model we envision:

- creation of a special query language adapted to kleenks themselves. While SPARQL[16] can be an elegant and efficient way to query RDF data, kleenks can be represented as RDF but this is an alternative representation. SPARQL lacks specialized primitives in order to touch on the unstructured data and social ratings and comments attached to kleenks
- defining scientometric metrics and algorithms to compute influence scores of authors based on new criteria after the `kleenk.com` platform gains enough traction
- implementation of algorithms that are able to extract generic knowledge from the Database of Trajectories in the form of public kleenks that can be reused from one deployment of ElderMonitor to another

Acknowledgments. Development of the ElderMonitor system has been sponsored by project ERRIC - Empowering Romanian Research on Intelligent Information Technologies/FP7- REGPOT-2010-1, ID: 264207. We are greatful to the scientific communities at University Politehnica of Bucharest and University of Montpellier for guidance and continuous exchange of constructive feedback.

References

1. Bizer, C., Cyganiak, R.: Quality-driven information filtering using the WIQA policy framework. Web Semant. 7, 1–10 (2009)
2. Bizer, C., Lehmann, J., Kobilarov, G., Auer, S., Becker, C., Cyganiak, R., Hellmann, S.: DBpedia - A crystallization point for the Web of Data. Web Semantics: Science, Services and Agents on the World Wide Web 7(3), 154–165 (2009)
3. Bollacker, K., Evans, C., Paritosh, P., Sturge, T., Taylor, J.: Freebase: a collaboratively created graph database for structuring human knowledge. In: Proceedings of the 2008 ACM SIGMOD International Conference on Management of Data, pp. 1247–1250. ACM (2008)
4. Botts, M., Percivall, G., Reed, C., Davidson, J.: OGC® sensor web enablement: Overview and high level architecture. In: Nittel, S., Labrinidis, A., Stefanidis, A. (eds.) GSN 2006. LNCS, vol. 4540, pp. 175–190. Springer, Heidelberg (2008)
5. Costa, R., Carneiro, D., Novais, P., Lima, L., Machado, J., Marques, A., Neves, J.: Ambient assisted living. In: 3rd Symposium of Ubiquitous Computing and Ambient Intelligence 2008, pp. 86–94. Springer (2009)
6. Dividino, R., Sizov, S., Staab, S., Schueler, B.: Querying for provenance, trust, uncertainty and other meta knowledge in RDF. Web Semant. 7, 204–219 (2009)
7. Gutierrez, C., Hurtado, C.A., Vaisman, A.: Introducing Time into RDF. IEEE Trans. on Knowl. and Data Eng. 19, 207–218 (2007)
8. Haklay, M., Weber, P.: Openstreetmap: User-generated street maps. IEEE Pervasive Computing 7(4), 12–18 (2008)
9. Haque, O.: Pachube (2004), http://www.pachube.com
10. RDF Primer (February 2004), http://www.w3.org/TR/rdf-primer/
11. Ismail, A.-A., Florea, A.M.: Multimodal indoor tracking of a single elder in an aal environment. In: ISAMI 2013 - 4th International Symposium on Ambient Intelligence (2013)
12. Jøsang, A., Ismail, R., Boyd, C.: A survey of Trust and Reputation Systems for Online Service Provision. Decis. Support Syst. 43, 618–644 (2007)

13. Mazzieri, M., Dragoni, A.F.: A Fuzzy Semantics for the Resource Description Framework. In: da Costa, P.C.G., d'Amato, C., Fanizzi, N., Laskey, K.B., Laskey, K.J., Lukasiewicz, T., Nickles, M., Pool, M. (eds.) URSW 2005-2007. LNCS (LNAI), vol. 5327, pp. 244–261. Springer, Heidelberg (2008)
14. Najork, M., Heydon, A.: High-performance web crawling. In: Handbook of Massive Data Sets, vol. 4, p. 25 (2002)
15. Petrie, C., Bussler, C.: Service agents and virtual enterprises: A survey. IEEE Internet Computing 7(4), 68–78 (2003)
16. Prud'Hommeaux, E., Seaborne, A., et al.: Sparql query language for rdf. W3C recommendation, 15 (2008)
17. Ramos, E.: Arduino basics. Arduino and Kinect Projects, 1–22 (2012)
18. Schenk, S.: On the Semantics of Trust and Caching in the Semantic Web. In: Sheth, A.P., Staab, S., Dean, M., Paolucci, M., Maynard, D., Finin, T., Thirunarayan, K. (eds.) ISWC 2008. LNCS, vol. 5318, pp. 533–549. Springer, Heidelberg (2008)
19. Sheth, A., Henson, C., Sahoo, S.S.: Semantic sensor web. IEEE Internet Computing 12(4), 78–83 (2008)
20. Shotton, J., Fitzgibbon, A., Cook, M., Sharp, T., Finocchio, M., Moore, R., Kipman, A., Blake, A.: Real-time human pose recognition in parts from single depth images. In: 2011 IEEE Conference on Computer Vision and Pattern Recognition (CVPR), pp. 1297–1304. IEEE (2011)
21. Zimmermann, A., Lopes, N., Polleres, A., Straccia, U.: A General Framework for Representing, Reasoning and Querying with Annotated Semantic Web Data. Elements, 1437–1442 (2011)

The Status Quo of Ontology Learning from Unstructured Knowledge Sources for Knowledge Management

Andreas Scheuermann[1] and Jens Obermann[2]

[1] University of Hohenheim, Information Systems 2, Schwerzstraße 35,
70599 Stuttgart, Germany
andreas.scheuermann@uni-hohenheim.de
[2] SAP Deutschland GmbH & Co. KG, Hasso-Plattner-Ring 7
69190 Walldorf, Germany
jens.obermann@sap.com

Abstract. In the global race for competitive advantage Knowledge Management gains increasing importance for companies. The purposeful and systematic creation, maintenance, and transfer of unstructured knowledge sources demands for advanced Information Technology. Ontologies constitute a basic ingredient of Knowledge Management; thus, ontology learning from unstructured knowledge sources is of particular interest since it bears the potential to bring significant advantages for Knowledge Management. This paper presents a study of state-of-the-art research of ontology learning from unstructured knowledge sources for Knowledge Management. Nine approaches for ontology learning from unstructured knowledge sources are identified from a systematic review of literature. A six point classification framework is developed. The review results are analyzed, synthesized, and discussed to give an account of the current state-of-the-art for contributing to an enhanced understanding of ontology learning from unstructured knowledge sources for Knowledge Management.

Keywords: Ontology Learning, Knowledge Management, Literature Review.

1 Introduction

In the global race for competitive advantage the ultimate success of companies increasingly depends on effectively and efficiently exploiting knowledge. This knowledge is often distributed, heterogeneous, and contained in various types of knowledge sources. The purposeful and systematic creation, maintenance, and transfer of knowledge are subject of Knowledge Management (KM). KM depends on non-technical aspects but increasingly draws upon the use of technical properties such as advanced Information Technology (IT). Such IT could significantly benefit from the use of Semantic Technology and particularly ontologies provide dedicated means to enhance the future challenges of Knowledge Management [1-2].

However, constructing ontologies (from scratch) is a non-trivial and complex task, which requires considerable efforts regarding costs, time, and labor. Ontology construction involves experts from the area of ontology engineering and experts from the particular domain of interest. Experts are typically scarce and acquiring the relevant

E. Mercier-Laurent and D. Boulanger (Eds.): AI4KM 2012, IFIP AICT 422, pp. 72–94, 2014.

knowledge from a human domain expert is rather difficult due to the nature of human knowledge (e.g., implicit and procedural knowledge) and miscommunications. Despite ontologies bear the potential to significantly contribute to the further advancement of Knowledge Management, there are several obstacles specifically with regard to ontology construction, extension, and refinement that constrain a widespread adoption and use of ontologies in KM.

To overcome these obstacles, ontology learning represents a promising but yet not fully exploited approach to enable the (semi-)automatic construction, extension, and refinement of ontology. Ontology learning principally allows to (semi-) automate parts of the non-trivial and complex task of ontology construction and, thus, to significantly reduce cost, time, and labor expenses. That is, ontology learning appears to be an ideal solution to leverage ontologies for advancing KM not only from a technical but also from an economic perspective.

Unfortunately, huge amounts of knowledge exhibit a high relevance for companies but their representational form lacks a clear structure and organization [3]. This unstructured knowledge aggravates (semi-)automatic machine-readability and interpretability; thus, the use of approaches such as ontology learning. For instance, the wide adoption of Social Media on the World Wide Web (WWW) increased the number of unstructured knowledge sources dramatically. Social Media in terms of Facebook, Twitter, Blogs, and further types of these applications contain plenty of unstructured knowledge, which can be of major significance for company purposes such as marketing, product development, consumer studies, customer relationships, advertising, recruiting, etc. Despite the inherent characteristic features of this knowledge type hamper the use of (semi-)automatic approaches, increase the number of errors and demand for human intervention, exploiting semi- and unstructured knowledge sources for reasons of competitive advantage gains more and more significance.

The objective of this paper is to give an account of the current state-of-the-art in order to contribute to an enhanced understanding of ontology learning from unstructured knowledge sources for Knowledge Management. Therefore, this paper describes, analyzes, and assesses extant ontology learning approaches with regard to their capabilities to process unstructured knowledge sources for reasons of Knowledge Management. Thus, this paper extends and refines [4-6] in the matter of unstructured knowledge sources and Knowledge Management.

The remainder of this paper is organized as follows: Section 2 introduces ontology learning for knowledge management, which covers basic constructs from the areas of Knowledge Management, ontology, and ontology learning. Section 3 characterizes the review strategy, presents the classification framework, and introduces the identified ontology learning approaches. Section 4 presents the review results and critically reflects on them. Finally, Section 5 draws the conclusion.

2   Ontology Learning for Knowledge Management

2.1   Knowledge Management

Knowledge Management gains increasing importance for the competitiveness of companies and, thus attracted growing attention from both industry and academia.

KM essentially deals with cultural, organizational, human, and technical issues covering three processes of creating, maintaining, and transferring various forms of knowledge in an intra- and inter-organizational context [7]. These three overarching processes can be further decomposed into a coherent and consistent set of six Knowledge Management core processes [8]: (1) knowledge identification, (2) knowledge acquirement, (3) knowledge development, (4) knowledge distribution, (5) knowledge use, and (6) knowledge preservation (Fig. 1).

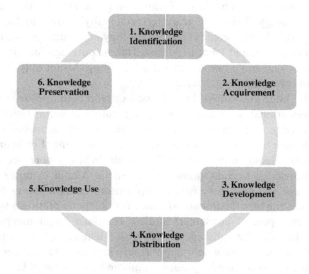

Fig. 1. Knowledge Management Core Processes

Subsequently, the constructs constituting the Knowledge Management core processes are briefly characterized:

1. *Knowledge identification* concerns the characterization and specification of the knowledge relevant for the organization.
2. *Knowledge acquirement* elicits and collects the identified knowledge.
3. *Knowledge development* augments and combines the acquired knowledge for creating new knowledge.
4. *Knowledge distribution* provides appropriate means to distribute and make the knowledge available.
5. *Knowledge use* depicts the exploitation of the knowledge for accomplishing the organizational goals.
6. *Knowledge preservation* is responsible for long-term knowledge storage.

Despite various cultural, organizational, and human factors exert an influence on the Knowledge Management core processes, the focus is on technical issues of KM and specifically ontology learning. To elaborate on ontology learning for KM, it is reasonable to understand the potential roles and benefits of ontologies in KM.

2.2 Ontology

The term ontology originates from philosophy and denotes the discipline of philosophy that concerns "the science of what is, of the kinds and structures of objects, properties events, processes, and relations in every area of reality" [9]. With the beginning of the late 1980s and early 1990s, ontology attracted growing attention and became subject of research in Computer Science and Artificial Intelligence (AI). AI research deals with formal representations of real world phenomena and reasoning about these phenomena. In a literal sense, AI research *borrowed* the term ontology from philosophy [10], equipped it with a computational meaning, and, thus, coined the term "formal ontology" (or computational ontology).

In the following, AI research studied ontology for its purposes, most notably in the context of knowledge engineering and knowledge representation, and contributed to several definitions. The most prominent definition stems from [10-11] and defines ontology as "an explicit specification of a conceptualization". A refinement of this definition provides [11] in terms of requiring the specification to be formal and the conceptualization to be shared. Based on this, [13] concisely and comprehensively points out the characteristics features of formal ontology by defining ontology as "a formal, explicit specification of a shared conceptualization of a domain of interest".

— *Conceptualization* depicts an abstract representation of some (real-world) phenomenon by having determined its relevant concepts, relations, axioms, and constraints.
— *Explicit* denotes the explicit (not implicit) definition of the type of concepts and relations as well as the axioms and constraints holding on their use.
— *Formal* indicates that the ontology should be readable and interpretable by machines, thus, formal excludes the use of natural language.
— *Shared* conceptualization reflects that an ontology captures consensual knowledge that is not private to an individual person but accepted by a larger group of individuals.

For reasons of the formal and explicit representation of consensual knowledge about a particular domain of interest, ontology draws upon the following set of basic modeling primitives [11]:

— *Classes* typically follow a hierarchical organization, which allows for applying inheritance mechanisms. Classes are used in a broad sense (types of anything); thus, they can be either abstract (e.g., intentions or beliefs), concrete (e.g., people or trees), elementary, or composite.
— *Relations* define the type of associations between classes and essentially distinguish between three types of relations: (1) unary relations, (2) binary relations, and (3) functions.
— *Axioms* model true statements. Ontology contains axioms (1) to constrain the knowledge, (2) to verify the correctness of the knowledge, and (3) to deduce new knowledge.

— *Instances* represent elements of a specific class whereas facts depict the relation between elements. Both instances and facts, i.e. any element of a domain of interest that is not a class refers to as individuals.

Against this background, the potential applications of ontologies spans a wide array but primarily aim at knowledge sharing and reuse, which includes (1) the formal specification of knowledge, (2) the structuring and organization of knowledge, and (3) the provision of a common terminology, i.e. interlingua [10],[13-16]. Regarding KM, the potential uses and roles of ontology primarily concern the Knowledge Management core process of:

— knowledge acquirement,
— knowledge development,
— knowledge distribution, and
— knowledge use.

Based on the definition of ontology and the clarification of its potential roles and benefits within KM, the subsequent section deals with ontology learning to narrow the scope and carve out its potential use and benefits for KM.

2.3   Ontology Learning

Ontology engineering is defined "as the set of activities that concern the ontology development process, the ontology life cycle, and the methods, tools, and languages for building ontologies" [17-18]. A closer inspection of this definition indicates that ontology engineering essentially covers the following five areas:

— the ontology development process,
— the ontology lifecycle,
— the methods for developing ontologies,
— the tools that support ontology development, and
— the (ontology) languages, which are applied in ontology development.

For elaborating on ontology learning, it is reasonable to focus on both the ontology development process and methods for developing ontologies. In particular, ontology development distinguishes between several different types of methods that deal with the creation of ontologies based on specific approaches: (1) methods for developing ontology from scratch, (2) methods for re-engineering of existing ontologies, (3) methods for ontology alignment and ontology merging, and (4) methods for ontology learning [17-18].

— Ontology development from scratch deals with newly developing ontologies, which means that large parts of the envisioned ontology are manually constructed whereas ontology reuse plays a minor role. Developing ontologies from scratch is required when ontologies of the particular domain of interest lack quality, availability, coverage, or not yet exist.

— Ontology re-engineering adapts preexisting ontologies according to specific re-quirements and covers the following steps: (1) retrieve the conceptualization of an ontology implementation, (2) transform it, i.e. extend, refine, and prune this con-ceptualization according to the given requirements, and (3) re-implement the (re-engineered) ontology.
— Ontology alignment (matching) and ontology merging methods generally aim at unifying preexisting ontologies. In particular, ontology alignment establishes vari-ous kinds of mappings between the ontologies and, thus, preserves the original on-tologies. In contrast to that, ontology merging generates a unified ontology from the original ontologies but does not preserve the original ontologies.
— Ontology learning (semi-)automatically acquires knowledge from knowledge sources to create, enrich, or populate ontologies. Ontology learning typically draws upon preexisting knowledge structures such as taxonomies or ontologies that al-ready capture parts of the domain of interest and presuppose the existence and availability of external knowledge sources.

This classification depicts that ontology learning bears the potential to significantly contribute to the further advancement of Knowledge Management. Ontology learning is capable to overcome impediments related to the construction, extension, and re-finement of ontologies with regard to costs, time, and human labor [4-5]. In particular, ontology learning has the potential to advance the following knowledge management core processes:

— knowledge acquirement and
— knowledge development.

However, to better understand the use and potentials of ontology learning for the two knowledge management core processes, it is reasonable to characterize ontology learning in more detail and classify existing approaches for ontology learning.

Characteristics
Ontology learning generally aims at automating ontology development with regard to acquiring knowledge from several types of knowledge sources and, then, constructing an ontology or components of an ontology (e.g., classes or properties). Therefore, ontology learning primarily draws upon constructs, methods, and techniques from the field of information extraction to elicit information, patterns, and relations from vari-ous kinds of knowledge sources as well as ontology engineering to construct the on-tology or its components. In essence, ontology learning pursues reductions in cost, time, and human labor, e.g., in terms of a reduced level of human interaction. [20],[25].

From a technical point of view, ontology learning combines the following two con-stituent components: (1) information extraction approaches and (2) (ontology) learn-ing approaches.

First, ontology learning principally distinguishes between two distinct approaches for information extraction: (1) rule-based approaches and (2) heuristics pattern ap-proaches [25]. Both approaches draw upon lexico-syntactic patterns, which allow for dealing with knowledge sources characterized by insufficient pre-encoded knowledge and wide ranges of data (e.g., text) [21]. Lexico-syntactic patterns aim at finding recurring and recognizable structures within data sets (e.g., text) without depending on sets of fixed terms of expressions, which need to be determined a priori.

Second, ontology learning incorporates learning algorithms, which essentially assess whether the extracted information entities fit the purpose and scope of the envisioned ontology. In case of a positive assessment, the learning algorithm adds the information entity as a new element to the ontology, that is, in terms of an ontology component [6],[22].

In principle, ontology learning differentiates from other existing approaches by its multidisciplinary applicability and the potential to exploit vast and heterogeneous knowledge sources [23].

Process

Ontology learning principally combines and integrates information extraction and ontology learning approaches. In addition to that, ontology learning approaches exploit the outcomes of numerous disciplines such as linguistics, statistics, heuristic and pattern matching, machine learning, or data mining for applying them on various types of knowledge sources to enhance the quality of the results. Based on that, ontology learning is a complex and multifaceted process. To point out the characteristics features of the ontology learning process, this paper refers to the ontology learning process proposed by [24].

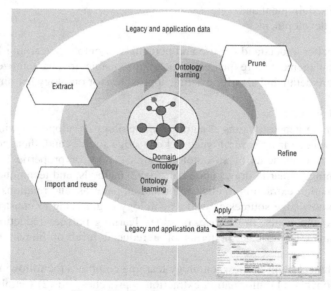

Fig. 2. Ontology Learning Process [24]

The ontology learning process shown in Fig. 3 is rather generic and encompasses the following four main activities:

— *Import and reuse* deals with mapping and merging preexisting knowledge structures.
— *Extract* concerns the creation of major parts of the ontology based on information extraction from various types of knowledge sources.
— *Prune* aims at tailoring the preliminary ontology to satisfy its purpose and scope according to specific requirements of the target application.
— *Refine* considers the completion of the ontology at a more detailed and fine-grained level.

After performing these four main activities of the ontology learning process, the target application provides a testbed and measure for validating and further refining the envisioned ontology. Further, this ontology learning process allows the ontology engineer to extend the ontology, i.e. to perform further iterations of the ontology learning process as well as to update and maintain the ontology in the course of the ontology lifecycle.

Classification
Ontology learning is an active area of research and, in accordance to that, literature yields several schemes for classifying ontology learning approaches based on multiple criteria such as type of preprocessing, preexisting knowledge structures, learning algorithms, learned ontology components, or degree of human interaction. In accordance to the purpose and scope of this paper, it is reasonable to classify ontology learning with regard to different types of knowledge sources. For instance, [24] classify ontology learning according to the following types of knowledge sources: free texts, dictionaries, semi-structured schemata, and relational schemata. Influenced by [24], this work categorizes ontology learning approaches based on the following three types of knowledge sources: (1) structured knowledge sources, (2) semi-structured knowledge sources, and (3) unstructured knowledge sources.

Next, each of these types of knowledge sources is briefly characterized:

— *structured knowledge sources* are tightly coupled to specific rules of a conceptualization, e.g., relational databases and the relational schema.
— *semi-structured knowledge sources* incorporate some rules of a conceptualization but also contain unstructured elements, e.g., HTML documents
— *unstructured knowledge sources* can be of any kind and lack particular rules or structure. The key characteristic features of unstructured knowledge sources are the high availability throughout all domains but also the lowest accessibility for ontology learning.

Against the background of these three types of knowledge sources, the scope of this paper covers semi-automatic and automatic ontology learning approaches from unstructured knowledge sources.

3   Methodology

3.1   Review Strategy

To identify the relevant ontology learning approaches in the literature, a structured and iterative approach was employed. A systematic search was used to retrieve publications (journal articles, conference and workshop proceedings, as well as technical reports) that reported on ontology learning. The search combines both a keyword-based and explorative search strategy to reach a maximum coverage and to accomplish high quality search results. The keyword-based search assembled multiple search strings (e.g., ontology learning, unstructured knowledge, etc.) in various forms for searching online databases (e.g., Google Scholar, Scopus, ACM Digital Library, etc.). The search strategy relied on citation count as a proxy measure to identify probable core publications. Since filtering based on citation count may exclude some relevant ontology learning approaches, an explorative search was used to find additional publications on ontology learning. Furthermore, the search strategy was iterative to both reduce the list of search results (e.g., adding constraints to the search query) as well as expand the list (e.g., adding alternative terms to the search query). Employing this review strategy resulted in a manageable list of potentially relevant ontology learning approaches. This list was then manually inspected by analyzing the abstracts and skimming the content, resulting in nine publications.

3.2   Classification Framework

The classification framework consists of six criteria for describing and analyzing the indentified ontology learning approaches. These six criteria stem from an analysis of literature in the area of ontology learning and are assessed relevant for reviewing ontology learning approaches with respect to unstructured knowledge sources and Knowledge Management. As such, these criteria are extrinsic in their nature and allow for an assessment from an objective point of view. In particular, the various criteria reflect descriptive constructs of the domain of ontology learning that focus both on methodological properties of the ontology learning approaches (Criteria 1-5) as well as on the resulting ontologies (Criterion 6). In the following, Table 1 depicts the classification framework and the six constituent criteria with example concrete measurements before each of these criteria is briefly characterized.

Table 1. Classification Framework

#	Criterion	Concrete Measurements
1	Objective	Purpose, scope, target application
2	Methodology	Statistical, logical, natural language
3	Technique	Supervised, unsupervised
4	Degree of Automation	Semi-automatic, (fully) automatic
5	Reuse of Knowledge Sources	Lexica, taxonomies, ontology
6	Ontology Components	Classes, relations, instances, taxonomies

Criterion 1: Objective
(Objective) aims to detect and analyze the primary goal of ontology learning in terms of the purpose and scope of the envisioned ontology based on the specification of the identified problem in the target application.

Criterion 2: Methodology
(Methodology) aims to detect and analyze the methodological approach that underpins ontology learning from unstructured knowledge. This criterion pays special attention to statistical and natural language processing (NLP) approaches for ontology learning as they frequently occur in literature and can be assessed promising for Knowledge Management.

Criterion 3: Technique
(Technique) aims to detect and analyze the technique for extracting information and learning; thus, this criterion specializes Criterion 2. For instance, it elaborates on the process of ontology learning in terms unsupervised or supervised.

Criterion 4: Degree of Automation
(Degree of Automation) aims to detect the degree of automation at which the ontology learning approach is supposed to operate. The degree of automation basically distinguishes between semi-automatic and (fully) automatic approaches for ontology learning and relates to economical advantages, which gain importance for knowledge management in fast changing business environments.

Criterion 5: Reuse of Knowledge Sources
(Reuse of knowledge Sources) aims to detect whether the ontology learning approach reuses preexisting (formal) bodies of knowledge, e.g., WordNet. This is especially interesting for KM as it can be assumed that there are already ontologies, which have to be extended or refined according to changing business demands. In addition to that, this criterion expresses the basic understanding of the ontology learning approach: building up ontologies from scratch or finding a preexisting knowledge structure as the starting point.

Criterion 6: Ontology Components
(Ontology components) aim to detect and analyze the ontology components, which essentially correspond to the results from information extraction and, then, become the subjects of learning. Ontology components typically correspond to classes, relations, axioms, and instances but might also cover taxonomies or further types of knowledge structures. This criterion highlights the envisioned results of ontology learning and maintains close relationships to Criterion 3 and Criterion 5. Criterion 6 is of particular importance for KM since it provides information about the envisioned ontology.

3.3 Identified Ontology Learning Approaches

Ontology learning from unstructured knowledge sources primarily distinguishes between two different types of approaches: (1) statistical approaches and (2) natural

language processing (NLP) approaches. The search result finally comprises four statistical ontology learning approaches and five ontology learning approaches based on
NLP (Table 2).

Table 2. Identified Ontology Learning Approaches

Authors	Type	Short Description
Agirre et. al (2000) [25]	Statistical	Enriching very large ontologies using the WWW
Faatz and Steinmetz (2002) [26]	Statistical	Ontology enrichment with texts from the WWW
Sanchez and Moreno (2004) [27]	Statistical	Creation of ontologies from web documents
Cimiano et al. (2005) [28]	Statistical	Learning of concept hierarchies from text corpora using formal concept analysis
Hearst (1992) [21]	NLP	Automatic acquisition of hyponyms from large text corpora
Kietz et al. (2000) [29]	NLP	Semi-automatic ontology acquisition from corporate intranets.
Gupta et al. (2002) [30]	NLP	Architecture for engineering sublanguages – WordNets
Alfonseca and Manandhar (2002) [31]	NLP	Extension of a lexical ontology by a combination of distributional semantics signatures
Narr et al. (2011) [32]	NLP	Extraction of semantic annotations from Twitter

In the following, the review describes and analyzes the nine ontology learning approaches based on the classification in statistical and NLP approaches as well as in
accordance to the chronological order of the year of development.

Statistical Approaches
Statistical ontology learning approaches that deal with unstructured knowledge
sources draw upon a common basic assumption. This basic assumption corresponds to
the distributional hypothesis [33]. The distributional hypothesis states that similar
words often occur in similar contexts and, thus, statistical patterns provide hints for
certain relations between words.

Agirre et al. (2000) Approach
[25] propose an automatic ontology learning approach, which deals with enriching the
WordNet database by using unstructured knowledge sources, i.e. the WWW. The
enrichment of WordNet is deemed necessary because of two major drawbacks: (1)
semantic variant concepts of words, which are related by topics, are not interlinked
(e.g., to paint and paint or sun cream and beach) and (2) the vast collection of word
meanings without any clear distinction. In this context, the proposed ontology learning approach primarily relies on word lists. Word lists describe the sense of the words

of interest. This sense is based on the idea that other specific words describe the context and, thus, express the meaning of the word of interest (indirectly and implicitly). Initially, the proposed approach queries (boolean search query) the WWW for documents (datasets), which contain the word of interest. Thereby, the higher the number of the words of interest in the retrieved documents, the higher the statistical likelihood that the document correlates with the topic searched for. To increase this likelihood, the search could explicitly include and exclude further descriptive constructs, i.e. words. Then, counting the occurrence of single words in the documents and using calculated distance metrics to hierarchically sort them results in topic signatures. These topic signatures are clustered and evaluated by means of a disambiguation algorithm. Thereby, clustering corresponds to a common technique to generate prototype-based and hierarchical ontologies. A predefined semantic distance algorithm works as a measurement to agglomerate terms or clusters of terms. The largest or the least homogeneous cluster is split into smaller subgroups by a divisive process to further refine the envisioned ontology.

Faatz and Steinmetz (2002) Approach
[26] introduce a semi-automatic ontology learning approach, which primarily aims at enriching preexisting ontologies. The proposed approach is illustrated with an example of a medical ontology. Similar to [25], [26] use a statistical approach to cluster words, which occur in a certain context to each other. In addition to that, this approach incorporates a set of predefined rules. This set of rules represents distance measurements, e.g., maximum word distance between two words in a document, which, in principle, should not be contradictory to already existing distance measures. The statistical similarity measurement generally relies on the Kullback-Leibler divergence [34], which was originally designed to test the probability distribution between statistical populations in terms of information. In particular, [26] use the Kullback-Leibler divergence to check the weighted probability of a given linguistic property w with respect to its fulfillment by a word x. This allows for assessing and minimizing the distance of the word of interest and the retrieved document in a way similar to an optimization problem.

Sanchez and Moreno (2004) Approach
[27] develop an automatic ontology learning approach, which exploits web documents as the primary knowledge source to create ontologies. Using the WWW for ontology creation might increase the probability that the ontology reflects the current state of practice or knowledge and, thus, is more complete. Similar to [25] and [26], [27] formulate queries to search for specific words of interest and constraint this search by criteria like the maximum number of returned results as well as by the use of filters for similar documents. Based on the initial search results, a first analysis according to predefined prerequisites is conducted for filtering relevant documents. Then, the application of statistical analysis techniques aims at further filtering the most relevant documents from this subset. The next step is to filter the results from the previous step by adding a new search word to refine the original search. The goal of the last two

steps is mainly to increase search depth. Moreover, the resulting taxonomies support finding new relations between ontologies.

Cimiano et al. (2005) Approach

[28] propose the adoption of Formal Concept Analysis (FCA) for ontology learning on an automated basis. The proposed ontology learning approach analysis documents by searching for sets of object attributes and, based on them, derives relationships and dependencies between the objects. The results of this search conform to nouns associated with several verbs as trailed attributes. These attributes define the context of the noun. The formal abstraction of the inherited nouns provides additional benefits to an end-user as the verbs provide a further foundation to enrich the envisioned ontology. The reason for this is potentially because of the more adequate description by a verb in contrast to a noun or hyponym.

NLP Approaches

Prior to characterizing the identified ontology learning approaches based on NLP, it is reasonable to note that literature lacks a clear and consensual distinction between statistical and NLP approaches for ontology learning. Despite ontology learning approaches draw upon statistics and linguistics to exploit unstructured knowledge sources, NLP approaches incorporate a more intuitive way of dealing with unstructured knowledge sources by using techniques such as pattern recognition [35]. In particular, ontology learning approaches based on NLP provide additional benefits with regard to knowledge-intensive domains, which require several constraints and rules within ontology learning. Such constraints and rules conform to lexical inventories, syntactic rules, or predefined knowledge structures [36].

Hearst (1992) Approach

[21] introduces an ontology learning approach, which uses the lexico-syntactic pattern extraction method to support the enrichment of preexisting patterns within the Word-Net database by searching large text corpora as a mining resource for suitable semantic patterns. A crucial prerequisite of this approach is that the English language has identifiable lexico-syntactic patterns, which indicate specific semantic relations in terms of is-a relations. In comparison to other approaches, the underlying text corpora have to fulfill only very little usage requirements. In particular, this means that only one instance of a relation has to be available in the knowledge source to decide whether the knowledge source is suitable or not. [21] uses a deterministic system to provide one or several hyponyms for each unknown concept, which all have a certain probability to be correct based on the unstructured knowledge source. To increase the suitability of the derived concepts, the lexico-syntactic patterns have to fulfill some criteria. That is, the lexico-syntactic patterns (1) need to frequently occur in the text corpora, (2) indicate the relation of interest, and (3) allow for a potential recognition without any prior knowledge of the domain of interest. Moreover, this approach allows for combinations with other techniques such as statistical algorithms for the purpose of refining the patterns.

Kietz et al. (2000) Approach
[29] essentially build on the approach proposed by [21] to introduce an ontology learning approach that allows for semi-automatically create ontologies from text corpora retrieved from corporate intranets. The proposed approach incorporates a learning method, which is based on a set of given core concepts similar to WordNet. This learning method further uses statistical and pattern-based techniques to refine the respective results. Then, the resultant ontology is pruned and restricted. In comparison to prior approaches, this (non-taxonomic) approach uses conceptual relations rather than manually encoded rules for the purpose of ontology creation. Moreover, this approach comprises a set of evaluation metrics to ensure a hegemonic ontology with respect to the target knowledge structure. However, these metrics are not conclusive enough to fully automate the process of ontology learning.

Gupta et al. (2002) Approach
[30] introduce an ontology learning approach, which primarily aims at speeding up the ontology learning process by using WordNet and, particularly, by creating sublanguages, i.e. so-called WordNets. The creation of these sublanguages results from an application of acronym extractors and phrase generators for analyzing knowledge sources for concept elements. For instance, concept elements are words, potential relations between words, and phrases. Then, potential relationships are analyzed again and proposed as candidates for being added to the envisioned ontology. Thereby, words and suitable relationships are clustered into groups and linked to the corresponding synsets in WordNet as WordNets. Finally, the last step focuses on maintenance of the retrieved concept elements and knowledge structures.

Alfonseca and Manandhar (2002) Approach
[31] introduce an automatic ontology learning approach to extend a lexical semantic ontology. The proposed algorithm searches the existing ontology for similarity to a synset for information extraction. For this purpose, [31] define several signatures for the word of interest, which are evaluated with regard to their semantic similarity to existing words within the preexisting ontology. The signatures conform to: (1) topic signatures, which define a list and the frequency of co-occurring words, (2) subject signatures, which inherit a list of co-occurring verbs, (3) object signatures, which contain a list of verbs and prepositions, (4) and modifier signatures, which consist of adjectives and determiners. Thereby, similar words should be assigned with similar signatures since they are represented in similar contexts. All the signatures are aggregated to an overall similarity value. For assessing the frequency, [31] use the method of [25] to achieve more accurate results. Thereto, the plain frequencies are changed into weights, which assess the support of a word in a specific context of a synset.

Narr et al. (2011) Approach
More recent research in the area of NLP extends the area of which text corpora are derived from. In this context, [32] introduce an ontology learning approach to extract information directly from Twitter messages. This approach refines the attempt to retrieve information from unstructured knowledge sources to a new and even more

demanding level. Besides the challenge of retrieving the correct semantic relation in the in the unstructured knowledge sources, the problems of misspellings, abbreviations, and colloquial speech in Tweets occurs. Therefore, a normalization of the text is necessary prior to initializing the process of extending or refining the ontology. In addition to enriching an ontology, annotations from the Twitter messages are included in the retrieved semantic structures. These annotations refer to as contextual relations like opinions.

4   Results and Discussion

This section synthesizes, summarizes, and discusses the main results of the review ontology learning approaches from unstructured knowledge for Knowledge Management.

4.1   Results Statistical Approaches

Prior to presenting the review results in detail for each of the four statistical ontology learning approaches, Table 3 provides a summary and overview of the main findings.

Table 3. Results Statistical Ontology Learning Approaches

	Objective; Methodology	Technique; Degree of Automation	Reuse of Knowledge Sources; Ontology Components
[25]	Ontology enrichment; (primarily) statistics	Harris' distributional hypothesis, topic signatures, clustering by statistical measures; automatic	WordNet ontology; classes and relations
[26]	Ontology enrichment; (primarily) statistics	predefined text resources, clustering and statistical information, similarity measures; semi-automatic	medical ontologies; classes and relations
[27]	Ontology enrichment, (primarily) statistics	Keyword-based information by key words; automatic	WWW; Classes
[28]	Ontology creation; (primarily) statistics	Formal Concept Analysis, Harris' distributional hypothesis; semi-automatic	domain experts select specific knowledge sources; classes and taxonomies

Agirre et al. (2000)

[25] focus on the problem of word ambiguity in order to enhance ontology learning. To enrich ontologies, [25] use Harris' distributional hypothesis as the foundation for measuring the relevance of the retrieved knowledge elements. These knowledge elements conform to classes and relations. The proposed ontology learning approach can be performed automatically and exploits WordNet as its underlying knowledge source.

Faatz and Steinmetz (2002)

[26] use clustering techniques and similarity measures to perform ontology learning with regard to classes and relations from the retrieved knowledge sources. Instead of using randomly assigned knowledge sources, [26] define several knowledge sources, e.g., documents, which already deal with the topic to provide the basis for the operations of the algorithm. The proposed approach can be categorized as semi-automatic, since suitable knowledge sources are selected a priori by human, i.e. manual intervention. Further, this ontology learning approach mainly reuses medical ontologies with respect to the target application area.

Sanchez and Moreno (2004)

[27] introduce an ontology learning approach that aims at creating new ontologies. Therefore, this approach primarily enriches preexisting ontologies by means of the inclusion of additional knowledge elements, e.g., from the WWW. In general, [27] use the technique of keyword-based information extraction as the first step. Then, the algorithm focuses on the automatic processing of the ontology components, i.e. classes.

Cimiano et al. (2005)

[28] draw upon FCA to create ontologies from scratch. In addition to that, this ontology learning approach builds on Harris' distributional hypothesis. As such, the proposed approach allows for deriving classes and taxonomies from knowledge sources. However, theses knowledge sources have to be manually selected in accordance to the specific topic at hand. As a result, it is reasonable to argue that this ontology learning approach operates semi-automatically.

4.2   Results NLP Approaches

Before presenting the review results in detail for each of the five ontology learning approaches based on NLP, Table 4 provides a summary and overview of the main findings.

Table 4. Results Ontology Learning Approaches based on NLP

	Objective; Methodology	Technique; Degree of Automation	Reuse of Knowledge Sources; Ontology Components
[21]	Ontology enrichment; (primarily) NLP	lexico-syntactic patterns; automatic	WordNet; classes and hyponym-hypernym relations
[29]	Ontology creation; (primarily) NLP	statistical and pattern-based techniques; semi-automatic	GermaNet, WordNet; classes, is-a relations
[30]	Ontology enrichment; (primarily) NLP	Retrieval of sublanguages – WordNets – and adding synsets; semi-automatic	WordNet; WordNets
[31]	Ontology enrichment; (primarily) NLP	Information signatures; automatic	WordNet; objects, classes and hyponym-hypernym relations
[32]	Ontology enrichment; (primarily) NLP	Several NLP techniques; automatic	None; annotations and contextual relations

Hearst (1992)

The ontology learning approach proposed by [21] aims at enriching existing ontologies by exploiting knowledge sources not limited to specific domains. [21] uses lexico-syntactic patterns for retrieving classes and hyponym-hypernym relations. Furthermore, this approach reuses WordNet as its underlying knowledge source. The approach incorporates algorithms that are supposed to work in an automatic way.

Kietz et al. (2000)

[29] introduce an ontology learning approach, which takes an application-driven perspective since its main target corresponds to exploiting companies' intranets as the primary knowledge source. This approach is capable to retrieve classes and *is-a* relations from corporate intranets. Because of the nature of the intranets, this approach operates only semi-automatically. It reuses GermaNet and WordNet as the two major ontologies that underpin ontology learning.

Gupta et al. (2002)

[30] draw upon WordNet but essentially create sublanguages so-called WordNets for the purpose of enriching an upper ontology with regard to more domain-specific knowledge elements. The rationale underpinning this approach is to derive complete WordNets based on the assumption that the domain expert has selected suitable knowledge sources. This approach is capable of updating single WordNets without the need of dealing with the entire ontology. Nevertheless, this approach demands for human intervention and, thus, can only be performed semi-automatically.

Alfonseca and Manandhar (2002)

[31] develop an ontology learning approach, which aims at enriching preexisting ontologies of a domain of interest by exploiting predefined knowledge sources. The proposed approach works automatically without supervision as it generates information signatures based on a set of criteria. In addition to that, carrying out this approach requires large knowledge sources for generating adequate signatures for a unique identification of the envisioned ontology components.

Narr et al. (2011)

[32] propose an ontology learning approach with the goal to enrich preexisting ontologies by exploiting Twitter. The derived ontologies can be enriched with annotations and contextual relationships depending on accompanying words or hash-tags in the Twitter feeds. This approach is supposed to operate completely automatic.

4.3   Discussion

Ontology learning essentially distinguishes between two different approaches, i.e. underpinning methodologies in terms of statistics and NLP. The majority of these approaches aim at ontology enrichment, i.e. extending, refining, or populating preexisting ontologies instead of creating new ontologies from scratch. This observation implies that the majority of the reviewed ontology leaning approaches presupposes an existing knowledge structure, i.e. a taxonomy or an ontology as a starting point. For instance, the ontology learning approaches proposed by [27-28] primarily draw upon statistics and constitute the two exceptional cases. This circumstance may be due to fact that there is a higher likelihood of errors when an ontology is constructed from scratch since there is a severe lack of respective guidelines and possible comparisons to similar structures. In addition to that, [30] introduces an interesting ontology learning approach. That is, [30] aim at the creation of ontologies by means of constructing synsets (sublanguages of WordNet) but these synsets have to be connected to an upper ontology.

Furthermore, there are ontology learning approaches, which aim at the construction of *is-a* relations between classes. However, these approaches rather result in taxonomies than ontologies. Instead, a consideration of further types of relationships such as *part-of* relations seems to be largely disregarded. In contrast to that, the ontology learning approach proposed by [32] deal with enriching the retrieved relationships with additional attributes, which originate from the knowledge sources. Thereby, [32] rely on annotations by means of the extrapolation of contextual relationships. A closer inspection of the different methodologies (statistics vs. NLP) with regard to a historical dimension shows that the different ontology learning approaches evolve over time starting with the identification of rather simple ontology components to the more advanced extraction of complex ontology components from the underlying knowledge sources.

The majority of the reviewed ontology learning approaches exhibit a lack in providing explicit information about the performance, i.e. concrete performance measures. Instead, the authors report on the target applications and the use of the proposed ontology learning approach rather in terms of a proof of concept. In this context, lite-rature argues that an objective evaluation of the ontology learning approaches intro-duced by [21],[27], [30], and [32] is hardly feasible. In contrast to that, the remaining ontology learning approaches provide more detailed information about the perfor-mance results when evaluating their approaches. For instance, [25] evaluate their algorithm with regard to different levels of granularity. That is, [25] provide explicit information about how the algorithm performs on word disambiguation with the gen-erated topic signatures. The results show that the algorithm performs best with respect to a coarse level of granularity. In contrast to that, a more fine-grained level of granu-larity leads to a drastic decline in performance. Further, [26] report on similar results. Whereas the enrichment of some classes performs well, i.e. propositions are added to classes; other classes are not subject of enrichment at all. This difference might be due to the greater potential of the distributional meaning of some classes, e.g., medical doctor is too generic to provide a basis for achieving an adequate degree of quality. Similarly, [28] provide statistical performance measurements with regard to the appli-cation of their clustering technique. Thereby, the evaluation results show that the proposed ontology learning approach achieves a slightly higher (approx. 1%) degree of performance with respect to the retrieved classes and the precision than comparable approaches operating on two different domains. A further advantage of this approach is that the classes provide some additional description, which supports the users in better understanding the retrieved ontology. Moreover, [29] draw upon a pattern-based approach to obtain a basic ontological structure and, in this context, reached 76.29 % of correctly discovered relations. In addition to that, almost 50% of all dictionary entries are correctly imported into the envisioned ontology. At last, [31] compare different techniques for signature creation. The results show that only a combination of different signature methodologies for signature creation generates adequate results in terms of accuracy.

These observations allow for drawing the following conclusions. Some of the re-viewed ontology learning approaches operate (fully) automated and unsupervised. The remaining ontology learning approaches generate basic classes and provide rela-tions between these classes. However, there is still a demand for manual intervention to complete the ontologies with regard to the specific requirements of the target appli-cations. Manual interventions typically concerns the (pre-)selection of the knowledge sources or the manual evaluation of the retrieved ontology components, e.g., by a domain expert. This need for manual intervention aggravates a usage of the ontology learning approaches on a larger scale (e.g., inter-organizational Knowledge Manage-ment) because there is still considerable time, costs, and efforts required. This implies that automated and integrated activities that perform quality controls allow the appli-cation of ontology learning approaches in an up-scaling context such as Knowledge Management.

Based on that, this paper synthesizes the review results and their discussion by means of formulating eight hypotheses in the form of research questions. These eight research questions might provide a foundation to further develop ontology learn-ing approaches from unstructured knowledge sources for advancing Knowledge Management.

Hypothesis 1: How ontology learning approaches can support the knowledge management core processes most effectively?

Hypothesis 2: What ontology learning methodologies (e.g., statistics, natural language processing) and which combinations of them are most effective for Knowledge Management?

Hypothesis 3: What ontology learning techniques and which combinations of them are most effective for Knowledge Management?

Hypothesis 4: What degree of automation of ontology learning is most effective for Knowledge Management?

Hypothesis 5: What types of knowledge sources are most effective for reuse in Knowledge Management?

Hypothesis 6: What ontology components are most effective for Knowledge Management?

Hypothesis 7: What evaluation techniques and metrics are most effective for assessing the adoption of ontology learning for Knowledge Management?

Hypothesis 8: How to empirically study the actual use and the realized benefits of ontology learning in Knowledge Management?

This set of hypotheses suggest research to not only focus on technical advances in ontology learning from unstructured knowledge sources for Knowledge Management but also explicitly include empirical research to study behavioral issues in terms of the impacts of current ontology learning approaches to further enhance the understanding, and, thus, fertilize future research in this area.

5   Conclusion

The objective of this paper was to give an account of the current state-of-the-art in order to contribute to an enhanced understanding of ontology learning from unstructured knowledge sources for Knowledge Management. On the basis of a review strategy, this paper identified nine ontology learning approaches. Four of these approaches primarily draw upon statistics whereas the remaining five approaches rely on natural language processing. To analyze the nine ontology learning approaches, this paper applies a classification framework, which consists of six criteria. These six criteria stem from literature and, thus, reflect descriptive constructs of the domain of ontology learning from a Knowledge Management point of view.

A literature review for the broad and fine-grained category of ontology learning from unstructured knowledge sources for Knowledge Management is a difficult task because of the large amount and diversity of background knowledge needed for studying, classifying, and comparing these ontology learning approaches. Therefore, the first shortcoming of this research is the authors' limited knowledge in presenting an overall picture of this subject. Secondly, some ontology learning approaches were not included in this literature survey (due the survey's purpose and scope). Third, the classification framework provides a set of six constructs that represent key descriptive constructs of ontology learning from a Knowledge Management point of view. The classification framework could be further extended and detailed with respect to ontology learning as well as Knowledge Management.

The results of the review provides evidence that research on ontology learning from unstructured knowledge sources has the potential to significantly enhance the current state-of-the-art in Knowledge Management. There is still a large gap between the multifaceted nature and the advancements in the core discipline of ontology learning and the actual use in Knowledge Management. Therefore, this paper proposes to extend the classification framework with additional criteria dealing with both issues of ontology learning and Knowledge Management to be able to elaborate in a more precise and fined-grained way on the potentials of ontology learning from unstructured knowledge sources for Knowledge Management. Moreover, this paper suggests that future research should be focused on the usefulness and efficacy of ontology learning approaches from unstructured knowledge sources for which Knowledge Management is a well-suited example because of rather weak dependency of specific domains or industries and its high relevance to practice.

Acknowledgement. The work presented in this paper was partly funded by the German Federal Ministry of Education and Research under the project InterLogGrid (BMBF 01IG09010E).

References

1. Staab, S.: Wissensmanagement mit Ontologien und Metadaten. Informatik-Spektrum 25, 194–202 (2002)
2. Staab, S., Schnurr, H., Studer, R., Sure, Y.: Knowledge Processes and Ontologies. IEEE Intelligent Systems 16, 26–34 (2001)
3. McComb, D.: Semantics in business systems. Morgan Kaufman, Massachusetts (2004)
4. Hazman, M., El-Beltagy, S.R., Rafea, S.: A Survey of Ontology Learning Approaches. International Journal of Computer Applications 20, 36–43 (2011)
5. Shamsfard, M., Barforoush, A.: The state of the art in ontology learning: a framework for comparison. The Knowledge Engineering Review 18, 293–316 (2003)
6. Biemann, C.: Ontology Learning from Text: A Survey of Methods. LDV Forum 20, 75–93 (2005)
7. Alavi, M., Leidner, D.E.: Knowledge Management and Knowledge Management Systems: Conceptual Foundations and Research Issues. MIS Quarterly 25, 107–136 (2001)
8. Probst, G., Raub, S., Romhardt, K.: Wissen managen. Gabler Verlag, Wiesbaden (1998)
9. Smith, B.: Ontology. In: Floridi, L. (ed.) Blackwell Guide to the Philosophy of Computing and Information Blackwell 2003, pp. 155–166. Blackwell, Malden (2003)

10. Gruber, T.R.: Toward Principles for the Design of Ontologies Used for Knowledge Sharing. International Journal of Human-Computer Studies 43, 907–928 (1995)
11. Gruber, T.R.: A Translation Approach to Portable Ontology Specifications. Knowledge Acquisition 5, 199–220 (1993)
12. Borst, W.: Construction of Engineering Ontologies for Knowledge Sharing and Reuse, PhD Thesis, University of Enschede (1997)
13. Studer, R., Benjamins, R., Fensel, D.: Knowledge Engineering: Principles and Methods. Data and Knowledge Engineering 25, 161–197 (1998)
14. Motta, E.: Reusable Components for Knowledge Modeling. In: Case Studies in Parametric Design. IOS Press, Amsterdam (1999)
15. Guarino, N.: Formal Ontology and Information Systems. In: Proceedings of the First International Conference on Formal Ontology in Information Systems, Trento, Italy (1998)
16. Uschold, M.: Building ontologies: Towards a unified methodology. In: Proceedings of the 16th Annual Conference of the British Computer Society Specialist Group on Expert Systems, Expert Systems 1996, Cambridge, UK (1996)
17. Gómez-Pérez, A., Fernández-López, M., Corcho, O.: Ontological Engineering with examples from the area of Knowledge Management, e-Commerce, and Semantic Web. Springer, London (2004)
18. Corcho, O., Fernández-López, M., Gómez-Pérez, A.: Methodologies, tools and languages for building ontologies. Where is their meeting point? Data and Knowledge Engineering 46, 41–64 (2003)
19. Navigli, R., Velardi, P., Faralli, S.: A Graph-Based Algorithm for Inducing Lexical Taxonomies from Scratch. In: Proceedings of the 22nd International Joint Conference on Artificial Intelligence, Barcelona, Spain, pp. 1872–1878 (2011)
20. Sabou, M., Wroe, C., Goble, C., Mishne, G.: Learning domain ontologies for Web service descriptions: an experiment in bioinformatics. In: Proceedings of the 14th International Conference on World Wide Web, Chiba, Japan, pp. 190–198 (2005)
21. Hearst, M.A.: Automatic Acquisition of Hyponyms from Large Text Corpora. In: Proceedings of the 14th Conference on Computational Linguistics, Stroudsburg, PA, USA, pp. 539–545 (1992)
22. Cimiano, P., Mädche, A., Staab, S., Völker, J.: Ontology Learning. In: Staab, S., Studer, R. (eds.) Handbook on Ontologies 2009, pp. 245–267. Springer, Heidelberg (2009)
23. Buitelaar, P., Cimiano, P., Magnini, B.: Ontology Learning from Text: An Overview. In: Magnini, B., Buitelaar, P., Cimiano, P. (eds.) Ontology Learning from Text: Methods, Evaluation, and Applications, pp. 1–13. IOS Press, Amsterdam (2005)
24. Mädche, A., Staab, S.: Learning Ontologies for the Semantic Web. IEEE Intelligent Systems 16, 72–79 (2001)
25. Agirre, E., Ansa, O., Hovy, E., Martinez, D.: Enriching very large ontologies using the WWW. In: Proceedings of the ECAI Workshop on Ontology Learning, Berlin, Germany (2000)
26. Faatz, A., Steinmetz, R.: Ontology Enrichment with Texts from the WWW. In: Proceedings of the 13th European Conference on Machine Learning, Helsinki, Finland (2002)
27. Sanchez, D., Moreno, A.: Creating Ontologies form Web Documents. Recent Advances in Artificial Intelligence Research and Development 113, 11–18 (2004)
28. Cimiano, P., Hotho, A., Staab, S.: Learning Concept Hierarchies from Text Corpora using Formal Concept Analysis. Journal of Artificial Intelligence Research 24, 305–339 (2005)
29. Kietz, M., Volz, R., Mädche, A.: A method for semi-automatic ontology acquisition from a corporate intranet. In: Proceedings of EKAW 2000 Workshop "Ontologies and Text", Juan-Les-Pins, France (2000)

30. Gupta, K.M., Aha, D.W., Marsh, E., Maney, T.: An Architecture for Engineering Sublanguages WordNets. In: Proceedings of the First International Conference on Global WordNet, pp. 21–25 (2002)
31. Alfonseca, E., Manandhar, S.: Extending a Lexical Ontology by a Combination of Distributional Semantics Signatures. In: Gómez-Pérez, A., Benjamins, V.R. (eds.) EKAW 2002. LNCS (LNAI), vol. 2473, pp. 1–7. Springer, Heidelberg (2002)
32. Narr, S., DeLuca, E.W., Albayrak, S.: Extracting semantic annotations from Twitter. In: Proceedings of the Fourth Workshop on Exploiting Semantic Annotations in Information Retrieval, ESAIR 2011, pp. 15–16 (2011)
33. Harris, Z.S.: Mathematical Structures of Language. Wiley, New York (1968)
34. Kullback, S., Leibler, R.A.: On Information and Sufficiency. The Annals of Mathematical Statistics 22, 79–86 (1951)
35. Schütze, H.: Foundations of statistical natural language processing. The MIT Press, Massachusetts (1999)
36. Hahn, U., Marko, K.G.: Joint Knowledge Capture for Grammars and ontologies. In: Proceedings of the 1st International Conference on Knowledge Capture, pp. 68–76 (2001)

Knowledge Management Applied
to Electronic Public Procurement

Helena Lindskog[1] and Eunika Mercier-Laurent[2]

[1] Department of Management and Engineering, Linköping University, Sweden
Helena.lindskog@liu.se
[2] MODEME, Centre Magellan, Jean Moulin University, Lyon3, France
e.mercier-laurent@univ-lyon3.fr

Abstract. Public procurement is a knowledge-based process. It involves, amongst others the knowledge of needs and trends, knowledge of concerned products or services, on their evolution in time and knowledge about actors able to offer them. The knowledge of political and legal context should be also considered as well as the environmental and social impact. Electronic procurement aims in reducing the amount of paper, but also in quicker and more knowledgeable processing of proposals and decision taking. We consider procurement activity as a part of a global organizational knowledge flow. This work goal is to analyze the whole process, identify the elements of knowledge necessary for successful purchase processing, to study the contribution of AI approaches and techniques to support the above elements. It is also to position e-procurement in the organizational knowledge flow.

Keywords: Procurement, Public Procurement, e-procurement, Knowledge Management.

1   Public Procurement

Purchasing is one of the most important activities for any kind of organization. Axelsson and Håkansson [3] define three different roles for purchasing:

- The rationalization role – to buy at very competitive prices which will put pressure on supplier efficiency.
- The developing role – to monitor the technical development (product and process) in different supplier segments and to encourage the suppliers to undertake technical development projects.
- The structuring role – to develop and maintain a supplier structure with a high potential for both development and efficiency.

While purchasing is in many ways similar for both public and private sectors, public procurement is in almost all situations and countries regulated by a specific legislation, which is stricter than the one that regulates the private sector's purchasing activities. For example, in public procurement environment the Request for Proposal (RfP)

E. Mercier-Laurent and D. Boulanger (Eds.): AI4KM 2012, IFIP AICT 422, pp. 95–111, 2014.

after it has been published cannot be changed, there is a possibility to appeal for suppliers if they consider themselves of being unfairly treated in the tendering process and must be taken into consideration not only economical but also political goals such as environmental and societal. The closest similarity between public procurement and private purchasing is probably in the case of acquisitions of large investments, often called project purchasing [1], [4], [15] and [30].

Public procurement activities by European Union member states are based on the principles from the Treaty of Rome (1957) aiming for establishing the free market within the EU is the base for public procurement and follows five fundamental principles:

Non-discrimination – all discrimination based on nationality or by giving preferences to local companies is prohibited.

Equal treatment – all suppliers involved in a procurement procedure must be treated equally.

Transparency – the procurement process must be characterized by predictability and openness.

Proportionality – the qualification requirements must have a natural relation to the supplies, services or works that are being procured.

Mutual recognition – the documents and certificates issued by the appropriate authority in a member state must be accepted in the other member states [38].

Public procurement has great importance for the economy of any country, and for the European Union it accounts *"for almost one-third of government expenditure. In 2009, it amounted to 19.4% of GDP – or 2.2 trillion EURO – of all the income generated in the EU"* [41].

A considerable part of all purchasing activities on any national market is due to public procurement and corresponds to around 19.4% of the European Union's GDP: *"at the local/regional level public procurement can easily reach the double of that in terms of percentage of public expenditure. For the example, a study of public procurement across Baltic city metropolises(3) shows that public procurement accounts for 40% of the city budget in Helsinki and 30% in Stockholm"* - CORDIS Community Research and development of Information Service [40].

2   Electronic Public Procurement

Electronic procurement has over a number of years gained recognition in both private and public sectors. More and more parts of the procurement process are done electronically, even to carry out the whole tendering process electronically. Leukel and Maniatopoulos [20] define *"in a public sector context, e-Procurement as a collective term for a range of different technologies that can be used to automate the internal and external processes associated with the sourcing and ordering process of goods and services"*.

In Sweden, in December 2005, Verva[1] published a report for a national action plan of procurement stressing that both buyers and suppliers would benefit from electronic methods for procurement and that the whole procurement process from planning to billing should and could be done electronically. Sveriges Kommuner och Landsting (The Swedish Association of Local Authorities and Regions) is heading another important Swedish project - SFTI (Single Face to Industry) that aims to standardise the communication between public and private organisations. It has received international attention.

The Swedish research project KNUT (Electronic Public Procurement of Telecommunications Services), sponsored by the Swedish government agency Vinnova[2], was an attempt to develop electronically the missing parts of the whole public procurement process by in a systematic and structured way collect and analyze needs and incorporate the legacy system. This approach is of special importance in the public procurement environment, since after the publishing of the RfP, no changes can take place. When the pre-formal phases of the public procurement process are carried out electronically, the results can be directly transferred to the electronically produced RfP. One of the objectives of the project was to increase the number of SMEs participating in the public procurements [22].

The first parts of the procurement process to be standardized and electronically applied were ordering and billing. This is due to the relatively low complexity and limited number of solutions for these parts of the procurement process.

According to IDABC (Interoperable Delivery of European e-Government Services to public Administrations, Businesses and Citizens) [37] e-Procurement can benefit:

Public Administrations: e-Procurement should minimize the time and effort expended by administrations and contracting authorities for organizing public procurement competitions.

Businesses: It will also benefit enterprises keen to trade across borders, by giving them improved and easier access to public procurement opportunities across Europe.

Citizens: Making procurement procedures available to a larger audience of suppliers enables the public sector to purchase goods and services at more economically advantageous prices. Citizens will have reassurance that their administrations are spending money in a more cost-effective manner.

The implications of electronic public procurement and the objectives for using electronic public procurement are many and can be summarized as:

---

[1] Verva was one of the Swedish Government's central advisory agencies. Today, public coordination of framework contracts concerning products and services for the entire public sector in the fields of information and communications is carried out by Kammarkollegiet.

[2] Vinnova - (Swedish Governmental Agency for Innovation Systems) is a State authority that aims to promote growth and prosperity throughout Sweden. The particular area of responsibility comprises innovations linked to research and development. The tasks are to fund needs-driven research required by a competitive business and industrial sector and a flourishing society, and to strengthen the networks that are necessary parts of this work.

- **To reduce public sector spending.** In the context of public procurement, cost reduction can be divided into three types:
  - Overall
  - The reduction can be achieved by purchasing goods and/or services that correspond to the authorities' specific needs (not too much, which could unnecessarily increase costs, or too little, which risks not meeting the authority's current and future needs) or by changing internal processes using new technologies or other innovative approaches. One example can be increased usage of information communication technology, which may signify increased cost of purchasing in order to reduce the overall cost.
  - For specific service and/or goods
  - Standardized procedures and descriptions of products reduce the cost for the preparation of tenders. Electronic procurement makes it possible for more suppliers to be aware of and easier bid for government contract and/or through economy of scale in case of framework contract
  - Of the procurement process
  - By using models, standardized procedures for every phase of the public procurement process and concentrating on analysis of needs specific for the authority, thus, to reduce the amount of time and the number of staff involved in the process.
- **To increase the service level.** Usage of the same standardized procedures and description of goods and services makes it easier for the suppliers to know how to bid for the government contracts. Usage of a model for the analysis of needs and standardized Request for Proposal reduces the number of misunderstandings.
- **To increase the number of SMEs**
- **To reduce the dependency on consultants.** Electronic procurement gives the possibility for authorities to use the aggregate knowledge from earlier procurements in the same area and of similar type of authorities, thus, to reduce the need for external workforces, especially for less qualified type of information.
- **To increase competition.** Standardized procedures, models for structuring needs and requirements, and easier access to information about forthcoming public procurements and to electronic RfP facilitate the possibility for a bigger number of companies and from more EU countries to participate in public procurements
- **To rationalize and increase efficiency**. This is especially valid in case of carrying out the whole procurement process electronically. Even a partially electronic process such as for example e-Invoicing can give substantial gains.
- **To increase the possibility to aggregate knowledge.** Electronic procurement makes it much easier to collect statistics over existing procurements and analyze criteria, requirements, contracts and/or outcomes in order to attune new specifications and to avoid mistakes.
- **To increase the possibility to put pressure towards more standardization.** If the statistics based on a big number of procurements show similar difficulties in achieving satisfactory results depending on the lack of standards for specific functionality, there is pressure on standardization organizations to develop and prioritize standards that are in demand by the users.

- **To empower each agency.** Easy access to information about how to make an analysis of needs using appropriate models, specify requirements automatically based on analysis of needs and develop a Request for Proposal corresponding to an authority's needs gives the possibility to carry out the entire procurement process by the agency itself.

The most important conclusion is that carrying out the whole procurement process electronically can lead to considerable gains of rationalization and efficiency. The upgradeable and scalable model enables analysis of needs, collection of information about the legacy of currently valid contracts and a direct transformation of these results into the RfP. Thus, the whole process can be carried out electronically.

3   Analysis of a Public Agency Purchasing Activity

The purchasing activity of a public agency is presented in Figure 1.

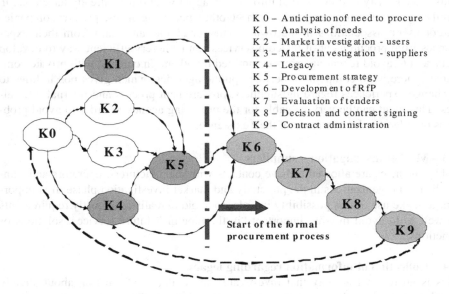

K 0 – Anticipation of need to procure
K 1 – Analysis of needs
K 2 – Market investigation - users
K 3 – Market investigation - suppliers
K 4 – Legacy
K 5 – Procurement strategy
K 6 – Development of RfP
K 7 – Evaluation of tenders
K 8 – Decision and contract signing
K 9 – Contract administration

Start of the formal
procurement process

Fig. 1. Public procurement – the purchasing process of a public agency [21]

The organizational buying process has been analyzed and structured by several researchers, among them [35], [29], [36] and [19]. Their research findings constitute the base for structuring and analysing the public procurement process of telecommunications services in the KNUT-project [22].

The public agency's buying process shown in Figure 1 is composed of ten phases and some of them can be carried out in parallel. The parts K1, K4 and K5 were developed in the KNUT project and K6, K7, K8 and K9 are the parts already available on the market.

K0 – Anticipation of need to start a procurement process. At this stage the organization, and especially its procurement department, observes the need of a new procurement (link with Figure 3). The absolutely most common reason to anticipate the need of the new procurement is the situation when the current contract is about to expire. If this happen close to the expiration date of the valid contract, it can be difficult to allocate enough time to carry out all necessary steps such as market investigations, analysis of needs, survey of legacy or choosing the procurement strategy.

K1 – Collection and analysis of needs

This is an internal activity in order to know what is needed in detail. Collection and analysis of needs often start with an analysis of the current situation and sometimes with a formulation of vision and strategy to achieve the vision. The vision can concentrate on "core" activities, improvement of the service level towards citizens and businesses, increased efficiency and reduction of costs.

K2 – Market investigation – users

This is an activity in order to find information about what others already have done in similar types of procurements. To meet other public agencies, private companies and/or users' associations in the own country or abroad and learn from their experiences from procurement of telecom services can be a very efficient way to develop RfPs and to avoid repeating errors committed by others. In contrast with private companies, there is no competition between public agencies, which gives possibilities to exchange experiences regarding suppliers, procurement process and internal difficulties. This input can be very valuable for the procuring agency in order to avoid problems or at least to be conscious of their existence.

K3 – Market investigation – suppliers

Public agencies are allowed to have contacts with manufacturers, operators and standardization organizations in the pre-study and market investigation phase. It is important to make use of this possibility in order to avoid unrealistic or costly requirements as well as to avoid missing important "in the pipeline" future services, solutions or functions.

K4 – Collection of information regarding legacy

This is an internal activity that investigates and collects information about already existing contracts and equipment within the organization. The most important parts of this investigation in case of telecommunications are legacies in form of ownership of properties, PABX[3]s, terminal equipment, and routers, and own networks such as building wiring or municipal broadband network. Other important parts are currently valid contracts on fixed connections, telephony services, switched board operators services, call center services etc. All these aspects must be taken into account in the development of the RfP.

---

[3] PABX – Private Automatic Branch Exchange.

K5 – Choice of procurement strategy

In this activity, the procuring organization investigates possible procurement scenarios and carries out the analysis of the consequences for each of these scenarios. The choice of the procurement scenario heavily depends on earlier undertaken investigations in K1, K2, K3 and K4.

In case of procurement of telecommunications, the KNUT project found three main scenarios:

1. Purchase of equipment,
2. Leasing of equipment
3. Service procurement (procurement of function)

Each of the main scenarios has several sub scenarios.

K6 – Development of Request for Proposal (RfP)

The development of the RfP is the central internal activity for public procurement. It includes structuring of mandatory and non-mandatory requirements, decision upon evaluation criteria, and often also contract proposal. Phases K1, K4 and K5 are input values for this activity. In the case of well carried out analysis of needs, legacy and choice of procurement strategy, the development of the RfP can be done automatically, i.e. electronically. With the development of the RfP starts the formal procurement process. The RfP cannot be changed after being published.

K7 – Evaluation of tenders

Tenders that do not comply with mandatory requirements are rejected and most of the evaluation will be concentrated on non-mandatory requirements and prices following the evaluation criteria. As a result one or several suppliers are chosen for decision taking.

K8 - Decision taking and contract signing

Decision taken by the procuring organization is valid only after giving during the stipulated time the possibility for the loosing tenderers to make a court appeal if they consider themselves being mistreated.

K9 – Ordering, invoicing, and follow-up

– After the contract is signed and up and running, the delivery and invoicing period starts depending on the type of goods or services. In case of framework contracts from a designated agency that procures on behalf of other public agencies, it is necessary to have a call-off contract with each specific agency that is calling off from the framework contract. The delivery and invoicing is to the calling-off agency. In order to learn from the specific procurement, both buyer and supplier should measure customer satisfaction and results/profits. This is an important and valuable input for decision making for tendering in other procurements in the same area.

The KNUT project aimed especially on the development of a model and a tool for the phases K1, K4 and K5 since the information from these phases can directly be transferred to already existing electronic procurement tools for the development of the RfP. The KNUT project developed the methodology and a tool for purchasing tele-communications services. The results of the project were tested in a real life procurement of telecommunications services in Swedish local community Lindesberg.

The experiences from this procurement could be used for procurements of tele-communications services by other entities and/or as a model for development of similar applications for other complex procurements. Possibly the most important learnt lesson from this the project and the test is that carrying out of the phases (K0 – K5) before the formal procurement phase starts are crucial in order to achieve the best results and it is also in these phases that the usage of Knowledge Management methods can of great help.

A Knowledge Management approach combined with electronic way to carry out procurement activities can play a great role in increasing the efficiency of the whole process [14].

4   Research Method

The research method we apply considers a whole cycle of life of knowledge related to procurement activity. This cycle includes understanding (existing elements and needs), modeling, choice of appropriate techniques and feedback integration. Amongst the various KM approaches those of bottom-up supervised by a top down [24] seems the most suited to study the knowledge flow of a procurement process. It consists in deep understanding of the procurement cycle of life from activity, involved actors and a related flow of knowledge points of view. The internal and external sources of knowledge are studied as well.

The KADS[4] way of thinking [5] will guide this analysis in aim to:

- determine a goal,
- analyze the knowledge involved in the procurement process,
- indentify the contextual knowledge (all external knowledge that apply as legal, environmental and others, necessary for understanding of all procurement aspects and their connections.
- define the actions (tactics) leading to the achievement of a given goal.

A general KADS structure is presented in Figure 2.

---

[4] Knowledge Acquisition Design Systems – European project Esprit 2.

Fig. 2. Problem solving using knowledge

KADS, conceived for effective designing of knowledge-based systems [32], takes into account the contextual knowledge, which is, in many cases, essential in decision making process. Initially designed to assist knowledge engineers and experts in building a conceptual knowledge models and built upon principles of genericity, modularity and reusability, KADS is also a way of thinking and problem solving. Conceptual knowledge models are independent of implementation [28] and can also serve for others applications. The goals are "translated" into a strategy and/or graph. Each leaf of this graph corresponds to a reasoning model drafted for a specific purpose. It can be generalized and instantiated for other similar reasoning according to principles described by Clancey [8]. The domain layer contains static knowledge expressed by hierarchically organized concepts and relations between them. Ontology is an example of such a knowledge model.

In this context, the strategy of a studied organization is a part of contextual knowledge. It can influence the way of problem solving by chaining the actions, organization of actors and/or of information system (top-down). An important point is the strategy of addressing the right actors the organization wants to respond to tenders. The RfP must be crafted to attract targeted businesses. If they want to attract SMEs the application format should be simplified and comprehensive.

At this step we will get a clear vision of knowledge related to the procurement process and its nature. The next step is the understanding of the real needs of those involved in the procurement process. The needs engineering method [23], [24], [25] is particularly useful for discovering their unexpressed needs. It consists in observing the users activity and working with them on elaborating the requirements of a future system. During this step new functions or services useful for users can be suggested. While the majority of applications and service providers are satisfied with expressed needs, the unexpressed ones are the potential source of innovation. Such a way of working "transforms" the users to "co-creators" of a future application; this fact is vital for appropriation of a new solution by them.

The Figure 3 presents the benefits of involving selected users into a co-construction of the future application.

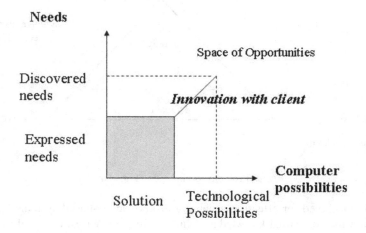

Fig. 3. Discovering of needs with future users

Traditional identification of needs and addressing them keeps participants in a small square; they have a little chance to innovate. Implication of clients allows both clients and service providers to reach the space of opportunities. It can lead to creation of new products and services.

Supervising by "top-down" means that we need to know the studied organization strategy to adapt our application to existing situation, but in the same time the feedback from the elaborating and use of the application can influence the strategy. In some cases an "innovation process management assessment" [25] may be introduced to argument the necessary adaptation and to provide a tool for systematic innovation management simultaneously. In reality many organizations and companies that consider themselves innovative are not managing the "knowledge innovation" process "from idea to values".

The analysis of a knowledge flow is fundamental for suited knowledge organization supporting the procurement activity in connection with the others organizational processes.

The KNUT project results are our starting point for this study.

5   The Role of Knowledge Management in Electronic Public Procurement

While there are many publications on e-Procurement and Knowledge Management we found only few connecting the both fields. The main effort is made on recording documents related to request for proposals, and past tenders into an organizational memory in aim to have quick access and a possibility to reuse existing knowledge [10], [8].

The MNEMOS project was, on our knowledge, the first that applied a Knowledge Management approach to a procurement process. Matra Marconi Space (MMS) activities were multidisciplinary combing knowledge about physics, electronics, satellites, information processing and other related fields. To assist MMS commercial engineers in relevant and quick answering the tenders by providing them an easy access to company knowledge was the main motivation for introducing KM through organizational memory [26].

Latter they added to the knowledge flow a skill management and decision support systems [27]. This project is a good example of bottom-up and incremental KM approach.

At present two main categories of approaches can be found – first emphasizes on management methods and organizational change and second focus on ICT, knowledge modelling and processing.

The first category discusses the importance of including procurement into an organizational strategy [18], managing knowledge and skills relative to the procurement process [12] and redesigning e-procurement as a new operating practice [14].

The second category focuses on management of the procurement process using traditional information technology and knowledge techniques as well. De Nicola [10] work is about knowledge modelling and processing and in particular they propose knowledge models such as ontology, while Vlahovic [33] research focus is on knowledge storing and processing.

De Nicola [10] describes also the interoperability between two different software applications and documents. Ontology is considered as a "common language" as well for applications as for involved various actors. A common language is one of the pillars of effective Knowledge Management.

Vlahovic [33] presents a system composed of database for storing information about calls for tenders and related documents. It is also used to track status of the call, either its expiry or cancelation if one is published. The information extraction techniques allow to access and retrieve information and accompanying documentation.

His knowledge base contains past tenders and feedback information supplied by client users. The analogy engine (case-based reasoning) provides information about preparing optimized proposals, estimating other characteristics of the tender and calculating possible expectations in terms of contract negotiation, ordering and payment. All of this information is made available to potential contractors through the client application to enhance their decision making procedures.

Quite whole KM cycle of life including identification, recording using models and processing is covered here:

Knowledge Management (KM) has been introduced as a new management method in the late 1980s [11], [31], [2] and a decade latter via ICT (Information and Communication Technology), mainly without taking into account the artificial intelligence approaches, techniques and experiences in building various knowledge-based systems. While one of the objectives of Artificial Intelligence (AI) has always been knowledge modelling and processing, the KM have been introduced to this field in early 1990s via Corporate Knowledge [7] and Organizational Memory concepts [9] Corporate Knowledge goal is to build an optimized knowledge flow for a given organization using conceptual knowledge modelling (Knowledge Models) and storage (Knowledge Repository), intelligent access to knowledge (Knowledge Navigator) using hypertext and semantic navigation in the knowledge repository and make it available for decision making (Corporate Decision) - [24].

The importance of external contributors (stakeholders), including clients for the organizational strategy has been better understood in the same period [2], [25].

By consequence, the definition of Knowledge Management we propose is following:

The organized and optimized system of initiatives, methods and tools designed to create an optimal flow of knowledge within and throughout an extended enterprise to ensure stakeholders success (Amidon, Mercier-Laurent, 1997).

According to this definition, AI plays an essential role in the optimizing of the knowledge flow and processing the knowledge elements influencing the success of all participants. AI techniques are effective for capitalization of knowledge elements to reuse, for collecting of "best" practices, feedback processing and decision making. AI helps in providing an intelligent guiding (tasks and reasoning models) to involved persons in accomplishing of the whole procurement process.

Information and Communication Technology will facilitate sharing of relevant elements amongst participants.

In the case of public procurement process, the related internal knowledge contains the elements such as needs, potential suppliers, technical knowledge, available technology, past projects and experience. In the majority of cases this knowledge is in the heads, sometimes it is shared by email. The elements of external knowledge are legal, political, environmental, economic and technological nature. This knowledge is spread over the web and documents.

The electronic procurement allow reducing paper, but also introducing the new way of thinking relative to usage of this media and instantaneous access to world base of information. Instead of reproducing the paper mechanism, a given organization can innovate in the way of preparing, diffusing and processing the proposals as well as in the way of capturing knowledge, opportunities in real time and for decision taking.

5.1   Knowledge Flow for e-Procurement

Each step of the process presented in Figure 1 needs internal and external knowledge to act and produces knowledge as well. Some elements of knowledge are shared by several steps. These steps organization could be considered as initial flow of knowledge. The process of procurement exchanges knowledge with other organizational processes and applications, such as services provided to citizens and enterprises, for example call for projects, electronic tax collection, healthcare, car registration and practically all internal processes.

A preliminary analysis of a knowledge flow related to e-procurement process is shown in Figure 4. The involved actors are organizations, procurement department, partners, suppliers, clients, citizens and businesses. Knowing them is vital for successful managing of procurement. All produce, have and use knowledge.

This flow is generic and works for purchase of equipment, leasing of equipment and service procurement as well.

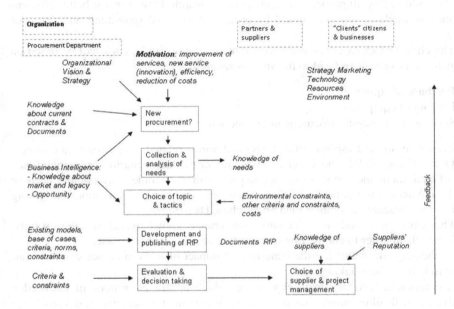

Fig. 4. Knowledge flow for procurement process

The anticipation and definition of needs involve the elements like knowledge on existing contracts and constraints such as end of current contracts, results, skills and other resources, legal and environmental constraints. It depends on organizational vision and strategy. Motivations of actors play an important role in the innovation process – they may detect a need for a new service or improvement of existing by adding for example the environmental aspects. Motivation by only reduction of costs may influence a new more effective organization or…relocation of services and lost of local jobs.

At this stage and all along the process the participants need the access to existing knowledge and support in finding the relevant information and opportunity watch (Business Intelligence). The AI techniques of knowledge discovery such as text mining and semantic search can be helpful. Business Intelligence (BI) is also useful in continuous discovering of new providers and services, laws, opportunities, practices and technology.

As mentioned before a collection and analysis of needs should be improved by adding "needs discovery" aspects [23]. It includes the involvement of selected users into the early stage of procurement process. In function of a type of organization it may include the knowledge about citizens businesses and their expectations.

Market investigation involves knowledge on similar types of procurement (known cases), feedback from experiences, users [34] and suppliers. Availability of all this knowledge can enhance the effectiveness of the whole process.

The information on legacy, environmental and other constraints to be considered can be collected by all participants and semantic search. However, for better efficiency the knowledge exchange should be organized to avoid spamming and waste of time.

The choice of knowledge-based procurement strategy and tactics will be based on knowledge of benefits related to the various scenarios:

- Purchase of equipment,
- Leasing of equipment
- Service procurement (procurement of function)

Corporate Social Responsibility (CSR) and norms related to environmental impact (ISO 26000 and 14001) encourage choosing rather the last scenario, if possible. Leasing of equipment and services of function procurement become more popular because of the environmental constraints. Some economists advice to focus more on leasing and service procurement rather than on purchase [16], [6].

The scenarios should also take into consideration knowledge about relevant business models in order to choose one or more that best suits a given case.

At the stage of evaluation the benefits and impact of a given choice can be simulated to help decision taking.

A continuous feedback from experience, which is also an attitude of knowledge cultivator, will allow improving the both e-procurement processing and knowledge management. A system of practice collection and processing, using for ex case-based reasoning (analogy) could be an added value. The opening to external knowledge, such as experience with suppliers and tools is vital.

The tasks chaining represented in Figure 1 may be considered as a generic reasoning model for e procurement process and tested in various fields.

The described knowledge flow is the first step of Knowledge Management approach. It should be validated by applying to KNUT project and tested on a real case.

5.2   Knowledge Management and KNUT Model/Tool

After understanding of the procurement and e-procurement processes specificities and getting a clear representation of involved actors and flow of knowledge, the next step will deal with knowledge modelling and a choice of appropriate tools.

One of the important prerequisites for the best usage of the KNUT model is the construction or adaptation from existing generic knowledge models for collection of information from already carried out procurements. The RfPs, procurement processes and contracts could be then compared as well as all comments taken automatically into account.

At this stage we will study existing ontologies. KNUT conceptual knowledge model can be built incrementally or adapted from existing. The use of knowledge modelling techniques will facilitate more effective RfP construction; a new RfP can be quickly composed with existing modules, as Lego™ toys. The phase of proposals evaluation may follow an appropriate reasoning model and use a decision support system and constraint propagation engine if apply.

The feedback form testing of KNUT model combined with Knowledge Management approaches and techniques will be integrated to improve the whole cycle of life.

With the collective, aggregated knowledge about procurements of specific goods or services (in case of KNUT model/tool, it deals with telecommunications services) KM techniques can not only speed up the process of development of a RfP but also to analyze and then improve both the model/tool and next procurements that use the model. It can influence more accurate choices.

6   Conclusions and Perspectives

Public procurement could be a first step in introducing a holistic knowledge management approach in organizations that are not yet practicing it. The described case is just a beginning of a larger project which could be followed by a PhD student using KNUT model and working on a real case in aim to study a genericity of knowledge models and reasoning related to electronic public procurement. A tool for assistance for procurement cycle of life will be prototyped and tested.

Knowledge Management approach will certainly increase the efficiency of the procurement process by organizing and optimizing the related knowledge collection, modelling and processing, including access and sharing. The reuse of existing knowledge components and experiences, as well as the quick access to relevant information will help more effective development of RfP. Knowledge-based decision support system may assist in the process of evaluation and in the choice of the best supplier.

The procurement process is just one element of organizational flow of knowledge, which has a potential of the integration of other processes into the whole flow of knowledge. It may impulse the systematic management of the innovation process. It can also influence the organizational strategy.

The AI approaches and techniques can bring a significant help in knowledge gathering, modelling, reusing as well as in discovering knowledge from data, text and image when apply.

To attract the SMEs, the whole procedure should be simplified to focus on essential in aim to encourage the SMEs to apply for tenders. A SME can not spend a month answering if it is not sure to gain the contract. Testing the elaborated model on some SMEs may be of interest in this case.

The experience in introducing the Corporate Social Responsibility in organizations may bring interesting feedback to e-procurement policies and process.

References

1. Ahlström, M.: Offset Management for Large Systems – A Multibusiness Marketing Activity. Linköping University, Studies in Management and Economics (2000)
2. Amidon, D.: The Innovation Strategy for the Knowledge Economics. Butterworth Heinemann (1997) ISBN 0750698411
3. Axelsson, B., Håkansson, H.: Industrial Procurement. LiberFörlag (1984)
4. Bonnacorsi, A., Pammolli, F., Tani, S.: The changing boundaries of system companies. International Business Review 5(1) (1996)
5. Schreiber, G., Wielinga, B., Breuker, J.: KADS, A Principled Approach to Knowledge-Based System Development. Academic Press (1993)
6. Buclet, N.: Concevoir une nouvelle relation à la consommation: l'Economie de fonctionnalité. In: Annales des Mines, pp. 57–66 (Juillet 2005)
7. CEDIAG Corporate Knowledge, internal Bull document (confidential), described in [23] (1991)
8. Clancey, W.J.: Heuristic classification. Artificial Intelligence 27 (1985)
9. Conklin, E.J., Star, S.L.: Organizational Memory. In: Proceedings of the Second European Conference on Computer-Supported Cooperative Work, ECSCW 1991, pp. 189–190 (1991)
10. De Nicola, A., Missikoff, M., Misceo, F.: A Core Business Ontology for eProcurement: a First Proposal. In: The Proceedings of itAIS 2005, 2nd Conference of the Italian Chapter of AIS (2005)
11. Drucker, P.: The New Society of Organizations. Harvard Business Review (September-October 1992)
12. Egbu, C., Vines, M.P., Tookey, J.: The role of knowledge management in e-procurement initiatives for construction organizations. In: Greenwood, D.J. (ed.) Proceedings 19th Annual ARCOM Conference, September 3-5, vol. 2, pp. 661–669. Association of Researchers in Construction Management, Brighton (2003)
13. European Commission. Directive 2004/18/EC of the European Parliament and of the Council of 31 March 2004 on the coordination of procedures for the award of public works contracts, public supply contracts and public service contracts (2004)
14. Federici, T., Resca, A.: Managing E-Procurement in Public Healthcare: A Knowledge Management Perspective. International Journal of Healthcare Delivery Reform Initiatives (IJHDRI) 1(1) (2009)
15. Gelderman, C.J., Ghijsen, P.W.T., Brugman, M.J.: Public procurement and EU tendering directives – explaining non-compliance. International Journal of Public Sector Management 19(7), 702–714 (2006)
16. Giarini, O., Stahel, W.R.: The Limits to Certainty, Facing risks in the new service economy-International Studies in the Service Economy. Kluwer, The Netherlands (1989)
17. Goldkuhl, G., Axelsson, K.: E-services in public administration. International Journal of Public Information Systems 3, 113–116 (2007)
18. Knudsen, D.: Aligning corporate strategy, procurement strategy and e-procurement tools. International Journal of Physical Distribution & Logistics Management 33(8), 720–734 (2003)
19. Kotler, P.: - Marketing Management Analysis, Planning, Implementation, and Control, 9th edn. Prentice Hall, USA (1997)
20. Leukel, J., Maniatopoulos, G.: A comparative analysis of product classification in public vs. private e-procurement. The Electronic Journal of e-Government 3(4), 201–212 (2005)

21. Lindskog, H.: Process of Public Procurement of Telecom Services, The Buyer's Perspective. In: Proceedings of the 7th ISOneWorld Conference, Las Vegas (2008)
22. Lindskog, H.: KNUT Elektronisk offentlig upphandling av telekommunkationstjänster, slurapport, Vinnova (2010)
23. Mercier-Laurent, E.: From Data Programming to Intelligent Knowledge Processors: How Computers Can Improve the Global KM Flow. Cutter IT Journal 17(12), 33–39 (2004)
24. Mercier-Laurent, E.: Rôle de l'ordinateur dans le processus global de l'innovation à partir de connaissances, Mémoire d'Habilitation à Diriger les Recherches en Informatique, Université Lyon 3 (2007)
25. Mercier-Laurent, E.: Innovation Ecosystems. Willey-ISTE (2011) ISBN: 978-1-84821-325-8
26. MNEMOS. Comment Matra Marconi Space batît sa mémoire technique, |L'Usine Nouvelle n° 2543 (Avril 04, 1996), http://www.usinenouvelle.com/article/gestion-de-projetcomment-matra-marconi-space-batit-sa-memoire-techniquele-constructeur-de-satellites-construit-metier-par-metier-un-systeme-de-capitalisation-des-connaissances-reutilisables-obj.N78526
27. MNEMOS (1998), http://www.eurekanetwork.org/project/-/id/1093
28. Newell, A.: The knowledge level. Artificial Intelligence 18 (1982)
29. Robinson, P.J., Faris, C.W., Wind, Y.: Industrial Buying and Creative Marketing. Allyn and Bacon Inc., Boston (1967)
30. Roodhooft, F., Van den Abbeele, A.: Public procurement of consulting services: Evidence and comparison with private companies. International Journal of Public Sector Management 19(5), 490–512 (2006)
31. Savage, C.: 5th Generation Management: Integrating Enterprises through Human Networking. The Digital Press, Bedford (1990)
32. Dolenc, N., Libralesso, J.-M., Thirion, C., Gobrecht, A., Lesaffre, F.-M., Hellelsen, M., Lalhier, M., Lenuet, D., Steller, J.-M.: The SACHEM Project: Blast Furnace Operating Support System; Ambition and Stakes, Development and First Results. In: 3rd European Ironmaking Congress, Gent, Belgium, September 16-18 (1996)
33. Vlahović, N.: Public Knowledge Base System for Public eProcurement: A Conceptual Model. In: The Proceedings of the 5th WSEAS International Conference on Management, Marketing and Finances (MMF 2011), pp. 251–256. WSEAS Press, Athens (2011) ISBN: 978-960-474-287-5
34. von Hippel, E.: Learning from Lead Users. In: Buzzell, R.D. (ed.) Marketing in an Electronic Age, pp. 308–317. Harvard Business School Press, Boston (1985)
35. Webster, F.E.: Modeling the Industrial Buying Proces. Journal of Marketing Research 2, 370–376 (1965)
36. Wind, Y., Thomas, J.R.: Conceptual and Methodological Issue in Organizational Buying Behaviour. European Journal of Marketing 14, 239–286 (1980)
37. http://ec.europa.eu/idabc
38. http://europa.eu/publicprocurement
39. http://www.peppol.eu
40. http://cordis.europa.eu/fp7/ict/pcp/key_en.html
41. http://ec.europa.eu/internal_market/publications/docs/public-procurement_en.pdf

Distributed and Collaborative Knowledge Management Using an Ontology-Based System

Weronika T. Adrian, Antoni Ligęza, Grzegorz J. Nalepa, and Krzysztof Kaczor

AGH University of Science and Technology, Poland
{wta,ligeza,gjn,kk}@agh.edu.pl

Abstract. Semantic annotations and formally grounded ontologies constitute flexible yet powerful methods of knowledge representation. Using them in a system allows to perform automated reasoning and can enhance the knowledge management. In the paper, we present a system for collaborative knowledge management, in which an ontology and ontological reasoning is used. The main objective of the application is to provide information for citizens about threats in an urban environment. The system integrates a database and an ontology for storing and inferring desired information. While a terminology of the traffic danger domain is described by the ontology, the location details of traffic conditions are stored in the database. During run-time, the ontology is populated with instances stored in the database and used by a Description Logic reasoner to infer new facts.

1 Introduction

One of the important research fields of Artificial Intelligence (AI) is the area of Knowledge Representation and Reasoning (KR&R) [5]. The Semantic Web [3] initiative is sometimes perceived as the new incarnation of AI, tackling some of its problems and challenges. Although this worldwide project is not aimed at constructing intelligent machines, it has resulted in development of several effective KR&R methods. Representation of knowledge is done on a few levels of abstraction. For single objects, attributes and relations to other objects (resources) are defined, by use of semantic annotations. These attributes and relations are organized into semantic vocabularies for various domains. Classification of objects and classes definition using their interdependencies is done with use of ontologies [6] of different expressiveness and formality level. Stating logical axioms about classes enable automated reasoning and inferring conclusions about single objects. There is an ongoing research on integrating ontologies with higher-level representation of rules. Semantic applications can make use of this multilevel knowledge representation and exhibit semi-intelligent behavior.

Web-based information systems have been widely used to facilitate communication and distribution of information in a rapid and efficient way. Whether through official news portals or social systems like Facebook or Twitter, people inform each other about the events or dangers. Using GIS systems [14] that allow to store, represent and search geographic information, users can add location metadata to the information they provide or get useful data based on their localization (e.g. by the use of a GPS). One of the area which still needs a careful attention from the information systems is the local safety of citizens in the urban environment.

E. Mercier-Laurent and D. Boulanger (Eds.): AI4KM 2012, IFIP AICT 422, pp. 112–130, 2014.

Projects such as Wikipedia has demonstrated that people are willing to cooperate if they find it worthwhile and the system is easy to use. Collaborative knowledge engineering and management can be enhanced by employing intelligent techniques, for example by using formal knowledge representation. However, a system interface must remain simple. An interesting and promising example of such a combination are semantic wikis [9,1], in which teams can collaboratively build and manage formally specified knowledge in an intuitive fashion and with little technical knowledge.

In this paper, we present a system for collaborative knowledge management enhanced with semantic knowledge representation and reasoning. The main objective of the system is to gather knowledge about threats of various sorts within a defined urban area. The system should serve the local community and the police. Our proposed solution combines social software features (commenting, ratings etc.) with a strong underlying logical representation of knowledge entered by users. The application employs AI methods, namely a domain ontology of traffic dangers and conditions, and a Description Logic (DL) [2] reasoner to infer knowledge from facts explicitly present in the system.

The rest of the paper is organized as follows: in Section 2 the motivation for our research is given with references to selected previous works. Section 3 gives an overview of selected existing solutions and related work. In Section 4, basic assumptions for the system are specified. Section 5 gives an overview of the system, including its functionality, architecture, a threat ontology, the integration of an ontology and a database in the system, the reasoning in the system and the user interface. The implementation is briefly discussed in Section 6. Evaluation of the approach is sketched in Section 7. The paper is summarized in Section 8 and future work is outlined in Section 9.

2   Motivation

Within the INDECT project [1] several problems related to security and intelligent information systems are investigated. Task 4.6 of the project focuses on development of a *Web System for citizen provided information, automatic knowledge extraction, knowledge management and GIS integration* [8]. The main objective of our research is to develop a semantically enriched environment for collaborative knowledge management. Local communities should be able to quickly share information about current traffic dangers and threats, for instance closed roads, holes in the pavements and streets, dangerous districts or events that impede a regular traffic. The system proposed within the task should be a sort of a community portal that allows citizens to participate and cooperate in order to improve the security in the urban environment. Within the task several initial system prototypes have been developed [7,13] and the current work consists in integrating the best solutions into the final system.

The system should use some sort of intelligent processing to provide possibly most useful knowledge to the users. To this end, a Knowledge-Based System (KBS) should be proposed, with a formalized knowledge representation and reasoning mechanisms. Categorization of threats and possibility of inferring new facts based on the ones entered

---

[1] See http://indect-project.eu.

by users is a desired feature. To enhance the automated knowledge processing of the system, semantic technologies for GIS were analyzed and discussed in [10].

While a threat domain ontology can be the same for various locations, different system installations will vary depending on the locations they work in. Abstract knowledge can and should be shared across applications boundaries to facilitate change management. On the other hand, the system should be robust and easily adaptable to local conditions, so the access to the actual data should be optimized.

The system should encompass social features, such as possibility to comment on, discuss and rate information entered by other users. This way, the users can gain or loose credibility and the community can indirectly control spam information. The user interface (UI) should be intuitive and easy to use, potentially adaptable to various hardware platforms including desktop and mobiles. Encompassing these requirement should provide a useful intelligent system for improving urban safety.

3   Threat Information Systems – An Overview of Existing Solutions

In this section, we give a brief overview of the existing approaches and solutions for threat information systems. Crime Mapping systems were originally a class of systems that map, visualize and analyze crime incident patterns using Geographic Information Systems (GIS). This name has been later extended to incorporate all applications that aid in improving the public safety. This include natural disasters monitoring systems which are often designed for specific regions and the scope of their functionalities is usually limited to the specific types of disasters that are most common and most dangerous in those regions, systems monitoring threats on the roads and crime monitoring systems. A detailed survey of the existing crime mapping systems is given in [15].

Ubiquity of the Internet allowed the Crime Mapping class systems to be available not only for specialized units, but for everyone with Internet access, thus allowing the improvement of public safety.

Crime Mapping systems can be divided into categories based on the nature of threats they focus on. The INDECT Crime Mapping class system developed at the AGH University does not specialize in any of them. Instead, it attempts to track threats in all of those categories.

3.1   Categorization of Crime Mapping Systems

Crime Mapping is a very extensive class of systems. To facilitate analysis and comparison of its representatives, several factors can be separated that the systems can be categorized by. The following categorization and the list of systems are not exhaustive, but should give an overview of the state of the art in this area.

Types of threats. This seems to be the most important criterion, since the system is chosen by user based on kind of threats they are interested in monitoring or learning about. Crime Mapping systems focus on:

- Natural disasters: Earthquakes, Fires, Floods, Dry weather, Storms (e.g. thunderstorms, hurricanes, etc.), Tsunami, Tornados, Volcanic activity.
- Threats caused by a man: 1) Crimes: numerous types of criminal activity, e.g. robberies, assaults, car or house break-ins, sex crimes, etc., 2) Industry level: larger scale disasters caused by technology, e.g. chemical spills, toxic fumes, radiation, etc., 3) Infrastructure-type (e.g. old buildings, slippery stairs)
- Transportation risks: 1) Hazards: various places or situations that may cause a risk to the driver, e.g. potholes, sharp curves, road bumps, etc., 2) Disruptions: not as much dangerous places, but more an inconvenience for people travelling, e.g. road works, traffic jams, narrowings or speed limits.

Geographical range. Crime Mapping systems vary in area they cover. This also is an extremely important factor, as user will be looking for a system that covers the area of their interest. They are divided into following categories:

- Global: systems spanning the whole planet;
- Local: limited only to some area. Depending how the range boundaries are defined, they can be limited: geographically, for example, a system monitoring fires in only one forest or warning about tornados on some specific continent, or socially, depending by social structure, e.g. from single city quarter, through the whole city to an entire country or even several of them.

Availability. Crime Mapping systems can be also divided depending on who the system is available to. The significance of this factor is that users need to have means to access the system if they are to use it. Categories are:

- Publicly available: many systems are open for browsing for everyone, without even the necessity of registering or logging in.
- With authorized access: users need to register with the system and log in to learn the information it offers. Registration itself could be open for everyone or somehow limited – for example, a registration fee could be collected.
- Restricted: only people satisfying some defined conditions could be accepted as users, e.g. inhabitants of monitored area, members of an organization or employees of a company.

Data Source. Finally, Crime Mapping systems vary in where the data collected and presented comes from. The source of information matters, because it has impact on its quality and credibility. Data can come from:

- Agencies, cooperating with the system, e.g. law enforcement or university;
- Experts, analyzing data and providing the results to the system;
- Automated monitoring, collected by various measuring or observation apparatus (e.g. seismic sensors or cameras), often subjected also to processing or analysis, which itself also can be automated;
- Users – some systems allow users to provide data to the system, or even depend on that greatly.

3.2 Natural Disasters Information Systems

Natural disasters monitoring systems are often designed for specific regions and the scope of their functionalities is usually limited to the specific types of disasters that are most common and most dangerous in those regions. For example, the area of Great Britain has several different systems for warning about floods. Among others, there are: National Flood Hazard Mapping[2] in Wales, Managing Flood Risk and Flood Warnings[3] in Scotland and Risk of Flooding from Rivers and Sea[4] in London and its vicinity. Similarly, there is a California-Nevada Fault Map[5] (see Fig. 1) , collecting information about earthquakes in the western states of USA, where those are a frequent occurrence due to the proximity to the San Andreas Fault.

Another system, developed as part of U.S. Geographical Survey's (USGS) Earthquake Hazards Program[6] is available on the Internet to aid reducing earthquake hazard in the USA. However, their area of observations is not limited to the US only. The scientists behind the program study and keep track of earthquakes all around the world, providing not only local but also global information. This proves that aside from those regional systems for warning about national disasters there also are ones working globally. Other examples of such systems are Seismic Monitor[7], also gathering information about earthquakes around the world, and Global Flood Map[8].

3.3 Road Threats Information Systems

Another area where technological advancement is progressing constantly is the transportation. For common citizen especially important from the safety point of view is personal transport – car technology and road infrastructure.

GPS navigation devices become increasingly popular, and they not only serve as tools for finding optimal routes and guide the driver to their target, but often they also take into consideration and keep track of dangerous spots on the road, requiring the driver to be more cautious or avoid it completely. Places where, for example, accidents happen more often due to potholes or poor visibility, are sometimes included in maps the devices use, so that they inform the driver when they are approaching the danger.

Systems like that already exist. They collect information of such statistically risky places, but also keep track of other, temporary difficulties, like road works, narrowings, traffic jams or accidents. More often than in case of natural disasters monitoring systems these cover only some local areas – there is no actual global transport threats and difficulties monitor.

The examples of such systems are: Traffic Information Highways Agency (reporting bad weather, speed reductions, accidents and road works in England)[9], Travel News

---

[2] See: http://www.floodmaps.ie
[3] See: http://go.mappoint.net/sepa
[4] See: http://www.environment-agency.gov.uk/homeandleisure/floods
[5] See: http://earthquake.usgs.gov/earthquakes/recenteqscanv
[6] See: http://earthquake.usgs.gov/earthquakes
[7] See: http://www.iris.edu/seismon
[8] See: http://globalfloodmap.org
[9] See: http://www.highways.gov.uk/traffic/traffic.aspx

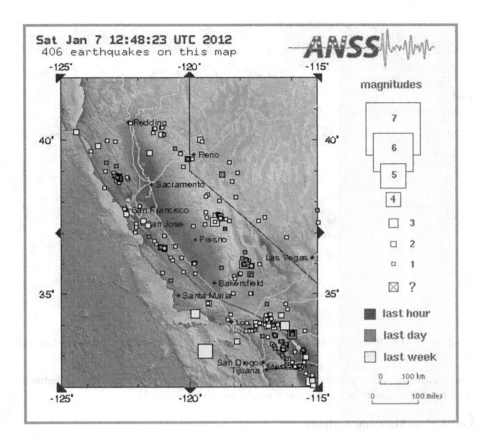

Fig. 1. California-Nevada Fault Map. Source: `http://earthquake.usgs.gov/earthquakes/recenteqscanv`.

Scotland (accidents, road works, other difficulties)[10], TravelMidwest.com[11] (road capacity, road works, accidents, speed cameras, etc. in Chicago and several other cities and areas around Midwestern states). NAVTEQ[12] is one of the few of such services that attempt to provide traffic information from all around the world, yet it only provides information about capacity and delays, not about threats or accidents.

Similar Polish service with traffic information, "Serwis dla kierowców" (Service for Drivers)[13], available on the website of General Directorate of National Roads and Motorways (GDDKiA), bears comparison with Traffic England. Although the interactive map is a little more difficult to use (mouse roller does not work as zoom in and out, drag and drop map moving sometimes fails), the road network this tool covers is much

---

[10] See: `http://www.bbc.co.uk/travelnews/scotland`
[11] See: `http://www.travelmidwest.com`
[12] See: `http://www.traffic.com`
[13] See: `http://www.gddkia.gov.pl/pl/10/serwis-dla-kierowcow`

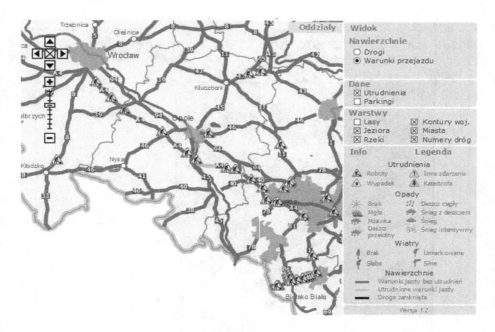

Fig. 2. Service for Drivers. Source: http://www.gddkia.gov.pl/pl/10/serwis-dla
-kierowcow.

more dense and is not limited only to motorways. Moreover, user can switch between
clear road map and information about road capacity (see Fig. 2).

3.4   Crime Mapping Systems

The name of Crime Mapping system class comes from the original idea for publicly
available systems providing information about crimes and threats in urban area. The
possibilities for what such systems could incorporate and the vast amount of functionalities they could provide are growing along with the development of the Internet. Crime
Mapping systems gain much in credibility and accuracy of presented data when they
cooperate with law agencies and police departments. Since this way the agencies aid in
increasing public safety, profits from such cooperation are mutual.

Because law differs between parts of the world, such systems are mostly local, vary-
ing in range from one police unit (e.g. Crime Tracker[14] for Jefferson Parish, Louisiana,
USA), through a province or a county (Cornwall Crime Explorer[15] or Arizona Crime
Search[16]) to a whole country (Crime Reports[17] or Crime Mapping[18], both of which span
over USA and Canada). Sadly, there are no global Crime Mapping systems.

---

[14] See: http://crimestats.jpso.com/crimetracker/externalmanager/
index.html
[15] See: https://www.amethyst.gov.uk/crime_atlas/atlas.html
[16] See: http://www.azcentral.com/CrimeMaps
[17] See: https://www.crimereports.com
[18] See: http://www.crimemapping.com

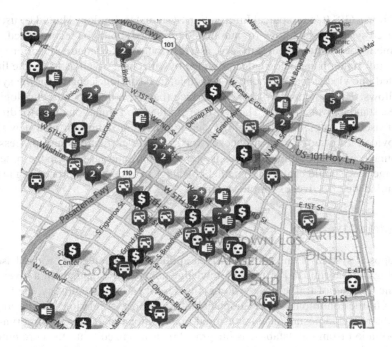

Fig. 3. Interactive map with crime markers. Source: http://www.crimemapping.com

The systems present the threats in a visual form on a map and provide various output channels, e.g. e-mail notifications, text messages or even Twitter alerts. They operate on mobile devices and make use of their GPS systems. The apparent lack, however, is that the information presented to the users is strictly that which was entered. The original contribution of our approach is to supply the system with intelligent processing techniques based on ontological reasoning. Moreover, our approach aims at encompassing various kinds of threats by using a threat ontology.

4   A Conceptual Model for the System

The main focus of our research was on tools to process the information provided by citizens via a specialized website. In fact, a Web System software for citizen provided information, automatic knowledge extraction, knowledge management and GIS integration is to be developed. This task is intended to complement other work oriented towards automated information extraction from existing web resources by building an Internet-based, distributed information acquisition and automated knowledge management system.

Such a system should combine a CMS (Content Management System) system with a KMS (Knowledge Management System) incorporating intelligent information processing tools based on knowledge engineering. It should allow storing and retrieving of partially analyzed investigations. For spatial information processing and information presentation a GIS (Geographical Information Systems) technology should be used and logic-based systems technology for automated inference should be incorporated.

The main goal of the system is to serve as a distributed knowledge acquisition system for data, information and knowledge provided by citizens, as well as to enable limited automated knowledge management. In principle, the working scenario for the systems is as follows. The system offers a web interface (based on thin-client technologies; in practice a standard web viewer). The interface offers various functionalities for different types of users. The main functionality refers to enabling definition of a new threat. The provided knowledge is then checked for syntactic correctness and processed in an automatic way. The ultimate result is stored in the internal knowledge base. The knowledge base should enable automatic knowledge extraction and processing in order to maximize the effectiveness of the system.

5 System Overview

The proposed system is an ontology-driven application. It integrates a database and an ontology for storing and inferring knowledge about traffic dangers in a given area. While the abstract of traffic danger domain is described by the ontology, the location details of traffic conditions and geographical information (e.g. relations among concrete streets, districts and postal codes) are stored in a relational database. During run-time, the information from the database is integrated (synchronized) with the core ontology (the terminology is populated with instance data stored in a database). The synchronization is done automatically at the application start and at any time on a user demand. The synchronized ontology is then used by a DL reasoning engine to infer facts about chosen area. The deduction is based on definitions of threats which depends on specific traffic conditions present in specific locations.

5.1 Functionality and User Roles

The main objective of the proposed system is to provide citizens with a real-time data about dangers occurring in a chosen area. Part of this information is entered into the system by so-called *trusted users*. The rest is automatically inferred based on the axioms of the threat ontology and instance data of current conditions (facts).

Three kinds of users are distinguished within the system. *Regular users* can browse the system knowledge and ask questions about specific locations and dangers. They address the system with dynamic questions and get results of inferred traffic dangers. *Trusted users* can modify the information stored in the database, e.g. they can update the locations of traffic conditions occurrences. The information is validated and stored in the database. Updated knowledge can be used for dangers deduction process, after *synchronization* with the ontology. Finally, the *experts* can modify the core ontology.

5.2 Architecture and Data Flow

The system is divided into three functionally different layers:

1. a web dashboard layer dedicated to the interaction with users (through browser clients),
2. a platform layer which is the core of system responsible for processing knowledge, and
3. a storage layer, where all the data is stored, in a database and an ontology (see Figure 4).

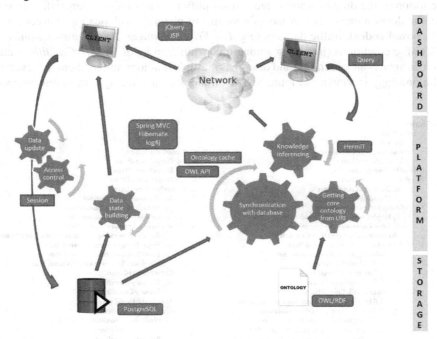

Fig. 4. Data flow in the system

All users can interact with the web-based dashboard for querying system, to get desired information. The main logic of the system (presented in Fig. 4 as three cogged wheels) consists in: downloading the core ontology (*"Getting core ontology from URI"*), synchronizing the core ontology with the current data uploaded by trusted users (*"Synchronization with database"*), and inferring the ontology dependencies (*"Knowledge inferencing"*).

For working with most recent data, provided by trusted users, the *synchronization* mechanism integrates core ontology, describing the abstract of traffic dangers, with specific real time data. The process is executed for the first time on application start, i.e. the first request to the server while accessing the main page of the system. This functionality is also available on demand. After synchronization, the populated ontology is cached in memory and used for inferencing.

A single installation of the system (for instance for a single city) has its own database, in which the information about streets, districticts and actual conditions are stored. The *core ontology* on the other had can be shared by several installations of the system. It is accessible by an URI and can be stored on local or remote server.

5.3 Traffic Danger Ontology

As noted in [11], "In recent years the development of ontologies has been moving from the realm of Artificial-Intelligence laboratories to the desktops of domain experts.". Sharing common understanding of the knowledge domain is one of the most critical reason for developing ontologies. Explicit domain assumptions provide a clear description of the domain knowledge and simplify the knowledge extensibility. In our case, the domain ontology consists of concepts of geographical locations (streets, districts, postal codes), traffic dangers (e.g. *LowFrictionDanger*, *RoadConstructionDanger*), traffic conditions (including among others a hierarchy of *WeatherCondition*s and *RoadConstructionCondition*s) and describes multiple relations among them. An excerpt of the ontology is shown in Figure 5. The ontology enable the system to reason upon

Fig. 5. Traffic Danger Ontology: Asserted class hierarchy

stored facts and answer the questions of the following types:

- What traffic dangers can be encountered within a specific area?
- Is there any danger within area of specific postal code or specific district?
- What kind of dangers are connected with specific atmospheric conditions?
- Are there any dangers connected with specific condition (e.g. low friction) in a specific area?
- What are the sub-areas of a specific location?
- Are there any traffic conditions provided for a specific location?

In order to answer these questions either a semantic reasoner is used (which performs classification of concepts within the ontology) or appropriate DL queries are constructed. Based on the definitions of *TrafficDangers* in the ontology and information about actual condition occurences, implicit knowledge may be deduced (what kind of danger results from given conditions in a selected area).

5.4 Integration of the Ontology and the Database

While the abstract domain knowledge is expressed by the ontology axioms, the operational knowledge of the system is stored in a relational database. The database schema can be observed in Figure 6. The knowledge stored in the database consists of the locations structure and the actual traffic conditions in these locations. Specifically, the locations of the traffic conditions occurrences are defined by postal codes. The postal codes are connected to streets, which in turn are connected to districts. For instance, one can add an information that a particular street is under construction (a *RoadConstructionCondition* or one of its subclasses occurs) or that there is a specific weather condition in a specific district.

One of the most important aspects of the system is the possibility of an integration of data from the database and the ontology. Upon the *synchronization* process, the core ontology is cached and populated with the data from the database becoming a *synchronized ontology*. While the core ontology describes a terminology of traffic danger, the synchronized one is related to a specific environment and used for reasoning. Consequently, synchronized ontology can differ between the various environments where the system is deployed. For example, traffic conditions information for Cracow can vary significantly from those in Montpelier. Although it is possible to have a single installation of the system and synchronizing the ontology at once with all global data, it can result in system overloading and decreasing performance while inferring dependencies.

5.5 Reasoning in the System

Reasoning in the system is provided by invoking a DL reasoner on a synchronized ontology. The sequence diagram (see Figure 7) the required steps for the reasoning process. Once the trusted users have provided traffic conditions facts, a regular user can check what threat they may expect in a specific area. Responding to the user request, the system imports the up-to-date facts into a locally stored ontology (synchronizes the ontology), and then query the ontology by posing appropriate DL queries. From a user

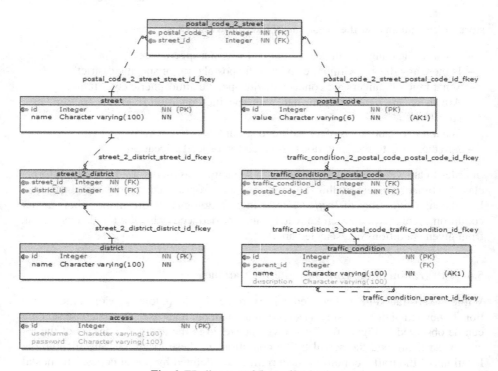

Fig. 6. ER diagram of the traffic database

perspective, a query is constructed by selecting a desired location through a web-based interface. Once the query is created, the DL reasoner is invoked to process it on the cached ontology. The inferred set of information is provided to the user. The reasoning takes relatively little time given the ontology having less than 100 classes. However, no benchmark testing has been done yet and it this is a subject for further work.

5.6   User Interface

The web-based interface of the system allows its users to create dynamic questions, and get the results about inferred traffic dangers. The prototype implementation [12] uses simple forms by use of which the users can construct questions for the system, e.g. a user can choose a desired location from a drop-down list and ask what threats may be encountered in this particular area (see Fig. 8).

Full development of a Graphical User Interface (GUI) with a map component is in progress. There is a process going on to integrate the logical layer of the system with an interface that uses maps and provides social features for the community of users. A fully-fledged GUI with an interactive map on which the users can navigate and filter threats by location, date, severity etc. has been developed (see Fig. 9), but is not yet fully integrated with the logical layer. In this version, a spatially-enabled database will be used which allows to store geographical data in an efficient way. The usability of the system is expected to increase, due to the possibility of visually choosing an area of interest (see Fig. 10) and the social features like rating threats and discussing them.

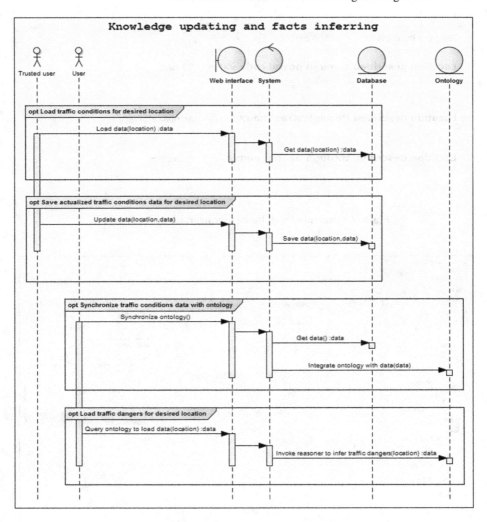

Fig. 7. Sequence diagram for updating and inferring data

6   Implementation and Deployment

The ontology has been developed in a top-down process with the Protégé [19] editor integrated with the HermiT DL Reasoner [20]. The ontology is provided in different formats (OWL2 XML [21], RDF/XML [22] or OWL2 Manchester Syntax) [23]). The synchronization is

---

[19] See http://protege.stanford.edu/
[20] See http://owlapi.sourceforge.net/
[21] See http://www.w3.org/TR/owl2-xml-serialization/
[22] See http://www.w3.org/TR/rdf-syntax-grammar/
[23] See http://www.w3.org/TR/owl2-manchester-syntax/

| Dangers by location | Any questions ? | About |

Location described through postal code value: 30-081

Possibility of pulling out of road.
Traffic congestion is higher than usual.

Location described through street name: ArmiiKrajowej

Vehicles speed on road can be higher than usual.

Location described through district name: Prokocim

Should be safely.

Fig. 8. An excerpt of web-based user interface of the system

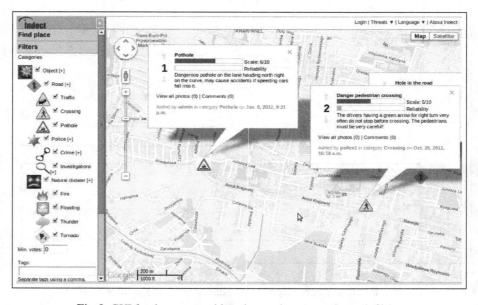

Fig. 9. GUI for the system with an interactive map and search filters

based on the OWL API library [24] and provides up-to-date information (cache in memory) for the HermiT DL Reasoner.

The ontology can be stored on local or remote server and is accessed by an URI. The cooperation with a database is provided through the Hibernate ORM [25] technology. The simple form-based user interface has been built with the JavaServer Pages (JSP) [26] and

---

[24] See http://owlapi.sourceforge.net/.

[25] See http://www.hibernate.org/

[26] See http://www.oracle.com/technetwork/java/javaee/jsp/index.html

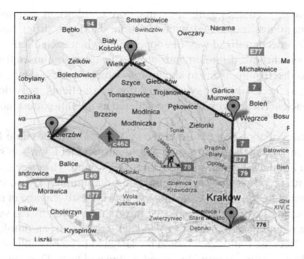

Fig. 10. GUI for the system: a map with selected area

jQuery JavaScript Library [27], while requests from users and appropriate responses, are controlled by Spring MVC [28]. For logging the results of particular operations, log4j Java-based logging utility [29] is used. PostgreSQL [30] is choosen as SQL database. The application has been written in Java using the Eclipse Java IDE [31]. Dependencies management and versioning is the task of Apache Maven tool [32]. All these technologies are free software or open source.

7 Evaluation

With respect to the criteria defined in Section 3, the system can be categorized as:

- General-purpose: it is designed to provide information about a wide variety of threats,
- Local: it is specifically aimed at being used in small communities (neighborhood, city, etc.)
- Publicly available (with limited functionality) and with authorized access (for more advanced features),
- Depending on users as main data providers.

   The system has several advantages which make it suitable for being used in the aforementioned local environment. The architecture of the system, with loose coupling of the

---

[27] See http://jquery.com/
[28] See http://static.springsource.org/spring/docs/3.0.x/
[29] See http://logging.apache.org/log4j/
[30] See http://www.postgresql.org/
[31] See http://www.eclipse.org/
[32] See http://maven.apache.org/

database and ontology, enables using the same core ontology in various installations. Synchronized ontologies (populated with real time data) can differ between various environments. This decentralized way of cooperation, when each client have cached in memory its own synchronized-on-demand ontology instance, is chosen for performance optimization reasons. Comparisons to situation in which single instance of ontology is the centralized part, accessible for synchronization to all clients, provide obvious performance drawbacks. This is why it was considered as an anti-pattern and depreciated by design.

The web-based, collaborative nature of the system makes it possible for citizens to communicate with each other, discuss and rate threats, and let them – to some extend – control the quality of the information entered into the system. The effectiveness of using the system depends largely on the engagement of the community. The so-called *network effect* is an important factor, because the more people honestly engage in the knowledge management process, the better the quality of information given by the system.

The architecture and design principles, especially the use of an ontology, have also their drawbacks. Because ontologies should be designed to be reusable, it is required to spent relatively lots of effort to provide a good design and tests. Domain experts should be involved in developing these tasks in parallel with programmers, to provide short iterations, as results of quick responses for every inconsistencies in ontology (irrelevant hidden relationships, domain descriptions mistakes or usability problems).

The data in the system is currently acquired from users. However, the system would benefit from incorporating some knowledge from external data sources, e.g., weather forecast services etc.

8   Summary

AI techniques may be successfully used in various applications for Knowledge Management. Using an ontology in a KM system allows to store abstract data, share it across several installations and manage changes in a centralized way. A loose coupling of the ontology with a relational database allows to store concrete data about conceived area in a database and populate the ontology with instance data during application run-time. Embedding a Description Logics reasoner enable the system to reason upon explicit knowledge entered by users and give back a useful response. A graphical user interface with a map component and social software features make the system user friendly and has a gradual learning curve.

To the best of our knowledge, there does not exist a crime mapping system that uses ontologies and DL reasoning to provide rich information based on knowledge gathered in the system. Although there exist numerous solutions for various danger information systems, none of them describe the threats in a formalized ontological way, relate weather or road conditions to the possible dangers and reasons about these dependencies. We believe that this is our original contribution compared to existing work.

9   Future Work

The system has been tested with several Web browsers and can be used on any device that support Web browsing. However, for mobile devices, some adaptations are needed.

The current prototype implementation has a limited user interface. The intended integration with a GUI providing interactive map and social features is not yet finalized. A possible direction for further development could be focused on extensions for heterogeneous application-to-application communication. The RESTful Web Services [33] can be considered. External systems would be perceived as software agents. Their tasks could be focused on periodic connections to the system, getting some information set, and creating statistics about the traffic dangers. The statistics could visualize frequencies of particular dangers on a specific area or classify the safety of the selected district.

Another important research thread is the *context-awareness* of the system. Using the system should be seamlessly incorporated into the daily routines of its users. Therefore, certain adaptations are considered [4] that will allow installations of the system to work on mobile devices in an adaptive way.

Acknowledgement. The research presented in this paper is carried out within the EU FP7 INDECT Project: "Intelligent information system supporting observation, searching and detection for security of citizens in urban environment" (http://indect-project.eu).

References

1. Adrian, W.T., Bobek, S., Nalepa, G.J., Kaczor, K., Kluza, K.: How to reason by HeaRT in a semantic knowledge-based wiki. In: Proceedings of the 23rd IEEE International Conference on Tools with Artificial Intelligence, ICTAI 2011, Boca Raton, Florida, USA, pp. 438–441 (November 2011), http://ieeexplore.ieee.org/xpls/abs_all.jsp?arnumber=6103361&tag=1
2. Baader, F., Calvanese, D., McGuinness, D.L., Nardi, D., Patel-Schneider, P.F. (eds.): The Description Logic Handbook: Theory, Implementation, and Applications. Cambridge University Press (2003)
3. Berners-Lee, T., Hendler, J., Lassila, O.: The Semantic Web. Scientific American (May 2001), http://www.sciam.com/article.cfm?articleID=00048144-10D2-1C70-84A9809EC588EF21&#38pageNumber=1&#38catID=2
4. Bobek, S., Nalepa, G.J., Adrian, W.T.: Mobile context-based framework for monitoring threats in urban environment. In: Dziech, A., Czyżewski, A. (eds.) MCSS 2013. CCIS, vol. 368, pp. 25–35. Springer, Heidelberg (2013)
5. Brachman, R., Levesque, H.: Knowledge Representation and Reasoning, 1st edn. Morgan Kaufmann (2004)
6. Guarino, N.: Formal ontology and information systems. In: Proceedings of the First International Conference on Formal Ontologies in Information Systems, pp. 3–15 (1998)
7. Ligęza, A., Adrian, W.T., Ernst, S., Nalepa, G.J., Szpyrka, M., Czapko, M., Grzesiak, P., Krzych, M.: Prototypes of a web system for citizen provided information, automatic knowledge extraction, knowledge management and GIS integration. In: Dziech, A., Czyżewski, A. (eds.) MCSS 2011. CCIS, vol. 149, pp. 268–276. Springer, Heidelberg (2011)

---

[33] See http://www.ics.uci.edu/~fielding/pubs/dissertation/rest_arch_style.

8. Ligęza, A., Ernst, S., Nowaczyk, S., Nalepa, G.J., Szpyrka, M., Furmańska, W.T., Czapko, M., Grzesiak, P., Kałuża, M., Krzych, M.: Towards enregistration of threats in urban environments: practical consideration for a GIS-enabled web knowledge acquisition system. In: Dańda, J., Derkacz, J., Głowacz, A. (eds.) MCSS 2010: Multimedia Communications, Services and Security: IEEE International Conference: Kraków, Poland, May 6-7, pp. 152–158 (2010)
9. Nalepa, G.J.: Collective knowledge engineering with semantic wikis. Journal of Universal Computer Science 16(7), 1006–1023 (2010), http://www.jucs.org/ jucs_16_7/collective_knowledge_engineering_with
10. Nalepa, G.J., Furmańska, W.T.: Review of semantic web technologies for GIS. Automatyka: Półrocznik Akademii Górniczo-Hutniczej im. Stanisława Staszica w Krakowie 13(2), 485–492 (2009)
11. Noy, N.F., McGuinness, D.L.: Ontology Development 101: A Guide to Creating Your First Ontology. Stanford University, Stanford, CA, 94305
12. Waliszko, J.: Knowledge Representation and Processing Methods in Semantic Web. Master's thesis, AGH University of Science and Technology (2010)
13. Waliszko, J., Adrian, W.T., Ligęza, A.: Traffic danger ontology for citizen safety web system. In: Dziech, A., Czyżewski, A. (eds.) MCSS 2011. CCIS, vol. 149, pp. 165–173. Springer, Heidelberg (2011)
14. Wilson, J., Fotheringham, A. (eds.): The Handbook of Geographic Information Science. Blackwell Publishing Ltd. (2008)
15. Żywioł, M.: Analysis and evaluation of crime mapping systems (2012)

Collective Intelligence for Evaluating Synergy in Collaborative Innovation

Ayca Altay and Gulgun Kayakutlu

Istanbul Technical University Department of Industrial Engineering Maçka,
34357 İstanbul, Turkey
{altaya,kayakutlu}@itu.edu.tr

Abstract. Collaborative innovation is an unavoidable need for the small and medium enterprises (SME) both in terms of economic scale and technological knowledge. Risks and the innovation power are analyzed for the wealth of collaboration. This paper aims to present the *synergy index* as a multiplier of the innovation power of research partners to construct a successful collaboration. The proposed index can be used with different number of companies in collaboration cluster and the synergy maximization is guaranteed by using a new particle swarm algorithm, *Foraging Search*. This paper will give the formulation and criteria of the synergy index in detail. A sample synergy index application for the Turkish SMEs will clarify the steps to follow.

Keywords: Innovation, SME, Synergy, Clustering, Foraging Search.

1 Introduction

Recently an article published in Scientific American illuminated one of the main differences between the humans and the animals as sharing the knowledge to create cumulative culture [1]. Though it is recently biologically proven, we have been using the concept of synergy in engineering since the very first project developed to create a team work. In the last few years international projects are run in collaboration by public and private authorities causing studies and discussions on synergy and conflict [2]. Companies are obliged to innovate for competition and are willing to collaborate for the unique product/processes/service only after defining the team with bigger chance of success [3]. Small and medium companies (SME) would like to gratify the collaborative innovation with less risk.

The main approach in the synergy literature is the extraction of factors that affect synergy in alliances using case studies [4,5] or statistical analyses [6,7]. These studies recommend building alliances based on the criteria that have the biggest effect on collaborations. Further quantifications are achieved with Multi Criteria Decision Making, where partners are selected using the criteria extracted in previous studies [8]. In the existence of strict goals of alliances, a number of mathematical methods are built. Majority of the researchers have exploited and developed recent mathematical models involving the goal programming [9] and multi-objective programming [10].

E. Mercier-Laurent and D. Boulanger (Eds.): AI4KM 2012, IFIP AICT 422, pp. 131–150, 2014.
© IFIP International Federation for Information Processing 2014

This study has the main objective of proposing a synergy index as a multiplier of the innovative power to be maximized for successful partnership. It will be presented that when both innovation capabilities and the risks are considered through internal and external influencers, the synergy created will avoid the failure. In order to determine the best team of companies, the possible companies are to be clustered based on all the criteria effective for synergy improvement. A collective intelligence approach, particle swarm optimization is selected to evaluate the collaborative synergy since it has the social component in parallel with the knowledge based evaluation [11]. However, the fact that the classical particle swarm method is based on balancing the exploration and exploitation at the particle level [12] would mean individual success of each company. An advanced new particle swarm algorithm, foraging search is based on creating balance of exploitation and exploration at the swarm level as well as particle level, which allows us to calculate the collaborative success [13].

This paper is distinguished and will make contribution to the research in three main points:

- Instead of choosing a partner as studied before, this study deals with grouping and clustering of the synergy creating SMEs.
- The criteria studied in this research combines the innovative power and risk criteria with the synergy which are depicted from the literature and selected by industrial experts.
- Algorithm used in this study is not based on a threshold as in goal programming, thus it allows the selection of partners even in vague and uncertain conditions.

This paper is so organized that a literature review on the collaborative innovation will be given in the next section and the synergy index function will be explained in the third section. Foraging Search algorithm that is used to maximize the synergy will be explained in the fourth section and the fifth section of the paper is reserved for the application. The conclusion and further suggestions will be summarized in the last section.

2   Synergy in Collaborative Innovation

Knowledge based collaboration is the fuel of innovation for the SMEs. They are known to be agile in change, but fragile in facing the economic fluctuations [14]. Collaborative innovation is mainly based on the synergy created by the partner companies. When it is on the virtual network an intelligent agent can take the role of a moderator. In private or public industries skill based clustering has been an effective tool to create synergy among the team workers [15,16]. However it is difficult to construct a creative task ground for the team members who come from different business cultures. Innovative capabilities of more than one company working together are established on both the knowledge and vision for internal and external alliance. Big companies succeed the collaboration by defining the performance focused on cross-business growth [17]. They might even improve the innovative capabilities by merger and acquisition [18]. SMEs on the other hand, see the research support as one of the external fund to be accessed [19] and they jump into any partnership even it might be quite risky. Chang and Hsu studied both managerial and environmental drivers of innovativeness for SMEs to show that internal and external factors are independent [20]. Global collaboration changed the collaborative strategies both in functional operations and collaborative activities [21]. The economic crisis has led research and development for innovation towards a new approach and perspective: innovation through new products/processes or knowledge is not enough beneficial unless the systems around them are not ready. This is a common issue among the developing and highly developed countries [22].

Literature surveys allowed us depict thirty-two innovative synergy factors representing either organizational approach or alliance approach. Previous research also shows that these criteria are mainly analyzed by constructing the clusters in the same geographical region by using the collective intelligence methods [23, 24].

Table 1. Organizational Features Effective in Collaboration Synergy

Factor	Information Resource	Reference
Organizational structure	Organizational Manual & Management Survey	Twardy (2009)[25]
Administrative Capacity		Margoluis (2008)[26]
Values & Company culture	Employee & Management Survey	Rai et al.(1996)[27]
Reward& compensation systems		Ding (2009)[28]
Performance culture		
Financial condition	Company Balance Sheet	Rameshan&Loo(1998)[29]
		Chen et al(2008)[30]
		Twardy (2009)[25]
		Ding (2009)[28]
Organizational resources	Company balance sheet & Management Survey	Margoulis(2008)[26]
		Rose et.Al. (2010)[31]
Technological Capabilities	Technology Assessment	Chen et. al(2008)[30]
Brand / Firm reputation	Sales Information	Ding (2009)[28]
Visions, Goal & Objectives	Employee & collaborator Survey	Margoluis (2008)[26]
		Gomes-Casseres (2003) [32]
Company Pace		Linder (2004)[33]
Type of Leadership		Margoulis(2008)[26]

Some of the factors found during the literature survey are very similar and most of them cannot be expressed in figures. Therefore a need to combine or discard the least influential ones is observed. A fuzzy cognitive survey is responded by one SME executive, one academic expert on SMEs and a strategy consultant for SMEs. Fuzzy cognitive analysis allows linking the factors in a positive or a negative relationship with a degree in the interval [-1,1]. The weight given for each criterion is found through the centrality calculated by using the sum of scores given in the column (inbound) of the criterion, and the sum of scores given in the row (outbound) of the criterion in the normalized relations matrix.

Organizational factors like the governmental support or country, and intangible alliance factors like past alliance experience are eliminated since they had weights lower than 1%. Hence the set of factors that will be used in the synergy survey are reduced to 22 criteria, which are shown in Table 1 and Table 2. The survey demonstrated that the highest importance is recorded for the structure of alliance or the clarity of roles with a weight of 6.21. The selected criteria are explored below in the rank of their weights. It is remarkable that the first seven criteria are intangible alliance criteria.

Structure of Alliance (Clarity of Roles): A tangible alliance criterion. Margoluis [26] discusses that for an alliance in order to be effective, individuals and companies should know their tasks in a complete manner.

Inter-organizational trust: Ramaseshan and Loo [29] proves that inter-organizational trust positively affects the alliance. It has also been claimed as one of the most effective criteria for the existence of collaborations [34].

Dysfunctional conflict: Dysfunctional conflict is defined as disputes that cannot be agreed on [29]. Unlike dysfunctional conflict, functional conflicts are disputes that can be agreed on. Ramaseshan and Loo proves that excessive number of dysfunctional conflicts can negatively affect the efficiency of an alliance.

Values and company culture: Twardy [25] denotes that collaborating companies are deemed to face cultural differences during the alliance initiation. Besides, [27] claims that these differences may occur even among the companies within the same country or the same industry. Company culture also includes the decision making mechanism which is analyzed under the Organizational Structure" and Type of leadership" topics". It is also claimed that in alliances different cultures are forced to find a common ground for the sake of alliance.

Communication, coordination and information sharing systems: Communication is defined as the ability to interact and share information in an apparent manner [26] and it is one of the alliance efficiency affecting criteria according to Ding [28].

Commitment capabilities to alliances: Ramaseshan and Loo [29] proves that as openness and commitment of companies increase, the efficiency of the alliance increases. It has been found to decrease the turnover rate and increase the lifetime and the accordance of an alliance.

Inter-organizational communication: Inter-organizational communication is defined as formal as well as informal sharing of meaningful information between firms" [29]. In alliances, it is possible that both human and the machine problems may arise.

Scope of the alliance: Eden [34] discusses that a restricted scope negatively affects the efficiency of the alliance. It is recorded that more effort is spent on resolving the conflicting scope ideas among the firms.

Funding Balance: Linder et. al. [33] and Twardy [25] state that expectations from the alliance have a big impact on the health of alliance. The decision of the funding regime should be clarified before the constitution of the alliance and firms should not avoid to contribute.

Attitude towards alliance: Attitude towards alliance denotes whether the company is willing and ready for alliance [32]. As the eagerness of the company increases, the probability of synergy increases.

Table 2. Alliance Features Effective in Collaboration Synergy

Factor	Information Resource	Reference
Scope of Alliance	Contract, Employee Survey	Eden (2007)[34] Margoluis(2008)[26]
Structure of the alliance (clarity of roles)		Margoluis(2008)[26]
Compatibility of vision/goals&objectives		Gomes-Casseres (2003) [32]
Funding balance		Linder et. al.(2004)[33]
Attitude towards alliance	Employee & Project Manager Interviews	Linder et. al.(2004)[33]
Inter-organizational communication		Rai et. Al.(1996)[27]
Commitment capabilities to alliances		Margoluis(2008)[26] Eden(2007)[34]
Communication, Coordination& information sharing	Management Survey	Chen et al(2008)[30] Twardy (2009)[25] Ding[28]
Dysfunctional conflicts		Rameshan&Loo(1998)[29]
Inter-organizational trust		Gardet & Mothe, (2012)[35]

Compatibility of vision, goals and objectives: The vision, goals and objectives of collaborating companies are expected to be compatible as well as clear [31]. Conflicting or irrelevant objectives may decrease the lifetime of alliances as in the scope criterion.

Organizational Resources: Organizational resources given to the service of the collaboration are listed as skilled personnel, trade contacts, machinery, efficient procedures and capital [31]. Most of the researchers state that allies are to be complementary in covering the resource needs. Since the amount of contribution differs by company, this property is considered as organizational property.

Organizational Structure: Twardy [25] states that the governance model of a company has more than 25% importance on the success of an alliance. The best condition for synergy is to balance the freedom and control in a collaboration.

Company Pace: Company pace denotes whether the collaborating company is able to adapt changes in a slow or fast manner [32]. It is possible to assign benchmark points for this criterion such as industry average, rivals or business partners.

Administrative capacity: Administrative capacity is defined as the capacity of the organization to manage grants, reporting procedures and administrative tasks" [26]. It is defined by the self-evaluation of the company in the following four areas: Management, Programming, Monitoring, Evaluation.

Brand, firm reputation: According to Ding [28], having a good reputation in the target geographical scope is one of the most important criteria in alliances. A good reputation may increase the eagerness to collaborate.

Financial condition: Financial condition is revealed as a very important factor in alliances discussed in various number of studies [25][28,29,30]. It can be summarized as the more the financial power of companies is, and the better the financial condition of the collaboration is, the synergy is improved".

Type of leadership: Leadership style heavily influences the decision making structure of an organization [26]. Type of leadership is not included in the organizational structure since the first indicates the implementation of decisions whereas the latter shows the participation in decisions.

Performance culture: Performance culture is the approach for measuring the success of the employees and the company regularly, in a planned and methodic way or just ad-hoc and intuitive. Cheung [36] implies that project performance measure culture has an effect on alliance debates. It is also recorded that integrating very different performance measure cultures is an issue, whereas if cultures are similar, it is more manageable to integrate.

Reward and compensation system: Rai et. al. [27] implies that applications in human resources, especially reward and compensation systems, have a big impact on the working capacity of collaborations. Moreover, he argues that difference in such systems may arise even in the same countries or industries. Different types of compensations may include base pay, commission, overtime pay, bonuses, profit sharing, stock options, ravel / meal / housing and other benefits such as dental, insurance, medical, vacation, leaves, retirement, taxes. Though it is an organizational feature the accordance of these properties increases the strength of alliance.

Technological Capacities : Chen et. al. [30] state that technological capabilities of companies within alliance should be complementary. Yet, they do not provide a list of technological resources to be met. Data gathered from the literature provide various resources for different industries. In this study we provide basic elements that are valid for all industries covering computer hardware, system integration and management tools, communication equipment and software, automated data processing, database management systems, management information systems, knowledge base and infrastructure.

Clarity of visions, goals and objectives: Margoluis [26] states that visions, goals and objectives should be common or at least shared between the partners. Besides, in order to share a vision, a goal or an objective, they must be clear and well understood by the collaboration team members [32].

All studies apart from Huang et al. [10] ignore the synergy phenomenon in their studies. The concept is integrated in all objectives of collaboration as a coefficient.

The above mentioned criteria are thoroughly analyzed in the model building and application phases. It is observed in literature that generally used methods to select partners can be summarized as follows:

- The statistical methods are used to measure the efficiency of existing collaborations. The methods are static, and do not consider the new collaborations that can emerge.
- Multi criteria decision methods are used to maximize the innovation power or determine the reasons for the risk without considering the exponential effect of the synergy.
- Mathematical methods are used to model non-linear effects with possible 2n-1 collaboration link for n companies causing computational difficulties.
- Meta-heuristic algorithms are generally used to model the multiple objectives with simpler mathematical models.

It is also observed that none of these methods are used for clustering approach.

3   Synergy Index

3.1   Synergy Index Formulation

Synergy is defined as the gratifying factor for the combined performances of the individual companies [35]. The better is the accordance within the alliance, the greater is the synergy. Hence, synergy is positively related with the accordance. In other words, the system that makes the alliance work has to be robust for a lifetime of an alliance. Reliability can be defined in good working synergy criteria when the expected life of collaboration is the concern. The expected lifetime of alliance can be calculated using Weibull distribution which is accepted as the best function of lifetime calculation in the reliability theory [37, 38]. Weibull distribution has the following features:
     Density function :

$$f(x) = \frac{\beta}{\alpha}\left(\frac{x-v}{\alpha}\right)^{\beta-1} \exp\left\{-\left(\frac{x-v}{\alpha}\right)^{\beta}\right\} \tag{1}$$

Cumulative function:

$$F(x) = 1 - \exp\left\{-\left(\frac{x-v}{\alpha}\right)^{\beta}\right\} \tag{2}$$

Where $x > v$ and α, β and v are Weibull parameters.
     Expected value:

$$E[X] = \alpha.\Gamma(1 + \frac{1}{\beta}) \tag{3}$$

The analogy between the synergy and the lifetime suggests $v \geq 0$, since we take the two, analogous $v = 0$ will be accepted. In the formula β is the shape parameter and α is the rate parameter. For one company case, $\beta = 1$, the distribution becomes the Exponential distribution. For $\beta = 2$, the distribution becomes the Weibull distribution but for $\beta > 5$ it is not any more the same distribution.
     Hence, distribution of synergy is modeled as the reliability of a system of n where $1 \leq n \leq 5$ components. Therefore, it is safe to accept β as the number of companies in the collaboration cluster. In physical and biological systems, synergy is modeled with an accelerating effect, which resembles the shape of exponential distribution [38]. This allows us take the shape parameter β to denote the *number of firms in collaboration*. It is also viable to emphasize that the collaboration of more than 5 companies are not practical in the business life. Though there are examples of more than 5 companies in European projects, two features of these teams are to be recognized: they are not all SMEs (sometimes a big company like SAP or IBM takes place in the team) and the team is built only for one project.
     Weibull distribution will be constructed for each company considering the synergy coefficients and the number of companies in collaboration as parameters. Inter-company synergy will assume to have $1 \leq n \leq 5$ firm(s) in alliance.

The parameter α resembles the strength of elements in the reliability analogy, which is equivalent to the *merged synergy coefficient* that will be calculated using synergy factors. The synergy index s can be defined as

$$s = \alpha.\Gamma(1+\frac{1}{\beta}) \tag{4}$$

α: the merged synergy coefficient
β: number of companies

The synergy index will be used in calculating the maximization of innovation power. It is known that in collaborations the innovation can be greater than the sum of the individual if the accordance is well established. Hence, we try to maximize the minimum synergy among the collaborating companies. Each collaborating group is important and the company left outside the group must be successful if included in collaboration.

It should also be clear for the collaborating companies that if the synergy factors are merged in a negative way, that is, if the companies are discordant, the synergy index will be negative showing no possible lifetime for collaboration clusters.

3.2   Sensitivity Analysis

The proposed synergy index is sensitive to the number of firms in alliance. As an example, there exists 2 collaboration clusters, one with 2 companies and the second with 3 companies. In case the merged synergy coefficient $\alpha=0.7$ for both clusters, 3-company-alliance gives a better s than the 2-company alliance. This can be considered as a parallel system. It is always safer to increase the number of parallel elements. In Figure 1, synergy index sensitivity of number of firms in alliance for $\alpha = 0.7$ is demonstrated.

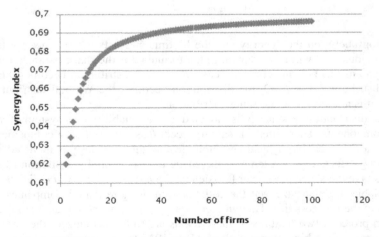

Fig. 1. Synergy index sensitivity for the number of firms

Synergy effect in innovation is shown to support the moral as well as causing improvements in project follow-up, creativity and technological intelligence when thresholds are taken into account [39]. The previous evaluations of synergy were mainly based on scoring because of the intangible factors.

4   Foraging Search

4.1   Motivation

The Foraging Search algorithm imitates the Animal Food Chain for optimization problems [40]. Animal Food Chain contains three groups: herbivores (plant eaters), omnivores (both plant and meat eaters) and carnivores (meat eaters). Herbivores are known as primary consumers, omnivores who feed on some specific plants and other herbivores are known as secondary consumers and lastly, carnivores who feed on specific herbivores and carnivores are known as the tertiary consumers. Herbivores are ultimate hunts of the food chain whereas carnivores are the ultimate hunters and omnivores, which are both hunters and hunts. According to the energy transformation, the energy transmitted through a food chain decreases as the number of consumers increase. The ratio of hunt and hunters depend on the ecological environment. In wild environments, the herbivore-omnivore-carnivore ratio can be 10:3:1 whereas in calm environments the related ratio can be 40:10:1. Additionally, it is also valid that in a food chain, the hunter is always faster than the hunt [41, 42].

The classical PSO algorithm employs one swarm and the related swarm is responsible for both exploration and exploitation[43].There is a new algorithm that implements two swarms of equal sizes clustering [44] separating the responsibilities for exploration and exploitation.

The Foraging Search uses three swarms, namely herbivores, omnivores and carnivores, to provide exploration by the herbivore swarm, exploitation by the carnivore swarm and exploration-exploitation balance by the omnivore swarm. Introduction of a food chain provides an incremental escaping ability which is modeled with first level and second level hunters. All fear and escape factors affect the speed of the animals, which the Foraging Search model embeds in the velocity update formula. Furthermore, this algorithm considers the environmental wildness which represents the complexity of the market. If the competition is harsh it is better to increase the wildness. That is why Foraging Search balances the exploration and exploitation at the swarm level.

4.2   The Clustering Algorithm

Each particle in the Foraging Search Clustering algorithm is represented by $k*d$ cluster centers where k is the number of clusters and d is the number of dimensions of the data points to be clustered. Likely, the velocity and speed updates are applied in order to locate optimum cluster centers.

Thirteen steps are followed:

Step 1. The environment is defined as calm, regular or wild.
Step 2. The herbivore : omnivore : carnivore (*h_number:o_number:c_number*)
ratio is determined.

- IF the environment is harsh: wild 10:3:1
- IF the environment is average: 25:6:1
- IF the environment is calm: 40:10:1

Step 3. Each particle is randomly initiated for each swarm, each particle is assigned random $c*d$ cluster centers where c is the number of clusters and d is the dimension of data points. The particles are named as x_{ijk}, the kth dimension of the jth cluster of the ith particle where $i= 1, ...$ h_number $\forall o\_number$ $\forall c\_number, j = 1, ..., c, k = 1, ..., d$.

Step 4. Data points are assigned to clusters using a distance metric (e.g. Euclidean distance, Mahalanobis distance, etc...).

Step 5. The quality of the clustering is measured by an objective function. The aim of clustering is building small clusters as dissimilar as possible. Consequently, the objective function may involve within cluster distances, among cluster distances or a combination of both measures.

Step 6. The best objective value and position for all particles, or particle bests, are determined for each particle in each swarm.

Step 7. The best objective value and position, or swarm bests are determined for each swarm.

Step 8. The best objective value and position of all swarms, or the global best is determined.

Step 9. The fear coefficients for herbivores are calculated.
Fear factors for herbivores:

$$pfho_i = 1 - \frac{d_{fho,i}}{d_{fho}^{\min}} \tag{5}$$

$$pfoc_i = 1 - \frac{d_{foc,i}}{d_{foc}^{\min}} \tag{6}$$

where
$i= 1,...,h\_number$

$pfho_i$: fear degree from omnivores of the ith herbivore (in the interval [0,1])
$pfhc_i$: fear degree from carnivores of the ith herbivore (in the interval [0,1])
$d_{fho,i}$: the distance of the ith herbivore to the nearest omnivore
$d_{fhc,i}$: the distance of the ith herbivore to the nearest carnivore
d^{min}_{fho}: the minimum distance for a herbivore to fear an omnivore
d^{min}_{fhc}: the minimum distance for a herbivore to fear an omnivore

Step 10. The fear coefficients for omnivores are calculated using the formula below:

$$pfoc_i = 1 - \frac{d_{foc,i}}{d_{foc}^{min}} \qquad (7)$$

where

$i = 1, \ldots, o\_number$

$pfoc_i$: fear degree from carnivores of the ith omnivore (in the interval $[0,1]$)

$d_{fho,i}$: the distance of the ith omnivore to the nearest carnivore

d^{min}_{fhc}: the minimum distance for an omnivore fear an omnivore

Step 11. The probability of being a hunt for omnivores is calculated as

$$pp_i = \frac{dc_i}{dc_i + dh_i} \qquad (8)$$

where

$i = 1, \ldots, o\_number$

pp_i: : the probability of omnivores being a hunter

dh_i: the distance of ith omnivore to the nearest herbivore

dc_i: the distance of ith omnivore to the nearest carnivore

Step 12. The velocities (v_{ijk}) of each particle are updated according to their swarms.

a. *Velocity Update for the Herbivore Swarm*

Since herbivores are ultimate hunt, their velocity update involves the escape from their first and second level hunters: omnivores and carnivores. The velocity update formula for herbivores is given below.

$$v_{ijk} \leftarrow wv_{ijk} + c_1 r_{1i}(y_{ijk} - x_{ijk}) + c_2 r_{2i}(\hat{y}_{ijk} - x_{ijk}) + pfho_i c_3 r_{3i} D(d_{fho,ijk})$$
$$+ pfhc_i, c_4 r_{4i} D(d_{fhc,ijk}) \qquad (9)$$

where

$i = 1, \ldots, h\_number$

v_{ijk}: the velocity of kth dimension of the jth cluster of the ith particle of the swarm

w: the inertia coefficient

c_1 and c_2: cognitive and social coefficients

r_{1i}, r_{2i}, r_{3i} and r_{4i}: random numbers for the ith particle in the interval $[0,1]$

y_{ijk}: personal best for the kth dimension of the jth cluster of the ith particle of the swarm

x_{ijk}: the position of kth dimension of the jth cluster of the ith particle of the swarm

$\hat{y}_{ijk}$: swarm best for the kth dimension of the jth cluster of the ith particle of the swarm

c_3: distance based coefficient of herbivores from omnivores

c_4: distance based coefficient of herbivores from carnivores

and

$D(.)$ is a measure of the effect that the hunter has on the hunt and it is formulated as

$$D(x) = \alpha e^{-\beta x} \tag{10}$$

where d is the Euclidean distance between the prey particle and the nearest hunter particle. α and β are positive constants that define the effect of distance to velocity.

b. *Velocity Update for the Carnivore Swarm*
Since herbivores are ultimate hunt, their velocity update involves independently chasing the nearest hunt. The velocity update formula for herbivores is given below.

$$v_{ijk} \leftarrow \left(\hat{y}_{ijk} - x_{ijk} \right) \tag{11}$$

where
$i = 1, \ldots, c\_number$
v_{ijk}: the velocity of kth dimension of the jth cluster center of the ith particle of swarm
r: random number in the interval [0,1]
$\hat{y}_{ijk}$: the position of the kth dimension of the jth cluster center of the nearest hunt to the ith particle of swarm
x_{ijk}: the position of the dimension of the jth cluster center of the ith particle of swarm

c. *Velocity Update for the Omnivore Swarm*
Since omnivores are both hunters and hunts, their velocity update involves the compound of both velocity update formulas whose ratio depend on the probability of being a hunter. The velocity update formula for herbivores is given below.

$$v_{ijk} = (1 - pp_i) \left(w v_{ijk} + c_1 r_{1i}(y_{ijk} - x_{ijk}) + c_2 r_{21}(\hat{y}_{ijk} - x_{ijk}) \right.$$
$$\left. + pfoc_i c_3 r_{3i} D(f_{foc,ijk}) \right) + pp_i \left(r(\tilde{y}_{ijk} - x_{ijk}) \right) \tag{12}$$

where
$i = 1, \ldots, h\_number$
v_{ijk}: the velocity of kth dimensionof the jth cluster of the ith particle of theswarm
w: the inertia coefficient
c_1 and c_2: cognitive and social coefficients
r_{1i}, r_{2i}, r: random numbers for the ith particle in the interval [0,1]
y_{ijk}: personal best for thek^{th} dimensionof the jth cluster of the ith particle of the swarm
x_{ijk}: the position of kth dimensionof the jth cluster of the ith particle of theswarm
$\hat{y}_{jjk}$: swarm best for thek^{th} dimensionof the jth cluster of the ith particle of the swarm
$\tilde{y}_{ijk}$: the position ofthek^{th} dimension of the jth cluster center of the nearest hunt to the ith particle of swarm
c_3: distance based coefficient of herbivores from omnivores
c_4: distance based coefficient of herbivores from carnivores
and

$D(.)$ is a measure of the effect that the hunter has on the hunt and it is formulated as

$$D(x) = \alpha e^{-\beta x} \tag{13}$$

where d is the Euclidean distance between the prey particle and the nearest hunter particle. α and β are positive constants that define the effect of distance to velocity.

Step 13. The particle positions for each particle in each swarm are updated using the formula below:

$$x_{ijk} = x_{ijk} + v_{ijk} \qquad (14)$$

where
x_{ijk} : the position of kth dimension of the jth cluster of the ith particle of theswarm
v_{ijk}: the velocity of kth dimension of the jth cluster of the ith particle of theswarm

5   Case Study

The synergy index is studied for a case of 51 SME companies in Thrace, Turkey. The companies are distributed in several industries as shown in Table 3.

Table 3. Industrial distribution companies in the case study

Industry	%	Industry	%
Food	17.6	Service	15.7
Clothing & Textile	13.7	Health	5.7
Machinery & Electronics	19.6	IT & Communication	7.8
Automotive	2.0	Construction	2.0
Chemical & Pharmaceutical	0.0	Furniture	2.0
Plastics	2.0	Metal	2.0
Publishing	2.0	Miscellaneous	7.9

A survey of 22 questions is run for 51 companies to figure out the approaches on 22 synergy factors. In order to measure the intangible alliance criteria, linguistic variables are presented in scenarios that would reflect the SME opinion. For example, since the firms do not know each other, they cannot be asked how much each trusts the others. Instead, it can be asked about how much they trust the alliance and how much they are willing or open to share as in the linguistic options that can be evaluated by the responder:

- We want to participate in collaborations but we do not have the experience
- We can contribute to alliances but our resources are limited.
- We are ready for collaborations that do not interrupt our daily processes.

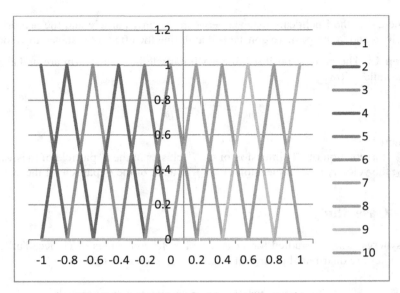

Fig. 2. Fuzzy numbers for 11-point likert scale

The questionnaire is constructed to score all twenty-two criteria with the above linguistic approach after receiving responses for more statistical information like how many white collar employees work for the company; would the size of the company be considered medium, small or micro or how many patents they have. Questions included different ranges of likert scales in order to represent the synergy criterion clearly. The scales of 5, 7 or 11 values are given in to present the choice between the two ends depending on the possibility of responses. The three samples given below represent different types of questions.

In order to ask for the attitude towards alliance the question is:

- *How does your company consider research collaboration?*

Ignored		Indifferent		Enthusiastic
1	2	3	4	5

The second sample represents the funding balance criteria:

- *How would your company prefer funding the research investments in collaboration?*

Partners with highest funds pay the highest percentage					Some should pay the short term and the others longterm investments					Each company pays his part and the common parts are defined in the contract
1	2	3	4	5	6	7	8	9	10	11

The third sample question asks about the vision, goal and objectives

- *Score validity of the following statements for your company*

	Not valid		Doubtful		Fully Valid
Written mission, goal and objectives are fully implemented and owned by the employees.	1		4		7
Written mission, goal and objectives are implemented but not owned by the majority of employees.	1		4		7
We have written the mission, goals and objectives but they are modified continuously and not owned by the employees.	1		4		7

Responses are clustered using the Foraging Search Algorithm and the synergy is calculated in clusters. Since the analogy of reliability is used for the synergy index, SMEs within a cluster act as a series system, that is, if one SME fails the collaboration has to be reconstructed in order to make it work. On the other hand, all clusters work independent of each other.

The case of no collaboration where none of the firms collaborate with each other, can be considered as a collaboration clusters where one firm exists in each cluster, which gives a synergy index of 0. Hence, the effect of synergy becomes $e^0 = 1$ for each firm, which means the strength of each firm equals to its own strength. It is plausible that for any innovation or other types of collaborations to be favorable, synergy in the cluster should be equal to or greater than 1, since the aim of the collaboration is creating positive synergy among partners. When the cumulative becomes -1 then there is negative energy, the power after collaboration is less than the company power alone.

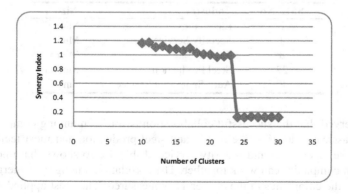

Fig. 3. Synergy Index Achieved based on Number of Clusters

When 2 clusters were run to have 29 and 24 companies each, it is observed that maximum synergy was created between SME 1 and SME 2. It was too crowded to be realistic in the business life. On the other hand, when beta constraint is restricted to be less than equal to 5 each cluster has 5 companies in 10 clusters as seen in Figure 3. In order to see the less crowded situations 11-30 clusters are also run. The best result is achieved by 11 clusters case with a synergy index scoring 1.18, meaning the life of collaboration is extended by 18%. The fact that repeated runs for each number of clusters gave the same exact results makes us believe this is the global optimum.

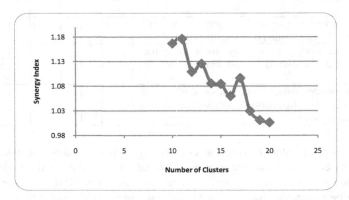

Fig. 4. Synergy Index change detailed for 10-20 Clusters

As detailed in Figure 4, the best objective value obtained is 1.18 with 11 clusters each having number of companies {5},{5},{5},{5},{4},{4},{5},{3},{5},{5} and {5}. Minimum synergy effect is obtained to improve 3% in 18 clusters. This means the life of collaboration is prolonged from 1 year to 1.03 years. The eleventh cluster only includes SME 2 as one of the most synergetic companies. Cluster 11 owns five companies from different industries in variety of sizes as shown in Table 4.

The correlation among the companies is found small enough to be ignored.

Table 4. Content of the most successful cluster

SME No	Industry	Size
2	Electronics	Micro
4	Security Service	Micro
8	Textile	Micro
27	Steel Production	Medium
40	Auto-Spare Part Service	Small

It is observed that the successful collaboration is foreseen among companies from the most classical industries like textile and steel production and most technological industries like electronics and security service. Table 4 also shows that micro, small and medium companies can work together. The correlation among the synergy criteria achieved by the companies in the cluster 11 is measured. The *t* test applied with 10 % significance showed that the correlation is too small to be ignored.

Therefore we can conclude for our case application with the following summary: unlike a generalized belief of industry and technology focus in collaboration, synergy is not only based on industry. All twenty-two criteria are evaluated by the respondent companies and the most critical influencers are evaluated as alliance approaches and balance of the resources. It is also observed that the micro companies give more importance to the human resource based criteria, whereas the medium size companies which have more opportunity for investment see issues on the collaboration critic factors.

It is experienced in business that the collaboration is more difficult as the number of partners increase. That is why this case is an initial study on measuring the collaborative innovation by using clustering method. The approach should be extended by relating the synergy effects on innovation power, innovation risks and financial changes. Only then we can propose SME s to collaborate with 3-4 more SMEof different size in different industries.

6   Conclusion and Suggestions

Innovative synergy is requested for collaborative research and development that is an obligatory process for the small and medium companies. This study proposes a synergy index that will help the SMEs to decide which companies will maximize the synergy if collaborated. The synergy is accepted as the life of collaboration which will be prolonged with robust partnerships.

The novelty of the paper is proposing a new approach to measure synergy for collaboration which is constructed and achieved by using a very new collective intelligence method, Foraging Search. Both the approach and the method have not been used before. The construction of survey on the intangible criteria is based on linguistic approach and therefore evaluated by using fuzzy measures. The number of companies in collaboration is restricted to 5 in order to avoid risks involved in increasing number of partners.

A case study is run for the 51 SMEs in Thrace, Turkey showed that the synergy is maximized when number of clusters is increased to 11, the best synergy is obtained with a group of five companies as 1.18, meaning that the life of collaboration will be increased by 18%. It is observed that the innovation is received with companies of different sizes and from a variety of industries. The business and alliance approaches of companies have a bigger role in synergy. This conclusion suggests that SMEs are to be trained to collaborate with the companies that strengthen their weak points.

The proposed approach is to be further developed by validity analysis through comparisons with different approaches and different methods. Further studies are developed to measure synergy in effect of economic development, innovation power maximization, and or minimizing the innovation risks. It is also suggested that the synergy calculation is to be validated for different countries and international collaborations. A further study on synergy will also be run to measure the strength of SME collaboration synergy in the supply chain of power games.

References

1. Yuhas, D.: Sharing the Wealth (of Knowledge): Cumulative Cultural Development May Be Exclusively Human, Scientific American, March 14 (2012), http://www.Scientificamerican.com (accessed: April 11,2012)
2. Tampieri, L.: The Governance of Synergies and Conflicts in Project Management: The Case of IPA Project RecoURB. Journal of the Knowledge Economy (2011) 1868-7873
3. Toppila, A., Juuso, L., Salo, A.: A Resource Allocation Model for R&D Investments: A Case Study in Telecommunication Standardization. International Series in Operations Research & Management Science 162, 241–258 (2011)
4. Das, T.K., Teng, B.S.: Partner Analysis and Alliance Performance. Scandinavian Journal of Management 19(3), 279–308 (2003)
5. Gardet, E., Mothe, C.: SME Dependence and Coordination in Innovation Networks. Journal of Small Business and Enterprise Development 19(2), 263–280 (2012)
6. Pangarkar, N.: Determinants of Alliance Duration in Uncertain Environments: The Case of the Biotechnology Sector. Long Range Planning 36(3), 269–284 (2003)
7. Wong, A., Tjosvold, A., Zhang, P.: Developing Relationships in Strategic Alliances: Commitment to Quality and Cooperative Interdependence. Industrial Marketing Management 34(7), 722–731 (2005)
8. McCutchen Jr., W.W., Swamidass, P.M.: Motivations for Strategic Alliances in the Pharmaceutical/Biotech Industry: Some New Findings. The Journal of High Technology Management Research 15(2), 197–214 (2004)
9. Hajidimitrou, Y.A., Georgiou, A.C.: A Goal Programming Model for Partner Selection Decisions in International Joint Ventures. European Journal of Operations Research 3(1), 649–662 (2002)
10. Huang, J.J., Chen, C.Y., Liu, H.H., Tzeng, G.H.: A Multiobjective Programming Model For Partner Selection-Perspectives of Objective Synergies And Resource Allocations. Expert Systems with Applications 37(5), 3530–3536 (2010)
11. Engelbrecht, A.P.: Fundamentals of Computational Swarm Intelligence. Wiley Interscience, New York (2005)
12. León-Javier, A., Cruz-Cortés, N., Moreno-Armendáriz, M.A., Orantes-Jiménez, S.: Finding Minimal Addition Chains with a Particle Swarm Optimization Algorithm. In: Aguirre, A.H., Borja, R.M., Garciá, C.A.R. (eds.) MICAI 2009. LNCS, vol. 5845, pp. 680–691. Springer, Heidelberg (2009)
13. Altay, A.: Collective Intelligence Model for Assessing Collaborative Innovation Power Including Risks, PhD. Dissertation, Istanbul Technical University, Industrial Engineering (2012)
14. Levy, M., Powell, P.: SME Flexibility and the Role of Information Systems. Small Business Economics 11(8), 183–196 (1998)
15. Khan, I.A.: Knowledge Groups: A Model for Creating Synergy Across the Public Sector Public Organization SME Flexibility and the Role of Information Systems Review, vol. (10), pp. 139–152 (2010)
16. Chen, G., Tjosvold, D.: Organizational values and procedures as antecedents for goal interdependence and collaborative effectiveness. Asia Pacific Journal of Management 25(1), 93–112 (2007)
17. Knoll, S.: Cross-Business Strategies, Dissertation-Universitat St. Gallen. Springer, Germany (2008)
18. Cefis, E., Mrsili, O.: Going, going, gone. Exit forms and the innovative capabilities of firms. Research Policy 41(5), 795–807 (2012)

19. Meuleman, M., DeMaesenerie, W.: Do R&D subsidies affect SMEs access to external financing? Research Policy 41(3), 580–591 (2012)
20. Chang and, Y.C., Hsu, C.J.: Ally or Merge – Airline Strategies After the Relaxation of Ownership Rules. Journal of the Eastern Asia Society for Transportation Studies (5), 545–556 (2005)
21. Lee, Y., Shin, J., Park, Y.: The changing pattern of SME innovativeness through business model globalization. Technological Forecasting and Social Change 79(5), 832–842 (2012)
22. Radas, S., Božić, L.: The antecedents of SME innovativeness in an emerging transition economy. Technovation 29(6-7), 438–450 (2009)
23. Brede, M., Boschetti, F., McDonald, D.: Managing Renewable Resources via Collective Intelligence. In: ModSim 2007, Christchurch, New Zealand (December 2007)
24. Brunker, D.: Collaboration and Other Factors Influencing Innovation Novelty in Australian Business, Commonwealth of Australia, Department of Industry, Tourism and Resources, DITR (2006)
25. Twardy, D.: Partner Selection: A Source of Alliance Success, Research Project, Eindhoven University of Technology and Zuyd University of Applied Science (2009)
26. Margoluis, C.: Healthy Relationships: Examining Alliances Within Population – Health – Environment Projects, World Wildlife Fund Report (2008)
27. Rai, A., Borahand, S., Ramaprasad, A.: Critical Success Factors for Strategic Alliances in the Information Technology Industry: An Empirical Study. Decision Sciences 27(1), 141–155 (1996)
28. Ding, J.F.: Partner Selection of Strategic Alliance for a Liner Shipping Company Using Extent Analysis Method of Fuzzy AHP. Journal of Marine Science and Technology 17(2), 97–105 (2009)
29. Ramaseshan, B., Loo, P.C.: Factors Affecting a Partner's Perceived Effective of Strategic Business Alliance: Some Singaporean Evidence. International Business Review 7(4), 443–458 (1998)
30. Chen, S.H., Lee, H.T., Wu, Y.F.: Applying ANP Approach to Partner Selection for Strategic Alliance. Management Decision 46(3), 449–465 (2008)
31. Rose, R.C., Abdullah, H., Ismad, A.I.: A review on relationship between organizational resources, competitive advantage and performance. The Journal of International Social Research 3(1), 488–498 (2010)
32. Gomes-Cassares, B.: Alliance Strategy: Fundamentals for Success. In: Management Roundtable Workshop (2003)
33. Linder, J.C., Perkins, S., Dover, P.: Drug Industry Alliances: In Search of Strategy, Accenture White Paper (2004)
34. Eden, L.: Friends, Acquaintances or Stranger? Partner Selection in R&D Alliances, Texas A&M University, Draft Working Paper (2007)
35. Gardet, E., Mothe, C.: SME dependence and coordination in innovation networks. Journal of Small Business and Enterprise Development 19(2), 263–280 (2012)
36. Cheung, Y.K.F.: A Study of Determinants of Effectiveness in Relational Contracting. Unpublished Master Thesis, Queensland University of Technology, Brisbane, Australia, M.C (2006)
37. Nelson, W.: Applied Life Data Analysis, New York. Wiley Series in Probability and Statistics (2004)
38. Ross, S.: A First Course in Probability. Prentice Hall, New York (2006)
39. ben Rejeb, H., Morel-Guimarães, L., Boly, V., Assiélou, N.D.G.: Measuring innovation best practices: Improvement of an innovation index integrating threshold and synergy effects. Technovation 28(12), 838–854 (2008)

40. Altay, A., Kayakutlu, G.: Animal Food Chain Based Particle Swarm Optimization. In: Ao, S.I., Gelman, L., Hukins, D.W.L., Hunter, A., Korsunsky, A.M. (eds.) World Congress on Engineering 2011, London, UK, July 6-8, vol. II, pp. 1094-1099 (2011)
41. Sulton, M.Q., Anderson, E.N.: Introduction to Cultural Ecology. Altamira Press (2004)
42. Chinsamy-Turan, A. (ed.): Forerunner of Mammals. Indiana University Press (2011)
43. Jarboui, B., Cheikh, M., Siarry, P., Rebai, A.: Combinatorial Particle Swarm Optimization (CPSO) for Partitional Clustering Problem. Applied Mathematics and Computation 192(2), 337–345 (2007)
44. Gras, R., Devaurs, D., Wozniak, A., Aspinall, A.: An Individual-Based Evolving Predator-Prey Ecosystem Simulation Using a Fuzzy Cognitive Map as the Behavior Model. Artificial Life 15(4), 423–463 (2009)

How to Understand Digital Studio Outputs: The Case of Digital Music Production

Karim Barkati and Francis Rousseaux

Institut de Recherche et Coordination Acoustique/Musique (IRCAM), France
`karim.barkati@ircam.fr`
Reims Champagne-Ardenne University, CReSTIC EA 3804 & IRCAM, France
`francis.rousseaux@univ-reims.fr`

Abstract. Digital studios trace a great amount of processes and artifacts. The important flow of these traces calls for a system to support their interpretation and understanding. We present our design and development of such a system in the digital music production context, within the *Gamelan* research project. This trace-based system is structured in three main layers: track production process, interpret collected traces according to a dedicated domain ontology, help querying and visualizing to foster production understanding. We conclude by discussing some hypotheses about trace-based knowledge engineering and digital music production understanding.

Keywords: Digital Music Production, Digital Artifact Preservation, Trace Engineering, Process Understanding, Digital Humanities, Digital Studio.

1 Introduction

1.1 Motivation and Objectives

From a social standpoint, the large and ever growing number of users of audio environments for personal or applied production makes the music production field one of the richest in evolution. However, the complexity of the production management is a well-known effect in the community and is often described as revealing an inconsistency between the tools used. Indeed, the industry provides tools that are more and more powerful but regardless of global usage: users combine multiple tools simultaneously or constantly alternate from one tool to another.

From a legal standpoint, there is a real problem of content tracking, given their multiple uses or changes in production. Till now, audio production systems have kept no operational tracks that would allow following up the rights associated with each element.

Indeed, music tool design mainly focuses on the making of the final product, because the very first aim of the studio is to provide the creator with efficient means to make and shape the musical object they came in the studio for. But

E. Mercier-Laurent and D. Boulanger (Eds.): AI4KM 2012, IFIP AICT 422, pp. 151–169, 2014.
© IFIP International Federation for Information Processing 2014

this requisite priority on creativity has overshadowed other needs that appear later: recovery and understanding. The *Gamelan* project aims at demonstrating that appropriately using knowledge management tools for trace-based systems [1,2], we now have both theoretical and practical means to build a system that can help understanding digital studio outputs, *i.e.* effective means to bring music production data and process to the Knowledge Level [3].

This paper describes how we designed and developed such a system upon a digital music production environment: the *Gamelan* "meta-environment". As far as we know, such a management and archiving system has not been built for music production before. It has been designed in three layers, as shown on Fig. 1:

1. Track production process (software events and files),
2. Interpret collected traces according to a domain ontology (DiMPO),
3. Help querying and visualizing to foster production understanding.

These three parts set the three central paper sections — Production tracking system, Trace interpretation system, and Querying and visualizing system — followed by Discussion and Conclusions.

1.2   Use Cases and Results

The *Gamelan* project embraces various creative practices related to its partners core business and expertise, who defined three main use cases.

IRCAM. *Recovery assistance and synthesis of information from one phase to another of a record.* Follow the recording and editing situation of the piece *Nuages gris* of Franz Liszt in the *Liszt as a Traveler* CD played by pianist Emmanuelle Swiercz. — Identify and represent the work sessions in two dimensions by time and by agent, all the events of one session (creation, update, export), and the dependencies of import and export files between sessions.

INA/GRM. *Identification of files that have contributed to the final version of a work.* Log every DAW operation of a composer during the composition of a jingle. — Ensure that the file called "Final-Mixdown" is actually the one that produced the latest audio files of the work; identify possible format changes (stereo, 8-channel, mp3); identify the intermediate versions; detect missing data and check information integrity are key features.

EMI Music. *Recovery and edit of past productions; Contributors listing.* Test the replacement of the drum from a recording traced by *Gamelan*. — Accurately identify which tracks to replay; substitute an identified track to another; replay the final mix session with the replaced tracks; identify contributors of the project.

Development results spread on several levels:

− an operational meta-environment with production tracking (*Gamelan Tracker*),
− a strongly-committed ontology for digital music production domain (DiMPO),

- a raw trace interpreter (*logs2dimpo*),
- a timeline visualizer (*GamelanViewer*),
- a query management application (*OwlimQueryManager*), with a set of queries related to the use cases.

1.3 Architecture Overview

The technical goal of the *Gamelan* research project is to create a software "meta-environment" (also called *Gamelan*), in the sense that it aims at producing knowledge over production environment utilization. It integrates some music production softwares and is able to describe the production workflow, from source to final product, at an abstraction level which is higher than the data level. For this purpose, methods from several fields were combined: trace engineering for the tracking system, and knowledge modeling and engineering for ontology design and the querying and visualizing system, as shown on Fig. 1.

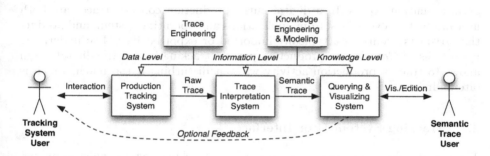

Fig. 1. *Gamelan* architecture overview

Gamelan promotes two categories of users: users of the tracking system, who generate traces while they interact with the digital tools of the studio during the production process, and users of these traces, at the other end of the whole system. If a user of the tracker is also user of the trace, then he or she simply get a feedback loop in the creative process, *e.g.* a live process evaluation.

With these two users, one can see the whole *Gamelan* architecture as a three-tiered system[1], made of three layers sequentially chained, corresponding to Ackoff's Data, Information and Knowledge levels [4].

The left-most region of Fig. 1 represents the trace collecting part of *Gamelan*, starting from the production activity of the tracking system user. This tracking module should respect the noninvasive constraint against creativity as much as possible. It feeds the system with raw traces which are precious but too difficult to exploit under this primitive form.

---

[1] Not to be confused with "client-server three-tier architecture".

After this raw trace point, an ontology becomes necessary for any further operation, as one leave the simple data level, providing a reference knowledge model. The DiMPO ontology, standing for "Digital music production ontology", has been elaborated during the project [5]. The main technical features of *Gamelan* meta-environment include at different levels: tracking, acquisition, ingestion, reasoning, requesting, browsing, file genealogy visualization, integrity and authority checking, and archiving. Besides, *Gamelan* relies on standard formats, such as: RDF[2], OWL[3], Sesame[4], SparQL[5] and OSC[6].

2   Production Tracking System

The first part of the meta-environment deals with raw traces of production, through automatic logging of user interaction events and contextual data asking. It involves the tracking system user, at data level, to collecting production traces.

We define *trace* as the recordings of computer-mediated activity from program execution events. In a digital music production context, traces are both user interaction event logs, from applications and operating system, and production artifacts themselves, typically imported or exported files. The underlying hypothesis of *Gamelan* on production process tracking is that the digital realm allows to track a production activity without disturbing it too much, which is often admitted[7].

2.1   Tracking System User Interface

The first development result is the production tracking system, which combines the *GamelanTracker* software and "gamelanized" production softwares, mainly Audacity. The development affects three layers:

- software and file system events tracking, based on messaging;
- production file movement monitoring and back-up recording;
- manual entry information collecting, via ontology-compliant user interface.

This part integrates musical and sound production softwares and has its own non-invasive user interface: instead of the common pop-up windows, we designed an unobtrusive menu, accessible from a small "Track on/off" checkbox icon, as shown on Fig. 2, top left.

---

[2] *Resource Description Framework*, a standard model for data interchange on the Web.
[3] *Web Ontology Language*, for authoring ontologies or knowledge bases.
[4] Sesame is a de-facto standard framework for processing RDF data.
[5] *SparQL Protocol and RDF Query Language*.
[6] *Open Sound Control* is a content format for messaging among digital devices.
[7] For instance see Dyke's thesis [6]: "The tracing of computer-mediated activity is a special situation in that it is both possible to be very specific in what is traced, and to do so without modifying the environment in a disruptive way."

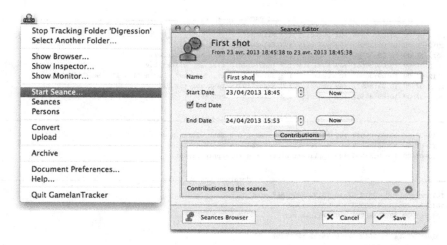

Fig. 2. *GamelanTracker* user interface (credit: INA)

2.2   Software Activity Tracking Implementation

Traces are to be mobilized in contexts that are never totally predictable and these inscriptions will report a reality that has evolved by itself. That is the reason why we designed a software activity tracking that is as agnostic as possible, through raw messaging, listening and logging.

The messaging part relies on an open-source standard commonly used in the computer music community: OSC (Open Sound Control[8]) developed at UC Berkeley [7], which is a communication protocol for modern networking technology, with a client/server architecture (UDP and TCP).

In order to produce usage data [8,9], we modified open-source domain production softwares, mainly Audacity[9], an open-source software for recording and editing sounds, written in C++. We added specific OSC messaging functions into several functions of interest, such as *open*, *save*, *save as*, *play*, *stop*, *cut*, *copy*, *paste*, etc. This way, each time the user performs an action through a user-level function call of the production software, our modified software sends a complete OSC message, built with the following: application name, application version number, time stamp, function name, plus specific function parameters if needed.

GamelanTracker, a corresponding tracking application, has been developed. It receives and logs every message broadcasted during production time from three possible sources:

- "gamelanized" applications, for action logs (`OSCMessages.txt`)
- File System, for file movement logs (`FolderState.txt`)
- Operating System, for application change logs (`CurrentApplication.txt`)

---

[8] http://opensoundcontrol.org
[9] http://audacity.sourceforge.net

```
─────────────────────────── OSCMessages.txt ───────────────────────────

2012-07-09 10:09:36546 +02 audacity 1.3 FileNew
2012-07-09 10:09:36553 +02 audacity 1.3 FileSaveAs  test.aup
2012-07-09 10:09:36560 +02 audacity 1.3 ImportAudio test.aup noise.wav
2012-07-09 10:09:36561 +02 audacity 1.3 ImportAudio test.aup clicks.wav
2012-07-09 10:09:36563 +02 audacity 1.3 Select "noise", "clicks"; Begin="1.931"; End="10.014"
2012-07-09 10:09:36571 +02 audacity 1.3 ExportAudio test.aup mix.aif
2012-07-09 10:09:36581 +02 audacity 1.3 FileClosed test.aup


─────────────────────────── CurrentApplication.txt ───────────────────────────

2012-07-09 10:09:36544 +02 ApplicationActivated net.sourceforge.audacity
2012-07-09 10:09:36582 +02 ApplicationActivated com.apple.dt.Xcode
2012-07-09 10:09:36593 +02 ApplicationActivated com.apple.finder


─────────────────────────── FolderState.txt ───────────────────────────

folder-state 0  2012-07-10 16:22:58961547 +02
2012-01-20 18:07:65253 +01  noise.wav
2012-01-20 18:07:65253 +01  clicks.wav
...
folder-state 21 2012-07-10 16:23:59005107 +02
2012-01-20 18:07:65253 +01  noise.wav
2012-01-20 18:07:65253 +01  clicks.wav
2012-07-10 16:23:59005 +02  mix.aif
2012-07-10 16:23:58980 +02  test.aup


─────────────────────────── Seances.txt ───────────────────────────

Demo     file://localhost/Users/Barkati/Music/Demo/
Recording    2012-01-20 15:59:28783242 +02   2012-01-20 19:59:39583242 +02
Alain Bonardi    Artistic director
Emmanuelle Swiercz  Pianist
Mix 2012-07-10 15:04:39889830 +02
Karim Barkati    Sound engineer
```

Fig. 3. Log files excerpts

GamelanTracker adds a reception time stamp and keeps track of every version of modified files in a backup folder for file genealogy analysis and preservation purposes. Fig. 3 shows excerpts of log files, reduced to fit in paper width (some timestamps and/or other information are truncated).

2.3   Manual Informing Issues

Software activity tracking is often not sufficient to fulfill our use cases. For instance, contributors listing (EMI use case) requires further contributor information that cannot be inferred from software traces. In these cases, at least some primary contextual information must be provided by a human operator, such as the user's name and the title of the work being produced (see `Seances.txt` excerpt on Fig. 3).

At first, production time seems to be the best time for asking the tracking system user to provide this information. But a design dilemma rapidly appears: on the one hand, the more contextual information feeds the system, the more informative the knowledge management can be, but on the other hand, the more a system asks the user to enter data while he or she is working, the more the user may reject the documenting system [10].

In our case, the balance between quantity and quality of information has to be adjusted in a close relationship with the ontology we have been incrementally developing with domain experts [11] and which is presented thereafter.

Temporal modalities have also to be anticipated in the information system, since the manual information can be entered during production time or temporally uncoupled, either by a producing user (*e.g.* a composer or a sound engineer) or by an external agent (*e.g.* a secretary or a curator).

3   Trace Interpretation System

This second part is hidden to both tracking system user and trace user. Nevertheless, it carries a crux task: interpret raw trace, to raise these traces from data level to information level. Firstly, a target representation language is required, calling for knowledge modeling. Secondly, an artificial interpretation program has to be designed and developed.

3.1   Knowledge Modeling

To formalize knowledge at stake, a domain ontology has been elaborated during the project, mainly by Antoine Vincent from UTC: DiMPO, standing for "Digital Music Production Ontology" [11]. Modeling digital music production knowledge required to form an analysis corpus first, because of the lack of written documents. Then, the preservation aim leads to ensure the robustness of the model, which we addressed with a differential method.

Music Production Knowledge. Usually, the modeling phase begins with a corpus analysis from a collection of candidate-documents selected on their relevance [12]. But in the case of digital music production, such a corpus does not exist, *i.e.* no written document can provide sufficient support to terms selection. Indeed, vocabulary, and consequently all the production process, relies on musical practices that are acquired more by experience than by teaching.

Thus, to achieve this essential phase of study, we needed to make up our own corpus, which is rather unusual in ontology making: several musical productions were followed to find out and adequately formalize invariants into an ontology.

With DiMPO, we do not seek to explain sound nor music (the *what*, as in MusicXML kind of languages) but the way it is produced (the *how*), *i.e.* a formal language for audio production process. This language is devoted to the representation of what we might call the "music production level", referring to the "knowledge level" of Allen Newell: we want to represent the work at the right abstraction level, neither too concrete because too technology dependent and therefore highly subjected to obsolescence, nor not concrete enough because information would be too vague to be usable [3].

Production Process Modeling. To create the DiMPO representation language and implement its operationalization, we applied the *Archonte*[10] method of Bachimont [13]. The modeling of digital music production followed three steps:

---

[10] ARCHitecture for ONTological Elaborating.

1. Normalization of the meanings of selected terms and classification in an ontological tree, specifying the relations of similarity between each concept and its parent concept and/or sibling concepts: we then have a *differential* ontology;
2. Formalization of knowledge, adding properties to concepts or constraining relation fields, to obtain an *referential* ontology;
3. Operationalization in the representation language, in the form of a *computational* ontology.

After a phase of collecting our corpus and selecting candidate terms, we took the first step in the form of a taxonomy of concepts, in which we strived to maintain a strong semantic commitment in supporting the principles of the differential semantics theory presented thereafter. This taxonomy has been performed iteratively, since it is tightly dependent on our participation in successive productions. Thus, at each new integration to the creation or the updating of a work, we flatten and question our taxonomy and term normalization, in order to verify that the semantic commitment is respected. For common features, we import standard ontologies, among which vCard[11] for standard identity information.

In order to ease incremental development and testing, we divided the ontology in two parts. The first part represents the model, with classes and properties, uploaded on a dedicated server `icm.ircam.fr`[12]. The second part contains model-compliant data sets, with "DiMPO individuals", uploaded on an OWL server `gsemantic.ircam.fr`[13] (an OpenRDF *Sesame* repository with the *OWLIM-Lite* engine).

The Differential Approach. The differential approach for ontology elaboration systematically investigates the similarity and difference relations between each concept, its parent concept and its sibling concepts. So, while developing this structure, we tried to respect a strong ontological commitment by applying a *semantic normalization, i.e.* by asking, for each concept c, the four differential questions of Table 1.

To carry out this semantic normalization task from a practical point of view, we used DOE[14] [14] and Protégé[15] softwares, for both taxonomy building, refining and exporting (RDFS, OWL, etc.). Fig. 4 shows an excerpt from DiMPO

Table 1. The four differential questions

1. $c \sim \text{parent}(c)$ — Why does this concept inherit from its parent concept?
2. $c \not\sim \text{parent}(c)$ — Why is this concept different from its parent concept?
3. $c \sim \text{sibling}(c)$ — Why is this concept similar to its sibling concepts?
4. $c \not\sim \text{sibling}(c)$ — Why is this concept different from its sibling concepts?

---

[11] http://www.w3.org/Submission/vcard-rdf
[12] http://icm.ircam.fr/gamelan/ontology/2013/04/03/DiMPO.owl
[13] http://gsemantic.ircam.fr
[14] http://www.eurecom.fr/~troncy/DOE/, *Differential Ontology Editor.*
[15] http://protege.stanford.edu/

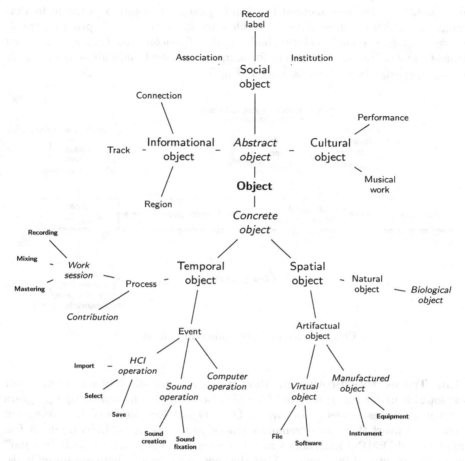

Fig. 4. Excerpt from the differential taxonomy (credit: UTC)

taxonomy. At the end of this recursive process, one obtains a domain-specific differential ontology, where the meaning of all terms have been normalized and that allows to develop the vocabulary needed for the next steps to reach the development of the representation language of the music production process.

As a result of the differential method, domain vocabulary mostly occurs in the leaves of such an ontological tree: *work, performance, version; connection, graphical object, track, region; association, enterprise, institute; musical score, instrument, brass, strings, percussions, winds; effect box, synthesizer; file, session file, program; create, delete, edit; content import, content export; listen, play, work session, current selection*; etc. A large set of properties completes this domain ontology.

3.2 Artificial Interpretation

Interpretation of raw traces according to the ontology yields "semantic traces" as interrelated ontological individuals, conformable to DiMPO. To perform this interpretation, we implemented the *logs2dimpo.pl* translation program in Perl language, which we chose for its text file parsing facilities. This program transforms raw logs into DiMPO individuals. Within *Gamelan*, this translator is called from *GamelanTracker*, and checks for uniqueness of each individual against a remote knowledge base when necessary (Fig. 5).

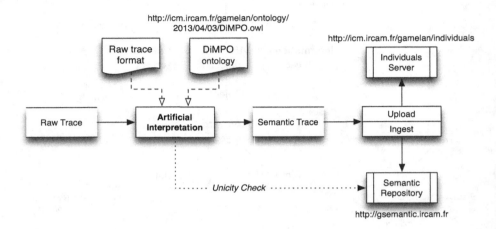

Fig. 5. Trace interpretation and management

Raw Traces Interpretation. Raw traces are not directly informative nor exploitable under this raw form of log files (see Fig. 3). The *logs2dimpo* program interprets theses traces according to DiMPO ontology and OWL language in order to convert them into "semantic traces", *i.e.* ontological individuals. A few interrelated DiMPO individuals are shown on Fig. 6 as "owl:NamedIndividual" elements, identified by a unique URI that ensures relations between individuals.

Uniqueness Checking. If a DiMPO individual produced by the translator is intended to be ingested into an existing semantic repository, then the translator shall check whether this individual is already recorded, to ensure individual uniqueness. A mechanism of index attribution recovers current indexes for each DiMPO class present in the semantic repository before individual numbering.

Individual and Ontology Servers. As production management may involve several users, we designed additional online features. For instance, before being ingested into the semantic repository, semantic traces are uploaded in a server dedicated to DiMPO individuals[16], in order to provide individuals with an internet location. Moreover, another server has been dedicated to DiMPO ontology versions[17].

---

[16] http://icm.ircam.fr/gamelan/individuals
[17] http://icm.ircam.fr/gamelan/ontology/2013/04/03/DiMPO.owl

Fig. 6. Some interrelated DiMPO individuals

4   Querying and Visualizing System

This third part aims at bringing production knowledge to the trace user, through knowledge engineering techniques. It has spread on several operational tasks: manage a server for the "semantic traces", deploy a semantic repository with reasoning capabilities from the ontology, and prototype use case queries.

4.1   Semantic Repository

A Sesame OpenRDF semantic repository has been installed from an Ontotext OWLIM-Lite version. It handles structured data storage and management, reasoning and querying.

Data Storage and Management. OWL/RDF data ingestion on the semantic repository is triggered by a short Java program integrated into *GamelanTracker* and using *Sesame* API. An online graphical interface allows repositories management at http://gsemantic.ircam.fr.

Reasoning. The OWLIM inference engine performs completion of facts through "total materialization" at load time. This reasoning strategy slows down upload but speeds up retrieval and querying, which is what we have chosen.

Querying. The semantic repository embeds a query engine accessible through HTTP. We use the SPARQL[18] language to write RDF queries against the semantic repository, with triple patterns syntax.

---

[18] SPARQL is an RDF query language, appeared in 2008 and well-suited for triples. Its recursive acronym stands for "SPARQL Protocol and RDF Query Language".

4.2   Triplestore Querying

The digital archival issue of provenance should be avoided or at least diminished upstream from the ingest step. The *Gamelan* meta-environment allows to detect crucial missing information by reasoning on the combination of software traces and user information, from expert knowledge. These features, important to the trace user, are partially carried out through production tracking and common knowledge management tools, such as domain ontology, query engine, and semantic repository. For example, one can query the semantic repository in order to check whether expected contributors and their roles on the project are well informed or not (EMI use case, results on Fig. 7).

```
SELECT ?Name ?Role
WHERE {
    ?subject        rdf:type                dimpo:ObjetBiologique .
    ?subject        vcard:fn                ?Name .
    ?subject        dimpo:intervientDans    ?contribution .
    ?contribution   dimpo:aPourContributeur ?subject .
    ?contribution   dimpo:aPourRole         ?roleID .
    ?roleID         rdfs:label              ?Role .
}
```

Name	Role
"Tristan Leblanc"^^xsd:string	"Développeur"^^xsd:string
"Laurent Vinet"^^xsd:string	"Beta-testeur"^^xsd:string

Fig. 7. Contributors checking

A query storage and management application has been developed to capitalize on and manage trace user queries: sets of queries are designed and managed in *OwlimQueryManager*, a user-friendly application developed on purpose, as shown on Fig. 8.

4.3   Time Axis Reconstruction

As we are dealing with production workflows, time axis reconstruction is essential to trace user understanding.

However, archiving music and sound production is generally limited to the rudimentary archiving of a final version (called "master version"), at the end of the production process. Whereafter it is clearly impossible to trace the production history from this single object, nor to take back and modify the process in a different perspective, as needed in *repurposing* EMI use case for instance. This led us to ensure strong timing properties through our trace-based system, not only time stamping user events from the production tools when emitting messages, but also independently time stamping a second time these events in the logging module when receiving messages. This allows to reconstruct the time axis of the production safely.

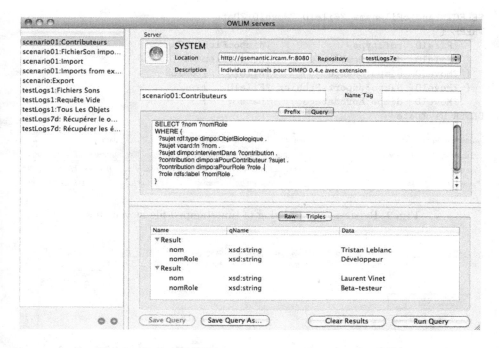

Fig. 8. *OwlimQueryManager* user interface (credit: INA)

For example, a typical query can retrieve and chronologically order audio files movements (imports and exports) in a musical project (results on Fig. 9).

4.4   Timeline Visualization

Furthermore, the *GamelanViewer* timeline visualization tool shown in Fig. 10 can draw a global view to help query results understanding, typically showing the genealogy of the files used during the production. For example, *Gamelan* can infer which files were used to compose a mixed file, hierarchically, and also deduce which is the "last mix" in a set of file; this kind of knowledge is of prime importance when a composer or a producer decides to remix a work years later, as pointed out in INA/GRM use case.

4.5   Production Patterns

When DiMPO ontology reached a decent and stabilized level, we entered a second phase of the ontological research: *production patterns* design. Production patterns define audio creation acts, such as editing, shown on Fig. 11 (in UML). The use of these patterns allows to represent a set of actions with a musical meaning, incorporating the vocabulary developed in the ontology.

```
SELECT ?AudioFilename ?FileID ?MoveID ?Date
WHERE {
    ?FileID   rdf:type                 dimpo:FichierSon .
    ?FileID   dimpo:nomFichier         ?AudioFilename .
  { ?MoveID   dimpo:source             ?FileID . } UNION
  { ?MoveID   dimpo:exporteFichier     ?FileID . }
    ?MoveID   dimpo:horodatage         ?Date .    }
ORDER BY ?Date
```

AudioFilename	FileID	MovementID	Date
"nuagesGris_extrait1_mono.wav"^^xsd:string	scenario01:FichierSon_1	scenario01:ImportAudio_1	2013-04-05T12:20:52.000
"nuagesGris_extrait2_mono.wav"^^xsd:string	scenario01:FichierSon_2	scenario01:ImportAudio_2	2013-04-05T12:20:55.000
"montage1.wav"^^xsd:string	scenario01:FichierSon_3	scenario01:ExportAudio_1	2013-04-05T12:22:14.000

Fig. 9. Retrieval and ordering of timestamped file movements

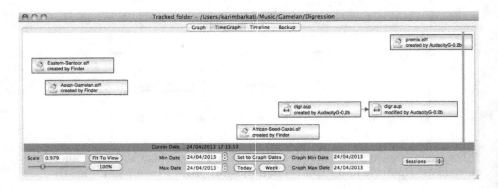

Fig. 10. Timeline visualization (credit: INA)

Our query patterns are grounded on these production patterns. Reuse of ontology vocabulary in production patterns eases their translation into query patterns, especially when using RDF-compliant query languages such as SPARQL, as we do onto our Sesame repository containing OWL individuals.

Here, knowledge can be viewed as bilocalized: on the semantic repository side for interrelated individuals of the semantic trace database, and on the query manager side for the formalized relations of the query patterns base. The more accurate production patterns are, the more useful derived query patterns can be, and the less the trace user has to know or to learn about the details of both the query language and the ontology.

5   Discussion

In this section, we discuss modeling, knowledge support, and time horizons of production process tracing.

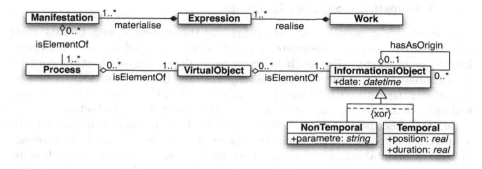

Fig. 11. A production pattern diagram for editing (credit: UTC)

5.1   Model Pervasiveness and Design Heuristics

As suggested in the architecture overview section (Sec. 1.3), apart from the operational tracking that has to remain agnostic, the domain ontology drives most functional modules of our system at each level:

Data — the semi-automatic collecting module, *i.e.* software activity tracking and manual informing design;

Information — the translation module that interprets raw data (both automatic usage data and manual user data) according to the ontology;

Knowledge — the semantic engine reasoning on the preprocessed information, and answering requests;

Understanding — the query manager module for data browsing, and the viewer module that provides graphical representations, such as timelines and file genealogy trees.

According to Ackoff's model [4], knowledge management depends on the ability to transform data and information into knowledge, a task where ontologies proved key tools [15,16], thanks to their semantic capabilities. That led us to undertake our semantic research in professional music knowledge modeling.

Yet, despite their power and thus their pervasiveness, ontologies remain human artifacts never elaborated without design heuristics. We developed a strongly-committed ontology incrementally, dipping into music productions with domain experts and submitting ontology drafts to them. This incremental approach continued during the next phases: during software development – with developers feedback –, and during tests and validation – with user groups feedback.

The differential approach we applied along the ontology development cycles balances the random part brought by heuristics but cannot eliminate it in any way. Ontology-driven knowledge management should be aware of this contingency dimension.

5.2   A Knowledge Support Language

The descriptive approach is not about keeping the content stored, because content is usually partial, incomplete or poorly defined (closed formats, imperfect knowledge of it, etc.). Rather, it is better to retain a *description* of the content that enables to reproduce it. The description may include the main points to reproduce, the author's intention to comply with [17], the graphical appearance, and any potentially informative element to the reader for reproduction.

So, the description of the content of a work is an approach increasingly adopted in response to the technical complexity (mostly digital) of content: instead of maintaining a technical object that we may no longer know how to reuse, we shall aim at constructing a description that allows to recreate this object with the tools we will have at hand when the time comes. Such a description necessarily introduces a deviation from the original. So the challenge is to minimize the impact of this difference on the integrity and authenticity of the work.

The main question is how to determine such a description language. The music score used in the so-called classical music, is a good example of such a description language. Instead of stepping on the impossible task to keep a musical object before recording techniques, musicians preferred to keep *the instructions to create it*. Now, the complexity of the works, the mutability and fragility of digital systems and objects imply that it is impossible to guarantee that a technical object will still be executable, readable or editable in the future.

Several approaches are possible, but some semiotic and logic work is necessary to identify such a description stage:

- Semiotic, because it is necessary to characterize the objects mobilized in a production, define their significance and propose an associated representation;
- Logical, since this representation must be enrolled in a language for operationalization in the proposed meta-environment.

The combination of these semiotic and logic approaches are key concepts to unlock knowledge possibilities of both the work as an artifact and the creation as a process.

5.3   Horizons of Production Process Tracing

As far as we know, music production process tracking has never been done yet, except for some isolated generative music programming under version control system (like cvs, svn or git). Regarding tracking, we distinguish between *user data* and *usage data*; the former corresponds to the manual informing data and the latter to the automatic tracking data.

As a meta-environment, *Gamelan* traces data during the production activity and utilizes formalized knowledge to exploit collected data, both during and after production time. This production tracing strategy aims for several beneficiaries and time horizons:

In the immediate time of production — The composer, audio producer, may turn back their own work during the production, to explore various options or correct the undesirable consequences. Use cases show needs for a selective offline "undo" instruction, to cancel a specific operation afterwards, even when the production software was quit. There is also, for the composer or the sound engineer, an opportunity to see and understand the overall work progress of composition or production during the process itself.

In the intermediate time of collection — The composer, or the institution that manages art works, may return on a given work to recreate it or reuse some parts of the content of the final work, which are usually no longer accessible.

In the long term preservation — The work becomes a memory and a relic, the challenge is to preserve the artistic and technical information to understand, interpret and re-perform, as in the case of contemporary works using real-time programs on stage.

6   Conclusions

Traditional places of creation generate final artifacts or art works that are closed: creativity is emphasized but the creation process is most often lost, locking both artifact structure recovery and process understanding. In this context, living labs often attempt to trace the creation process, by recording actions for usage study. But, be they artifacts or process recordings, how to understand digital studio outputs?

6.1   From Production Traces to Production Knowledge

We presented how we combined a trace-based architecture and an ontology-driven knowledge management system, the latter being built upon differential semantics theory for sustainability, in order to raise production activity traces from data level to information level, then to knowledge level. Technically, semi-automatic production tracking feeds an interpretation program which, in turn, feeds a semantic repository. The idea of such a production meta-environment, viewed as a trace-based system, meets clear needs in the community. As of now, *Gamelan* addresses intermediate artifacts preservation, file genealogy visualization, and contributors' identification. Moreover, our ontological work already points to the solution of various scientific challenges:

- Representation language for managing the production process;
- Description language for representing the content of a work, with the diversity of its components;
- Integration of both languages in a single control environment.

6.2   From Production Knowledge to Production Understanding

Digital studios and living labs produce a great amount of traces [18] that could be better understood – and thus more easily exploitable – using semantic trace strategies such as those developed within *Gamelan* for the case of digital music production, combining semi-automatic activity tracking with content and process modeling.

We presented how a knowledge management approach for digital music production workflows could be set up. This trace-based system already showed improving primary understanding, especially through visualizing interfaces. As we stated, further understanding would be of great utility at several time horizons: in the immediate time of production, in the intermediate time of collection, and in the long term of preservation.

Currently, our system can support trace interpretation only up to a certain point, which is style [19,20]. Meeting style understanding would need further modeling effort at higher level, which should be partially eased by our production patterns and the trace collecting and interpreting methods we developed. Further studies shall evaluate to what extent creation process style can be modeled.

Envision style modeling from semantic traces will require to rely on experts of art humanities at least, typically in our music production case on musicologists and composers.

Of course, approaching style understanding is of great interest [21,22]. Nevertheless, it may be perceived by creators as a provocative attempt to unraveling the mystery of art and creation. Then, we are entitled to wonder if art objects opacity regarding their making is not a consequence of a mystery will from creators. If it is the case, new understanding capabilities could be perceived both as a cure and a poison.

This is probably a first class concern of future Digital Humanities culture [23,24]. From our point of view, the advent of style pattern understanding would not reduce creative processes nor creativity potentials though, but rather most likely shift them.

Acknowledgments. The *Gamelan* project is funded by French National Research Agency. It started in 2009 and will end in 2013. The partners are:

- IRCAM (*Institut de Recherche et Coordination Acoustique/ Musique*),
- Heudiasyc – UMR 7253 CNRS UTC,
- INA (*Institut National de l'Audiovisuel*),
- EMI Music France.

References

1. Laflaquière, J., Settouti, L.S., Prié, Y., Mille, A.: Trace-based framework for experience management and engineering. In: Gabrys, B., Howlett, R.J., Jain, L.C. (eds.) KES 2006. LNCS (LNAI), vol. 4251, pp. 1171–1178. Springer, Heidelberg (2006)
2. Georgeon, O., Henning, M.J., Bellet, T., Mille, A.: Creating cognitive models from activity analysis: A knowledge engineering approach to car driver modeling. In: International Conference on Cognitive Modeling, pp. 43–48 (2007)

3. Newell, A.: The knowledge level. Artificial Intelligence 18(1) (1982)
4. Ackoff, R.: From data to wisdom. Journal of Applied Systems Analysis 16(1), 3–9 (1989)
5. Vincent, A., Bonardi, A., Bachimont, B.: Étude des processus compositionnels: Un langage pour représenter les processus de production sonore (2013)
6. Dyke, G.: A model for managing and capitalizing on the analyses of traces of activity in collaborative interaction. PhD thesis, ENS Mines (2009)
7. Wright, M., Freed, A., Momeni, A.: Opensound control: state of the art 2003. In: Proceedings of the 2003 Conference on New Interfaces for Musical Expression, National University of Singapore, pp. 153–160 (2003)
8. McLeod, I., Evans, H., Gray, P., Mancy, R.: Instrumenting bytecode for the production of usage data. In: Computer-aided Design of User Interfaces IV, pp. 185–195 (2005)
9. Smith, S., Schank, E., Tyler, B.: Instrumented application for transaction tracing, US Patent App. 11/092,428 (March 29, 2005)
10. Barki, H., Hartwick, J.: Measuring user participation, user involvement, and user attitude. MIS Quarterly, 59–82 (1994)
11. Vincent, A., Bachimont, B., Bonardi, A., et al.: Modéliser les processus de création de la musique avec dispositif numérique: représenter pour rejouer et préserver les œuvres contemporaines. Actes des Journées Francophones d'Ingénierie des Connaissances (2012)
12. Rousseaux, F., Bonardi, A.: Parcourir et constituer nos collections numériques. In: CIDE Proceedings, pp. 133–142 (2007)
13. Bachimont, B.: Ingénierie des connaissances. Hermes Lavoisier, Paris (2007)
14. Bachimont, B., Isaac, A., Troncy, R.: Semantic commitment for designing ontologies: A proposal. In: Gómez-Pérez, A., Benjamins, V.R. (eds.) EKAW 2002. LNCS (LNAI), vol. 2473, pp. 114–121. Springer, Heidelberg (2002)
15. Gruber, T.: Toward principles for the design of ontologies used for knowledge sharing. International Journal of Human Computer Studies 43(5), 907–928 (1995)
16. Fensel, D., Van Harmelen, F., Klein, M., Akkermans, H., Broekstra, J., Fluit, C., van der Meer, J., Schnurr, H., Studer, R., Hughes, J., et al.: On-to-knowledge: Ontology-based tools for knowledge management. In: Proceedings of the eBusiness and eWork, pp. 18–20 (2000)
17. Gaillard, L., Nanard, J., Bachimont, B., Chamming's, L.: Intentions based authoring process from audiovisual resources. In: Proceedings of the 2007 International Workshop on Semantically Aware Document Processing and Indexing, pp. 21–30. ACM (2007)
18. Følstad, A.: Living labs for innovation and development of information and communication technology: a literature review. The Electronic Journal for Virtual Organizations and Networks 10(7), 99–131 (2008)
19. Pachet, F.: The future of content is in ourselves. Computers in Entertainment (CIE) 6(3), 31 (2008)
20. Bonnardel, N., Zenasni, F.: The impact of technology on creativity in design: An enhancement? Creativity and Innovation Management 19(2), 180–191 (2010)
21. Carney, J.D.: The style theory of art. Pacific Philosophical Quarterly 72(4), 272–289 (1991)
22. Dubnov, S., Assayag, G., Lartillot, O., Bejerano, G.: Using machine-learning methods for musical style modeling. Computer 36(10), 73–80 (2003)
23. Giraud, F., Jauréguiberry, F., Proulx, S., et al.: Usages et enjeux des technologies de communication. Liens Socio (1970)
24. Wang, F.Y.: Is culture computable? IEEE Intelligent Systems 24(2), 2–3 (2009)

From Knowledge Transmission to Sign Sharing: Semiotic Web as a New Paradigm for Teaching and Learning in the Future Internet

Noël Conruyt, Véronique Sébastien, Olivier Sébastien,
David Grosser, and Didier Sébastien

LIM-IREMIA, EA 25-25, University of Reunion Island, 97490, Sainte-Clotilde, France
{noel.conruyt,veronique.sebastien,olivier.sebastien,
david.grosser,didier.sebastien}@univ-reunion.fr

Abstract. In the 21st century, with the advent of ultra high-speed broadband networks (1Gb per second), the Internet will offer new opportunities for innovators to design qualitative services and applications. Indeed, the challenge of such e-services is not only on the technological aspects of Internet with new infrastructures and architectures to conceive. The reality is also on its human and multimedia content delivery, with innovative philosophies of communication to apply in this digital and virtual age. In the context of Teaching and Learning as a human-centered design approach, we propose a new paradigm for thinking the Web, called the Web of Signs, rather than the Web of things. It focuses on the process of making knowledge by sharing signs and significations (Semiotic Web), more than on knowledge transmission with intelligent object representations (Semantic Web). Sign management is the shift of paradigm for education with ICT (e-Education) that we have investigated in such domains as enhancing natural and cultural heritage. In this paper, we will present this concept and illustrate it with two examples issued from La Reunion Island projects in instrumental e-Learning (@-MUSE) and biodiversity informatics (IKBS). This Sign management method was experimented in the frame of our Living Lab in Teaching and Learning at University of Reunion Island.

Keywords: Semiotic Web, Sign management, E-service, Education, Living Lab, Creativity Platform, Future Internet.

1   Introduction

The Future of Internet is not only a matter of technological, economical, or societal awareness; it is also grounded in individual, environmental and cultural values. Psychological, ethical, biological and emotional properties are indeed drivers of the Future Internet in a perspective of sustainable development of services with people. Although the Internet is the interconnection of networks of computers, it delivers interactive human-machine services such as the Web or Email [1]. The Web is an *information service* available on Internet with access to personalized documents, images and other resources interrelated together by hyperlinks and referenced with

E. Mercier-Laurent and D. Boulanger (Eds.): AI4KM 2012, IFIP AICT 422, pp. 170–188, 2014.

Uniform Resource Identifiers (URIs). Email is also a *communication service* available on the Internet. Nevertheless, Information and Communication Technologies (ICT) are not only oriented on technologies, but also convey human contents (data, information, and knowledge) that are communicated between end-users. At this upper level, co-designing e-services are means to connect producers and consumers of multimedia contents, in order that infrastructures of Future Internet meet user needs [2]. These principles have been adopted since 2006 by the European Network of Living Labs and are developed in the frame of corresponding literature [3].

Our idea is that in the Future Internet, we must not only pay attention to the *quantity* of information that is exchanged at higher speed between internauts (which is a techno-centric and economic perspective), but also to the *quality* of information communicated between people for them to be educated and aware of the richness and fragility of their environment. In the first case, users become stunned *prosumers* (producers and consumers of information), and in the second case they are simply *responsible citizens* (sensitive and educated people) in a closed world that must be preserved for the next generations.

In order to deliver such a holistic e-service in education, we introduce our methodology of Sign management in the first part of this paper. Then we explain how we organize the different types of Web that are part of the Semiotic Web, what makes its sense, and how to pass from Knowledge transmission to Sign sharing. This is illustrated with two examples taken from ICT projects for music education and biodiversity management. The conclusion emphasizes the need for repositioning human concerns at the center of technologies, and why we should favor the development of Living Labs philosophies.

2 Sign Management

The reality of Future Internet is that it supports both technological and content services over the physical network. But in the 21st century, the technology must be at the service of human content and not the contrary. Indeed with Web 2.0, we have entered an era where *usage* is the rule for making e-services. *Personalization* of product/services accessible throughout the Internet is becoming more and more important as innovation is opening [4] and democratizing [5]. But we will have also to manage the quality of information that is exchanged between people in order that knowledgeable persons can express their know-how and be acknowledged [6] for it. In the context of climate change, biodiversity loss, pollution and globalization, it is urgent that the Future of Internet enhances scientific voices at human level.

But this endeavor cannot be led only by managing knowledge of specialists with the technology of Semantic Web, so-called Web 3.0 [7]. Knowledge management is not enough for the Future Internet.

Firstly, knowledge cannot be managed because it resides between the ears of somebody (tacit knowledge). Only information that is transmitted between persons can be managed.

Secondly, Knowledge can be found in books written by specialists (explicit knowledge), but this is dead knowledge that cannot be updated. Knowledge is the result of a long experience of some experts that have experimented a lot of cases in the fields, and formed their know-how by compiling them in their mind. This know-how is living knowledge and it can be managed with multimedia contents (see below for music learning).

Thirdly, the response of ICT to tackle knowledge management is to propose Semantic Web as a solution. Indeed, this is necessary in the context of representing objects of knowledge in computers with formats coming from description logics (RDF, OWL), but it is not sufficient as far as this technology cannot capture the signification of these objects for different individuals, i.e. Subjects.

In the context of enhancing Knowledge with ICT, we propose Sign Management as a shift of paradigm for the Future Internet. It emphasizes the engineering and use of data, information and knowledge from the viewpoint of a Subject. This concept is derived from the pragmatic Peirce's theory of semiotics with a Sign's correspondence of the Subject to its Object. From this philosophical viewpoint, a Sign, or representamen, is something that stands to somebody for something in some respect or capacity [8]. From our computer science analysis, Data (Object) is the content of the Sign (something), Information, a multi-layered concept with Latin roots ('informatio' = to give a form) is its form, and Knowledge is its sense or meaning, i.e. no-thing. The notion of Sign is then more central than knowledge for our purpose of designing e-services.

In Figure 1, we define a Sign as the interpretation of an Object by a Subject at a given time and place, which takes into account its content (Data, facts, events), its form (Information), and its sense or meaning (Knowledge).

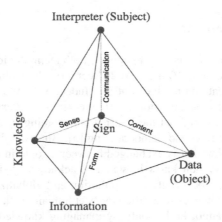

Fig. 1. The tetrahedron of the Sign

Then in Figure 2, we introduce Sign-ification, the continuous process of using Signs in human thinking for acquiring Objects interpreted by Subjects.

This signification process or Semiosis takes the different components of the Sign in a certain order to make a decision: first comes the Subject or Interpreter who is receptive to his milieu or "Umwelt" [9], and who cares about Information to act in a certain direction (volition), then occurs the searched Data (Object) to position himself in space and time (action), then Knowledge is activated in his memory to compare the actual situation with his past experiences and make an hypothesis for taking a decision (cognition). The Signification or the building of the sign communicates the process iteratively in a reflexive way (in order to memorize new knowledge) or communicates the resulting interpretation as information to its environment (by exteriorization).

Semiosis is similar to the working principle of inference engine that was modeled in expert systems: the evaluation-execution cycle [10]. The difference is that Signification integrates the Subject in the process, and this integration is therefore more meaningful to humans than to machines. The Subject operates on Signs in two phases: reflection and action. These phases are inter-linked in a reflexive cycle with a semiotic spiral shape including six moments: 1) to desire, 2) to do, 3) to know, 4) to interpret, 5) to know-how for oneself, 6) to communicate to others (Figure 2). The semiosis spiral is included in the tetrahedron of the Sign.

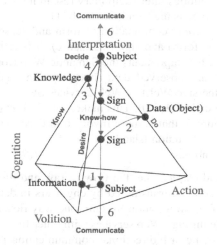

Fig. 2. The signification process for Sign management

Consequently, Signification is the key psychological process that makes sense for practicing usage based research and development with people by communicating data, information and knowledge.

Signification is the kernel of Semiotic Web although Representation is at the root of Semantic Web. Both are necessary to co-design e-services in the Future Internet, but from our experience, don't miss Sign management and Semiotic Web if you want to co-design e-services with end-users!

3   Semiotic Web

Making sense or signifying is a biological characteristic that cannot be eluded in the Future Internet. We are acting now on a limited planet and the objective is to render services to human beings and become responsible rather than serve oneself and consume even more energy and matter with the help of computers.

When an organism or an individual seeks for something, his attitude is to pay attention to events of his environment that go in the sense (direction) of what he searches. The primary intention of a microorganism such as bacteria is "good sense": it wants to capture information from the milieu to develop itself and stay alive [11]. Human development follows the same schema of self-organized living systems at more complex levels than these physiological and safety needs. They are those that have been defined in the hierarchy of fundamental individual needs: love, belonging, esteem, self-actualization [12]. As a consequence, we hold that before being able to make "true sense", i.e. adopt a scientific rationale, the objective of individuals is to respond to psychological needs (desire, pleasure, identity, etc.). This theory of human motivation is a natural and cultural hypothesis, which is corroborated by Umwelt [9], Activity [13] and Semiotic [8] pragmatic theories. These life and logical sciences are components of the Biosemiotics interdisciplinary research [14], which was introduced before the advent of Internet as the "Semiotic Web" [15].

Semantic Web is the *dyadic* combination of form and sense of the linguistic Sign [16], taken as a signifier (form) and signified (sense). It is rational. Semiotic Web is more generic and living. It complements the Semantic Web (form and sense) with the referents (content) that are observed data (interpretations) geo-referenced in a 3D information world (Immersive Web) as Web Services by subjects pertaining to communities of practice (Social Web 2.0). This makes our Sign management ecosystem a *tetrahedron* model (Figure 3) that is more involved in concrete life with end-users on a specific territory such as Reunion Island.

The Web of Signs combines:

1. The Web of *Data* and *Objects*, i.e. the flow of raw and digital contents produced by specialists (teachers) and transmitted by engineers in databases and knowledge bases in the frame of an Information System (one-way flow), but progressively becoming interoperable through Web services with other Information Systems,
2. The Web of *Subjects*, i.e. a bidirectional communication platform between users (teachers and learners) using different e-services within a community of practice to exchange interpretations of data and objects, and negotiate their value,
3. The Web of *Information* that is geo localized in attractive virtual worlds representing the real landscape (metaverses), and accessible at any time, anywhere, on any devices (mobiquity).
4. The Web of *Knowledge* for machines to communicate logically on the basis of a formal, open and semantic representation of data and objects,

At the University of Reunion Island, we have investigated each of these dimensions that are converging to form what we call the Semiotic Web. As the World is an Island and as Reunion Island is a small world, we designed our Living Lab as a small laboratory for Teaching and Learning Sciences and Arts by Playing [17]. Indeed, *edutainment* is one of the pillars of the Future Internet [18]. With game-based learning, we consider that we can play seriously to better know our environment and then better protect it.

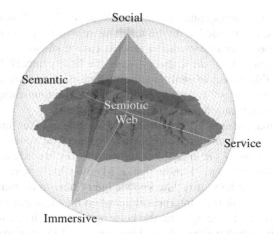

Fig. 3. The Situated Service, Social, Semantic and Immersive Web

For biodiversity management for example, we co-designed an Immersive Biodiversity Information Service (IBIS) for helping biologists and amateurs to access to forest and coral reef species information. This Teaching and Learning tool intends to use different modules dedicated to certain functionalities at different levels of data, information and knowledge and let them communicate by using Web Services [19].

In the spirit of Web 2.0 technologies, we participate to the ViBRANT FP7 project [20] that uses the Scratchpads for data sharing. Using a content management system (Drupal), Scratchpads 2.0 enables bottom up, collaborative work between all types of naturalists, from researchers to amateurs. This Social Web tool supports communities of taxonomists to build, share, manage and publish their data in open access.

For computer-aided taxonomy, we developed an Iterative Knowledge Base System platform called IKBS [21] with some taxonomists. It is based on a knowledge acquisition method and an observing guide for describing biological objects, i.e. the descriptive logics in life Sciences [22]. Our descriptive logics must not be confused with description logics (RDF, OWL) of the Semantic Web because they are the rules of thumb of experts for making descriptive models (ontologies) and describing cases. The objective of this Research tool in Biodiversity Informatics is to help biologists classify and identify a specimen correctly from an expert viewpoint by using onto-terminologies (ontologies + thesaurus).

4   From Knowledge Transmission to Sign Sharing

Knowledge is subjective in the paradigm of Sign management: it cannot be taken for granted without putting it into use, mediated and negotiated with other Subjects on a meeting place, which we called a Creativity Platform [23]. What can be managed is called descriptive or declarative knowledge: it is the communication of justified true beliefs propositions from one Subject made explicit. The formal interpretation process from observation to hypotheses, conjectures and rules is called signification of knowledge on the human communication side of the Sign. It is called representation or codification of knowledge on the machine information side of the Sign. Apart from being described, this interpretation process can be shown with *artifacts* to illustrate the description ("draw me a sheep", says the little prince!). Sign management wants to enhance this aspect of multimedia illustration of interpretations to facilitate transmission and sharing of knowledge through the communication of the Subject (see the fourth communication part of the sign in Figure 1).

In knowledge management, propositional knowledge is taken mostly in the sense of scientific knowledge, considered as objective in scientific books, and providing the know-that or know-what. Ryle in [24] has shown that this is confusing. In the sense of subjective knowledge taken as "I know that or I know what", there is the other sort of knowledge called know-how. It is "the knowledge of how to do things", i.e. what the subjects can show through their interpretations when they practice their activity (there is a difference between the recipe and the cooking of the recipe, isn't it?). And some people do the activity better than others. They are called the experts. As such, know-how is closer to data (Praxis) and information (*Techne*) than to knowledge (*Scientia*). Finally, know-how and know-that or know-what are different categories of knowledge and should not be conflated [25]. Knowledge synthesizes what makes sense in the head of skilled persons for doing well the tasks of their activity.

Starting from these differences of interpretations about the term of knowledge, and considering the domain of activity that we want to deal with, i.e. education with ICT, we prefer to focus on *managing interpretations*, and firstly the good ones from professors. Sign management manages live knowledge, i.e. subjective objects found in interpretations of real subjects on the scene (live performances) rather than objective entities found in publications (bookish knowledge).

In this context of managing know-how rather than knowledge, we have set-up our Living Lab in Reunion Island on the thematic of Teaching and Learning by Playing [26]. The sharing of expertise with ICT is our added value in education for some specific domains such as managing biodiversity, performing art (music, dance, etc.), speaking a language, welcoming tourists, or cooking. These niches can be enhanced with ICT in a sustainable manner by following some innovative methods. For example, sign or know-how management produces sign bases that are made of interpretations for knowing how-to-do things with multimedia content and not only knowing what are these things in textual Knowledge bases.

Finally, a Sign is a semiotic and dynamic Object issued from a Subject and composed of four parts, Data, Information, Knowledge and Interpreter. Our Sign paradigm uses a *fouradic* representation (a regular tetrahedron, see Figures 1 and 2) instead of the *triadic* sign representation that lets the Subject outside of the Semiosis process. All these subjective components communicate together to build a chain of significations and representations that we want to capture.

Sign management makes explicit the subjective view of doing arts and sciences. Our aim is to compare different interpretations of subjects about objects through transmitting and sharing them on a physical and virtual space dedicated to a special type of e-service, i.e. in instrumental e-learning or biodiversity informatics (see below). For the purpose of co-designing such a service with ICT, the Creativity Platform is the co-working, co-learning and communication space for researchers and developers, businesses and users, aimed at collectively defining the characteristics of e-services in order to ensure the most direct correspondence between expectations and use [27].

In its technical form (see Figure 4 on the right), the Creativity Platform includes a multimedia platform as the one that we find in television studios, but also includes a physical and virtual place to discuss ideas and projects, make models and prototypes, and experiment them in a synchronous (focus group) or asynchronous (video forum on the Internet) way.

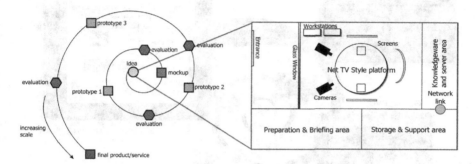

Fig. 4. The Creativity or Co-design Platform to experiment future products/services

Sign sharing makes use of the Creativity Platform by applying an iterative assessment process with end-users from the idea to the product/service through mock-ups and prototypes. We will now illustrate this method with examples in instrumental e-Learning and biodiversity informatics.

5   Sign Sharing in Music Teaching and Learning

Sharing Signs is particularly relevant in artistic fields, where a perfect synchronization between gestures, senses and feelings is essential in order to produce original and beautiful works.

In this frame, the @-MUSE project (@nnotation platform for MUSical Education) aims at constituting a Musical Sign Base (MSB) with the interactions coming from a community of musicians. This project benefits from the experience we accumulated in the field of instrumental e-Learning in Reunion Island, from various mock-ups to complete projects such as e-Guitare [23]. Figure 5 sums up our research process in this domain, based on a Creativity Platform.

While the different versions of e-Guitare were more centered on the teacher performance, the FIGS (Flash Interactive Guitar Saloon) service was more axed on the dialog between learners and teachers through an online glosses system. What principally emerged from these projects was the need to facilitate the creation and maintenance of new content on the platform. Indeed, while those projects required the intervention of computer scientists and graphic designers in order to create high-quality resources, @-MUSE aims at empowering musicians into creating and sharing their lessons by themselves, on the basis of a common frame of reference: the musical score.

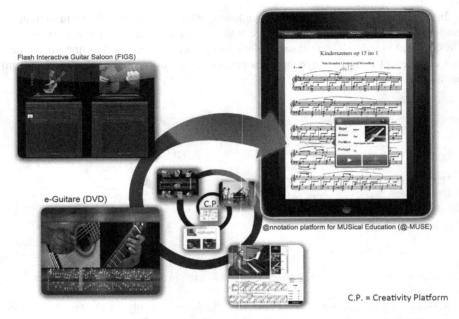

Fig. 5. Instrumental e-Learning services co-designed on a Creativity Platform (CP)

To do so, we designed a MSB. It consists in a set of annotated performances (specimen, or instance) each related to a given musical work (species, or class). This base can be used to compare various performances from music experts or students, and also to dynamically build new music lessons from the available content. To do so, we define a Musical Sign (MS) [28], as an object including a content (a musical performance or demonstration), a form (a score representing the played piece) and a sense (the background experience of the performer, what he or she intends to show) from the viewpoint of a subject (the creator of the Sign).

Figure 6 describes the composition of a MS that can be shared on the platform through a multimedia annotation. Indeed, the principle of @-MUSE is to illustrate abstract scores with indexed multimedia content on top of MusicXML format [33] in order to explicit concretely how to interpret them. Besides, as shown on Figure 6, multimedia annotations embed all three components of a Sign (data, information and sense). This procedure is inspired from a common practice in the music education field, which consists in adding annotations on sheet music in order to remember tips or advice that were validated during the instrumental practice [29].

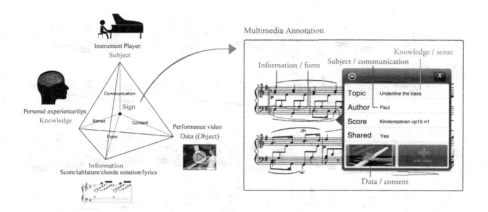

Fig. 6. The musical sign tetrahedron illustrated with a multimedia annotation on @-MUSE

Figure 7 presents an example of such practice on an advanced piece for the piano, where annotations indicate tips to overcome technical and expressive difficulties, and underline points to improve for the learner. Grounding the @-MUSE service on this practice insures a transparent and natural usage for musicians who already annotate their scores by hand, and additionally enables them to show what they mean using multimedia features. As such, @-MUSE empowers musicians into creating their own interactive scores, using for instance mobile tablets equipped with webcams (@-MUSE prototype [30]).

Naturally, our platform usage on mobile devices is particularly relevant as music is rarely practiced in a classroom, in front of a computer, but rather in informal situations (in front of a music stand, at home or with friends). Moreover, recent tablets featuring advanced tactile and multimedia characteristics facilitate the navigation within the score and the creation of high quality content on the platform.

Collaborative aspects are also essential in music learning, where one progresses by confronting his performances to others'. In this frame, managing Signs rather than Knowledge is particularly relevant, as there is no "absolute truth" in artistic fields: each interpretation can lead to technical discussions between musicians, and their negotiations should be illustrated with live performances to be shown, then understood. This is why we introduced the notion of Musical Message Board (MMB) in [28]. MMBs support discussions between musicians through a Glosses' system, leading to the creation of a thread of MS indexed on some parts of the score (a note, a musical phrase, a measure, etc.). In addition to these indexed multimedia annotations, what distinguishes this MS thread from a discussion on the piece is that each of the created Signs is indexed in context and can then be reused in different situations, for instance, on another piece of music presenting similar features. To do so, the MSB should be able to grasp the basic sense of the created MS, in order to organize itself, and provide advanced Sign sharing functionalities to users.

Fig. 7. Annotated score example (extract from "Jeux d'Eau" by Maurice Ravel)

Collecting MS on different pieces of music enables also the illustration of significant descriptive logics in order to organize the MSB. Descriptive logics of the semiotic Web are more meaningful than description logics of the semantic Web because they bring human interpretations (psychological annotations) on top of symbolic representations (formal notations). Indeed, in musical education, understanding the structure of a work is an important key to play it correctly. Musicology provides a guide for the musician to explore the piece in the finest details and to better assimilate it. But this structure can be lively exemplified with MS created by @-MUSE in the signification process of understanding the context of resolution of the musical piece.

Descriptive logics express the background knowledge of specialists who well understand the historical context of music playing. It often depends on the style or form of the considered piece, i.e. its classification. For instance, a fugue is based on a theme that is repeated all along the piece in different voices [30]. Underlining these themes within the score allows disposing of a framework to better analyze the corresponding performances and establish fruitful confrontations.

Figure 8 gives an example of an ontology based on descriptive logics (generic musical analysis).

This decomposition corresponds to the traditional way music teachers introduce a new piece to students [31]. After a short overview of the piece context (composer, style, mood), its characteristics patterns and difficult parts are identified and commented. This process can be recreated within the @-MUSE platform thanks to the characterization of descriptive logics adapted to each musical style.

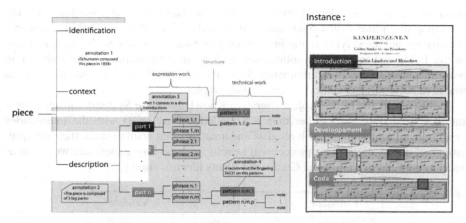

Fig. 8. The musical descriptive model supporting descriptive logics of the Semiotic Web

From the human-machine interaction point of view, it consists in proposing an "annotation guide" for each new piece, in order to obtain a complete interactive score at the end of the process. This method intends to guide users into the semiosis process described in Figure 2, by providing them a framework to communicate their own view of the considered piece and its characteristic features. In order to model these descriptive logics more formally, we proposed in [31] a Musical Performance Ontology based on the Music Ontology [32]. This ontology enables the automatic manipulation of concepts related to the piece structure, but also to gestural and expressive work. Tagging MS with these concepts and relations allows @-MUSE to automatically generate appropriate annotations on new pieces. Indeed, while machines can hardly deal with expressive and emotional information, they can provide basic information on specific patterns or unknown symbols, given a style or composer context. To do so, we designed a Score Analyzer [34] to automatically extract difficult parts within a given score, and to generate basic annotations. This prototype is based on the extraction of characteristic features of a score: chords, hands displacements, fingering, tempo, harmonies, rhythms and length. Work is in progress to measure the relevance of these estimations in comparison to human appreciations. As such, @-MUSE proposes an innovative service to share Musical Signs on a collaborative Web platform. The usage of multimedia and validated standards such as MusicXML empower users into illustrating specific parts of a musical work in a collaborative and reusable way. Perspectives of this research include further testing with musician collaborators from music schools, as well as work on decision support for automatic score annotation.

6   Sign Sharing in Biodiversity Informatics

Sharing Signs is also relevant in biodiversity management with ICT, in this specific domain called Biodiversity Informatics that applies computerized acquisition and processing methods to natural data, information and knowledge, in order to define, describe, classify and identify biological objects. More precisely, we focus on the scientific discipline called *Systematics* that deals with listing, describing, naming, classifying and identifying living organisms. Our natural objects are living specimens in the fields and in museum collections. Experts in Systematics at university or in museums have studied them intimately for years and are able to recognize their names that give access to more information in monographs.

In this frame, the IKBS project (Iterative Knowledge Base System) aims at constituting a Sign Base (SB) rather than a Knowledge Base (KB) with the interactions coming from a community of biologists and amateurs that want to share their interpretations of observations. This project will benefit from the long experience we accumulated in the field of Mascarene Corals and Plants identification [35].

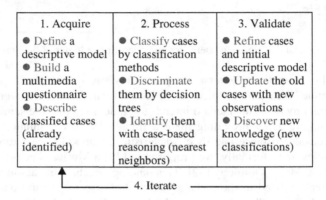

1. Acquire	2. Process	3. Validate
● Define a descriptive model ● Build a multimedia questionnaire ● Describe classified cases (already identified)	● Classify cases by classification methods ● Discriminate them by decision trees ● Identify them with case-based reasoning (nearest neighbors)	● Refine cases and initial descriptive model ● Update the old cases with new observations ● Discover new knowledge (new classifications)

4. Iterate

Fig. 9. Knowledge management cycle with IKBS

Figure 9 sums up our Knowledge transmission process in this domain, based on a Creativity Platform. It applies the experimental and inductive approach in biology, conjecture and test [36], with a natural process of knowledge management that is well suited to teaching from real examples. Indeed, IKBS has developed an original approach based on collection specimens' descriptions for helping specialists to discover new knowledge and classifications:

1. Acquisition of a descriptive model and descriptions,
2. Processing of this knowledge and case base for classification and identification purposes,
3. Experimentation, validation and refinement of cases and descriptive models,
4. Iteration.

For identification purpose, the expert controls the transmission process, which is detailed in Figure 10 for corals:

Current node of the decision tree ❶   ❷ Corresponding descriptive object and illustration

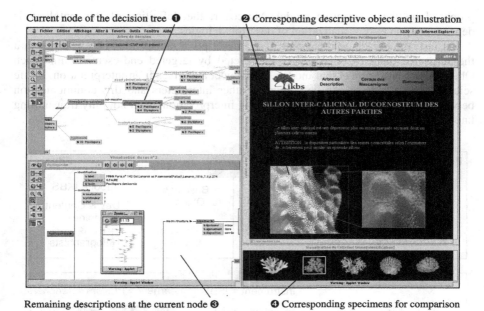

Remaining descriptions at the current node ❸   ❹ Corresponding specimens for comparison

Fig. 10. The identification process for corals

- The actual node of the decision tree or identification key is shown (e.g. inter-corallite's line),
- The referred question for this descriptive component and the illustrations of its possible values at this node are directly accessible (e.g. present or absent),
- One can leaf through the list of indexed cases at this node (e.g. cases of *Pocillopora* and *Stylophora*), in order to see the different values of the components and specimens,
- The pictures for the remaining objects at the current node are shown. The identification key may be useful to learn species' characteristics and improve one's ability to observe specimens in their natural surroundings or in a museum collection.

But the Learning problem from the end-user viewpoint is to *know how to observe* these objects in order to identify correctly the name of the species. This task is complex and needs help from the specialists who know by experience where to observe correctly the "right characters". By taking care of this knowledge transmission bottleneck, we enter the domain of Sign management for getting more robust results with end-users. Our idea of Sign management is to involve end-users with researchers and entrepreneurs for making them participate to the design of the product/service that they want.

The problem that we have to face with when making knowledge bases is that their usefulness depends on the right interpretation of questions that are proposed by the system to obtain a good result.

Hence, in order to get correct identifications, it is necessary to acquire qualitative descriptions. But these descriptions rely themselves on the observation guide that is proposed by the descriptive model. Moreover, the definition of this ontology is dependent upon easy visualization of descriptive logics.

At last, the objects that are part of the descriptive model must be explained in a thesaurus for them to be correctly interpreted by targeted end-users. Behind each Object, there is a Subject that models this Object and gives it an interpretation. In life sciences, these objects can be shown to other interpreters and this communication between Subjects is compulsory for sharing interpretations, and not only transmitting knowledge (Figure 11).

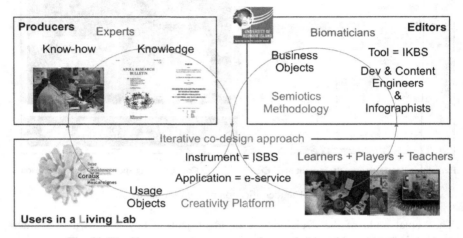

Fig. 11. The Sign management process for coral objects' interpretation

The challenge of Sign management for Science observation such as Systematics is to involve all types of end-users in the co-design of Sign bases for them to be really used (e-service). It is why we, as biologists and computer scientist (biomaticians), emphasize the instantiation of a Living Lab in Teaching and Learning at University of Reunion Island for sharing interpretations of objects and specimens on the table rather than concepts and taxa in the head of subjects: draw me a sheep, said the little prince !

7   Discussion

As shown in music and biodiversity Teaching and Learning, if we want to innovate with people, we should use the concept of Sign management rather than Knowledge management, because the paradigm shift is to pass from knowledge transmission to sign sharing by managing know-how.

Since several years in computer-aided systematics, we proposed a knowledge management methodology based on a top-down transmission of experts' knowledge, i.e. acquisition of a descriptive model and structured cases and then processing of these specimens' descriptions with decision trees and case-based reasoning. We designed a tool called IKBS for Iterative Knowledge Base System to build knowledge bases. But the fact is that Knowledge is transmitted with text, not shared with multimedia, and there is a gap between interpretations of specialists and end-users that prevents these lasts from getting the right identification.

More recently in instrumental e-Learning, we focused on the need to show gestural know-how with interactive multimedia contents to play correctly a piece of music, by annotating electronic scores with @-MUSE. This pedagogical approach is based on a gloss system on the Web that can be indexed in codified musical notation.

Today, we prefer to deliver a Sign management method for Teaching and Learning how to identify these collection pieces (specimens or scores) on a Co-Design or Creativity Platform. This bottom-up approach is more pragmatic and user-centered than the previous one because it implicates end-users at will and is open to questions and answers. The role of biological and musical experts is to show amateurs how to play, observe, interpret and describe these art and science works. The responsibility of semioticians (the new cogniticians) is to store and share experts' interpretations of their observation and playing, i.e. know-how rather than knowledge in sign bases with multimedia annotations for helping them to define terms, model their domain, and allow end-users to interpret correctly the objects.

As computer scientists and knowledge engineers, we want to design a new Iterative Sign Base System (ISBS) that will be the kernel of our Information Service for defining ontologies and terms, describing pieces work, classifying them with machine learning techniques, and identifying the name through a multimedia interactive questionnaire. The objective of such a tool is to become an instrument in users' hands for monitoring biodiversity in the fields with the National Park of Reunion Island, and music at home with the Regional Music Conservatory.

For achieving this, we stressed on the importance of reducing the gap between interpretations of teachers (specialists) and learners (amateurs) to get the right identification name and then access to information in databases, or to get the correct gesture that gives the right sound for playing music. This pedagogical effort must concretize itself on a Co-Design or Creativity Platform, which is the Living Lab meeting place for teachers, players and learners, and where these people can manipulate the objects under study, test the proposed e-services and be guided by experts' advices. The teacher is a *producer* who communicates his skilled interpretation of an activity at different levels of perception: psychological motivation, training action, and reasoning feedback. The players are designers-developers *editors* that produce multimedia contents of the expert tasks to perform a good result and index them in a sign base. The learners are *prosumers* (producers and consumers) who experiment the sign bases on the physical or virtual Co-Design Platform and tell about their use of the tool to domain experts, ergonomists and anthropologists, in order to improve the content and the functionalities of the mock-ups and prototypes.

Behind each Object to observe, play and describe, there is a Subject who expresses himself and interprets an object by adding his proper signification. This is why we differentiate the Semantic Web, which is the business object approach (the Web of things) represented "objectively" with some description logics (formal syntax for ontologies and cases), and the Semiotic Web that is the usage object approach (the Web of Signs) signified by some descriptive logics of the domain (meaningful process of performance), and which are more subjective. The purpose of the Semiotic

Web is to facilitate a consensus between community members, without forgetting that some interpreters are smarter than others in performing a Science or an Art. Their expertise will be visible if users show their interpretations of objects by multimedia artifacts (HD video, 3D simulation, annotated drawings or photos), and if other end-users can ask questions on their know-how and negotiate interpretations. It is why in the frame of natural and cultural heritage enhancement, we proposed to develop Teaching and Learning by Playing e-services with people in a Living Lab by using Sign management on a Co-design Platform at the University of Reunion Island [37].

8   Conclusion

In the post-industrial age of our digital society, designing new services on the Web is crucial for regional territories in order that they become more attractive, competitive, and also more sustainable in the global economy. But up to now, innovation is mainly seen as a linear technological downstream process, centered on enterprises (clusters) and not viewed as an iterative usage upstream process, focused on individuals (Living Labs).

The *form* of LL is attractive because it is an ecosystem based on democratizing innovation with people. User-centered design innovation means that some people, called lead-users, want to innovate for themselves. It has been shown that these persons make most of the design of new services, and only a few come from manufactures.

The *content* of LL is competitive because the best solutions from lead-users are experimented in real time by making situational analyses in "usage laboratories". Mock-ups and prototypes are tested and instrumented to get the best-customized-personalized products and services. For example, the game design (user interaction) and interfaces of 3D multimedia video games benefit greatly from the analysis of feedbacks coming from end-users in communities of practice. So, the success of the e-service does not depend only on the technical success: it has more to do with the quality of human-computer interaction provided with the technology.

At last, the *sense* of LL should be more sustainable, i.e. to render a useful and free service before being profitable, i.e. not only based on a monetary basis but also on trust and reputation. This characteristic is fundamental in the meaning of open access innovation to serve a mission within the scope of products and services made by publicly funded universities. The ultimate value would be to create a form of digital companioning in order to reposition human sharing at the core of technology race.

Acknowledgments. We would like to thank the French National Government, the Regional Council of Reunion Island and the European Union for supporting this research in the frame of the PO-FEDER 2-06 ICT measure: http://www.reunioneurope.org/UE_PO-FEDER.asp. We are also grateful to the FP7 Vibrant project (www.vibrant.eu) contract no. RI-261532. Period, Dec. 2010 to Nov. 2013: they gave us the opportunity to develop our vision of sign management for biodiversity monitoring. This paper was presented at the ECAI/IFIP Artificial Intelligence for Knowledge Management Workshop (AI4KM) of ECAI'2012 (http://www2.lirmm.fr/ecai2012/) on the 28th of August 2012 in Montpellier, France.

References

1. http://en.wikipedia.org/wiki/Internet
2. http://www.openlivinglabs.eu/news/when-infrastructure-meets-user-new-lovestory-making
3. http://www.ictusagelab.fr/ecoleLL/content/literature
4. Chesbrough, H.W.: Open Innovation: The New Imperative for Creating and Profiting from Technology. Harvard Business School Press, Boston (2003)
5. Von Hippel, E.A.: Democratizing Innovation. MIT Press, Cambridge (2005)
6. Keen, A.: The Cult of the amateur: How Today's Internet is Killing Our Culture, 228 p., Doubleday, New York (2007)
7. Lassila, O., Hendler, J.: Embracing "Web 3.0". IEEE Internet Computing 11(3), 90–93 (2007), doi:10.1109/MIC.2007.52
8. Peirce, C.S.: Elements of Logic. In: Hartshone, C.H., Weiss, P. (eds.) Collected Papers of C. S. Peirce (1839 - 1914). The Belknap Press, Harvard Univ. Press, Cambridge, MA (1965)
9. von Uexküll, J.: Theoretical Biology, pp. xvi+362. Kegan Paul, Trench, Trubner & Co., London (1926) (Transl. by D. L. MacKinnon. International Library of Psychology, Philosophy and Scientific Method)
10. Farreny, H.: Les Systèmes Experts: principles et exemples: Cepadues-Editions, Toulouse (1985)
11. Shapiro, J.A.: Bacteria are small but not stupid: cognition, natural genetic engineering and sociobacteriology. Studies in History and Philosophy of Biological and Biomedical Sciences 38(4), 807–819 (2007)
12. Maslow, A.H.: A Theory of Human Motivation. Psychological Review 50(4), 370–396 (1943)
13. Engeström, Y.: Learning by expanding: an activity-theoretical approach to developmental research. Orienta-Konsultit Oy, Helsinki (1987)
14. Barbieri, M.: Introduction to Biosemiotics. The new biological synthesis. Springer (2007)
15. Sebeok, T.A., Umiker-Sebeok, J. (eds.): Biosemiotics: The Semiotic Web 1991. Mouton de Gruyter, Berlin (1992)
16. Saussure de, F.: Nature of the Linguistics Sign. In: Bally, C., Sechehaye, A. (eds.) Cours de Linguistique Générale. McGraw Hill Education (1916)
17. University of Reunion Island Living Lab vision (2011), http://www.slideshare.net/conruyt/urlltl
18. New Media Consortium (2013), http://www.nmc.org/publications
19. Conruyt, N., Sébastien, D., Vignes-Lebbe, R., Cosadia, S., Touraivane: Moving from Biodiversity Information Systems to Biodiversity Information Services. In: Maurer, L., Tochtermann, K. (eds.) Information and Communication Technologies for Biodiversity and Agriculture, Shaker Verlag, Aachen (2010) ISBN: 978-3-8322-8459-6
20. Vibrant FP7 Project (2011), http://vbrant.eu/
21. Conruyt, N., Grosser, D.: Knowledge management in environmental sciences with IKBS: application to Systematics of Corals of the Mascarene Archipelago. In: Selected Contributions in Data Analysis and Classification. Studies in Classification, Data Analysis, and Knowledge Organization, pp. 333–344. Springer (2007) ISBN: 978-3-540-73558-8
22. Le Renard, J., Conruyt, N.: On the representation of observational data used for classification and identification of natural objects. In: New Approaches in Classification and Data Analysis, Studies in Classification, Data Analysis, and Knowledge Organization, pp. 308–315. Springer (1994) ISBN: 978-3-540-58425-4

23. Conruyt, N., Sébastien, O., Sébastien, V., Sébastien, D., Grosser, D., Calderoni, S., Hoarau, D., Sida, P.: From Knowledge to Sign Management on a Creativity Platform, Application to Instrumental E-learning. In: 4th IEEE International Conference on Digital Ecosystems and Technologies, DEST, Dubaï, UAE, April 13-16 (2010)
24. Ryle, G.: The concept of mind. Hutchinson, London (1949)
25. Callaos, N.: The Essence of Engineering and Meta-Engineering: A Work in Progress. In: The 3rd International Multi-Conference on Engineering and Technological Innovation: IMETI 2010, Orlando, Florida, USA, June 29-July 2 (2010)
26. http://www.slideshare.net/conruyt/living-lab-and-digital-cultural-heritage
27. Sébastien, O., Conruyt, N., Grosser, D.: Defining e-services using a co-design platform: Example in the domain of instrumental e-learning. Journal of Interactive Technology and Smart Education 5(3), 144–156 (2008) ISSN 1741-5659
28. Sébastien, V., Sébastien, D., Conruyt, N.: Dynamic Music Lessons on a Collaborative Score Annotation Platform. In: The Sixth International Conference on Internet and Web Applications and Services, ICIW 2011, St. Maarten, Netherlands Antilles, pp. 178–183 (2011)
29. Winget, M.A.: Annotations on musical scores by performing musicians: Collaborative models, interactive methods, and music digital library tool development. Journal of the American Society for Information Science and Technology (2008)
30. Sébastien, V., Sébastien, P., Conruyt, N.: @-MUSE: Sharing musical know-how through mobile devices interfaces. In: 5th Conference on e-Learning Excellence in the Middle East, Dubaï (2012)
31. Sébastien, V., Sébastien, D., Conruyt, N.: An Ontology for Musical Performances Analysis. Application to a Collaborative Platform dedicated to Instrumental Practice. In: The Fifth International Conference on Internet and Web Applications and Services, ICIW, Barcelona, pp. 538–543 (2010)
32. Raimond, Y., Abdallah, S., Sandler, M., Giasson, F.: The Music Ontology. In: Proceedings of the International Conference on Music Information Retrieval, ISMIR (2007)
33. Castan, G., Good, M., Roland, P.: Extensible Markup Language (XML) for Music Applications: An Introduction. In: The Virtual Score: Representation, Retrieval, Restoration, pp. 95–102. MIT Press, Cambridge (2001)
34. Sébastien, V., Sébastien, D., Conruyt, N.: Constituting a Musical Sign Base through Score Analysis and Annotation. The International Journal on Advances in Networks and Services (2012)
35. http://coraux.univ-reunion.fr/, http://mahots.univ-reunion.fr/
36. Popper, K.R.: La logique de la découverte scientifique. Payot (eds.) Press, Paris (1973)
37. http://www.openlivinglabs.eu/livinglab/university-reunion-island-living-lab-teaching-and-learning

Author Index

Adrian, Weronika T.   112
Altay, Ayca   131

Barkati, Karim   151

Conruyt, Noël   170

Dinu, Razvan   53

Ferber, Jacques   53
Florea, Adina Magda   53

Golubev, Konstantin M.   1
Grosser, David   170

Ismail, Andrei-Adnan   53

Kaczor, Krzysztof   112
Kayakutlu, Gulgun   131

Ligęza, Antoni   19, 112
Lindskog, Helena   95

Mercier-Laurent, Eunika   95

Nalepa, Grzegorz J.   112

Obermann, Jens   72
Owoc, Mieczysław   38

Potempa, Tomasz   19

Rousseaux, Francis   151

Scheuermann, Andreas   72
Sébastien, Didier   170
Sébastien, Olivier   170
Sébastien, Véronique   170
Stratulat, Tiberiu   53

Weichbroth, Paweł   38

Printed in the United States
By Bookmasters